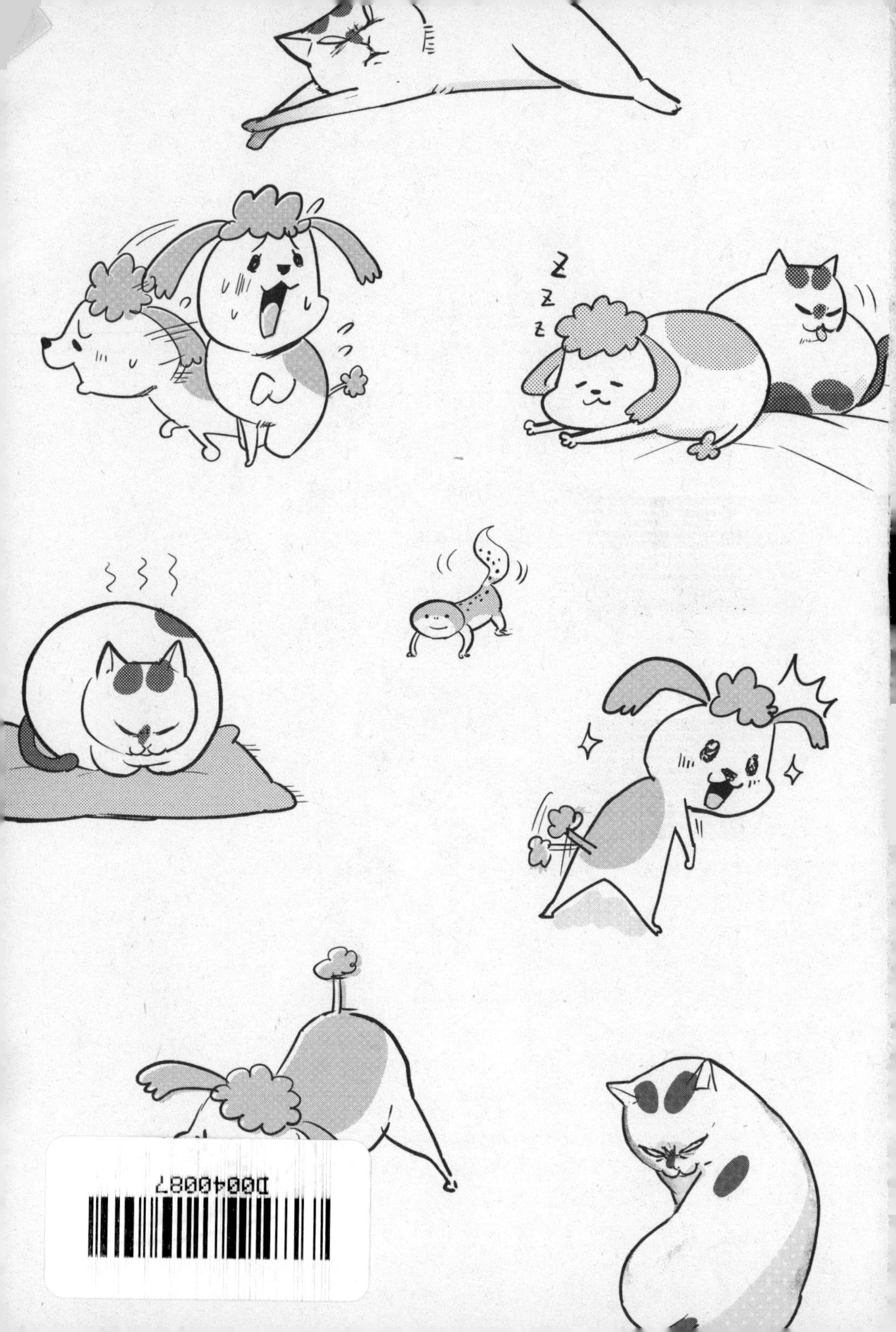
Z Z Z

This is Volume 2.
Neither Inu nor Neko
have any idea they've
been in 2 volumes of
manga, and are sleeping
as usual.

Hidekichi Matsumoto

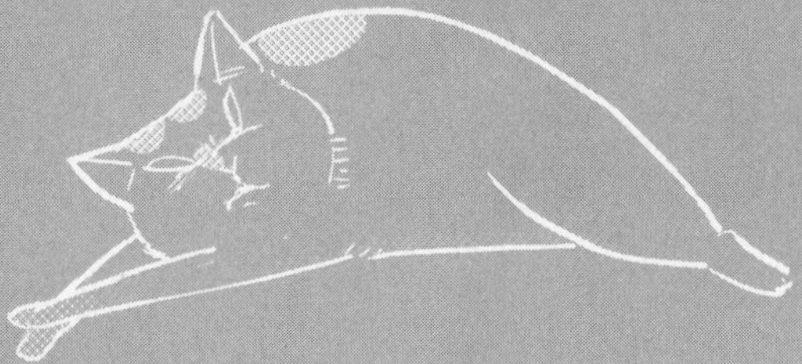

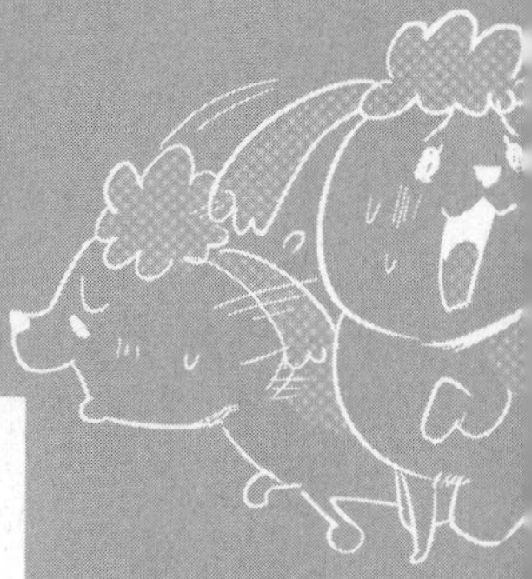

With a Dog AND a Cat, Every Day is Fun

2

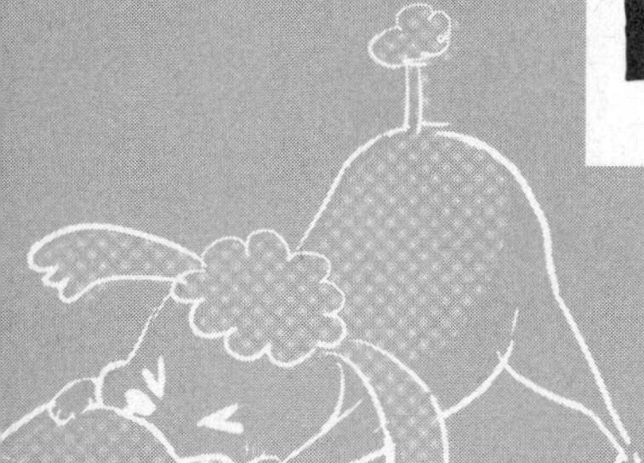

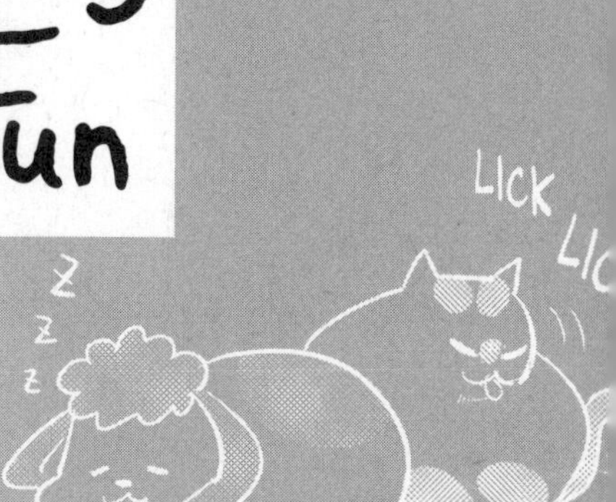
LICK
LIC
Z
z
z
z

Hidekichi Matsumoto

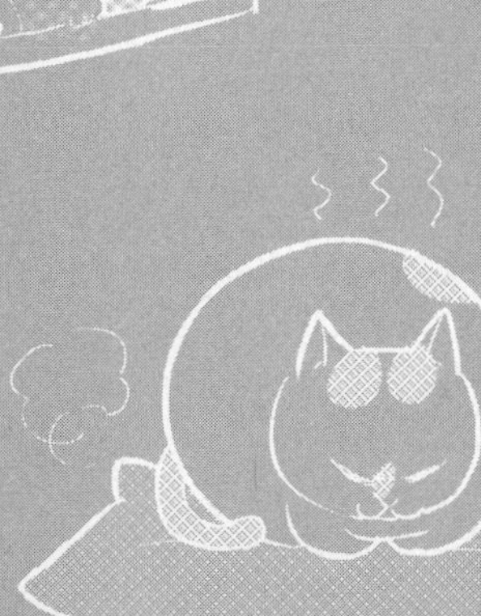

CAST

INU-KUN

Loves Neko. Even when he doesn't like something, if you sing and dance, he soon forgets about it.

NEKO-SAMA

A fearsome face. A cool customer. His passion for theft is staggering.

HIDEKICHI MATSUMOTO

Manga artist. Loves animals.

MOM

Hidekichi's mother. Holds the #1 ranking in the Matsumoto household.

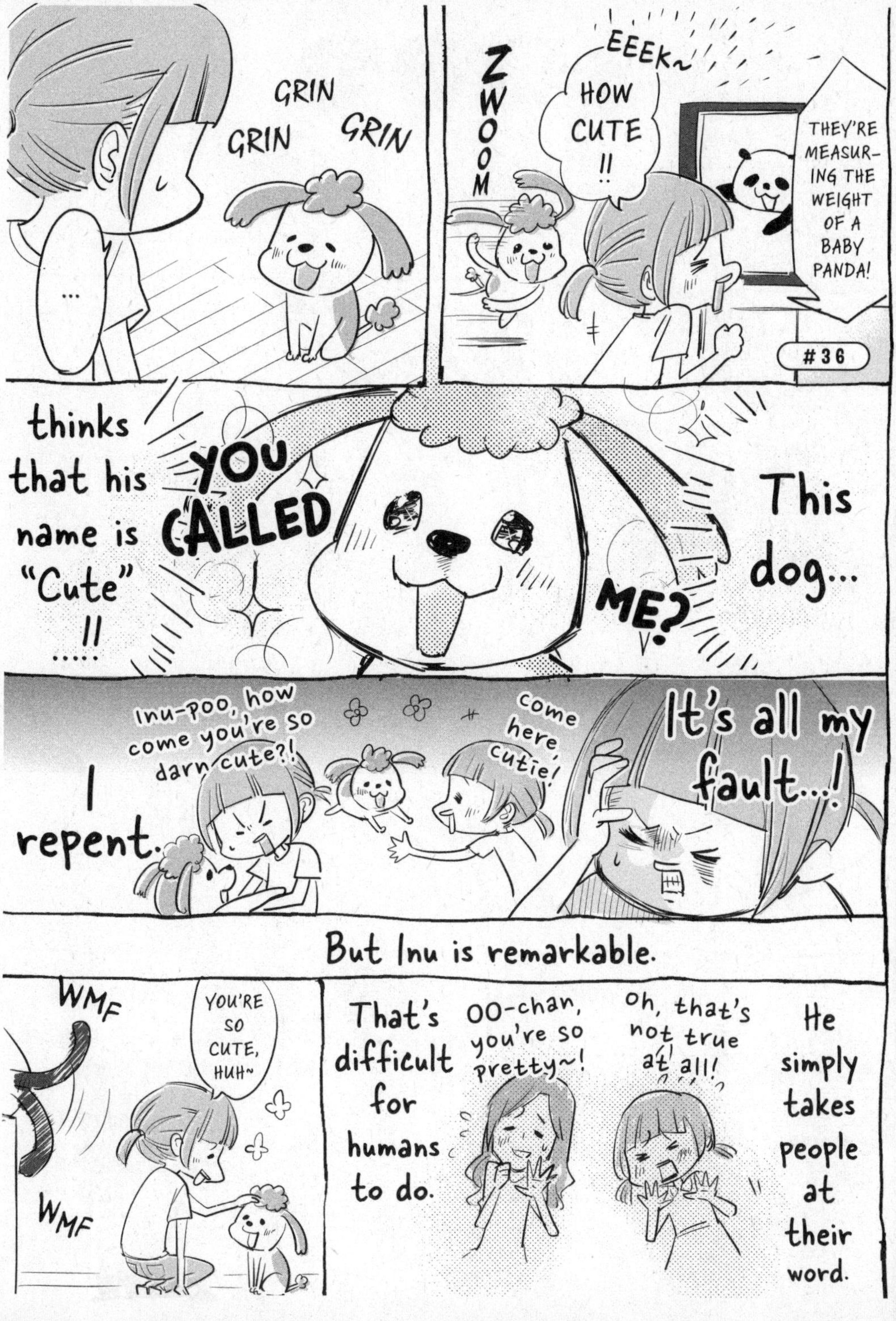
#36
THEY'RE MEASURING THE WEIGHT OF A BABY PANDA!
EEEK~
HOW CUTE !!
ZWOOM
GRIN
GRIN
GRIN
...
This dog...
YOU CALLED ME?
thinks that his name is "Cute" !!
.....
It's all my fault...!
Come here, cutie!
Inu-poo, how come you're so darn cute?!
I repent.
But Inu is remarkable.
He simply takes people at their word.
Oh, that's not true at all!
OO-chan, you're so pretty~!
That's difficult for humans to do.
YOU'RE SO CUTE, HUH~
WMF
WMF

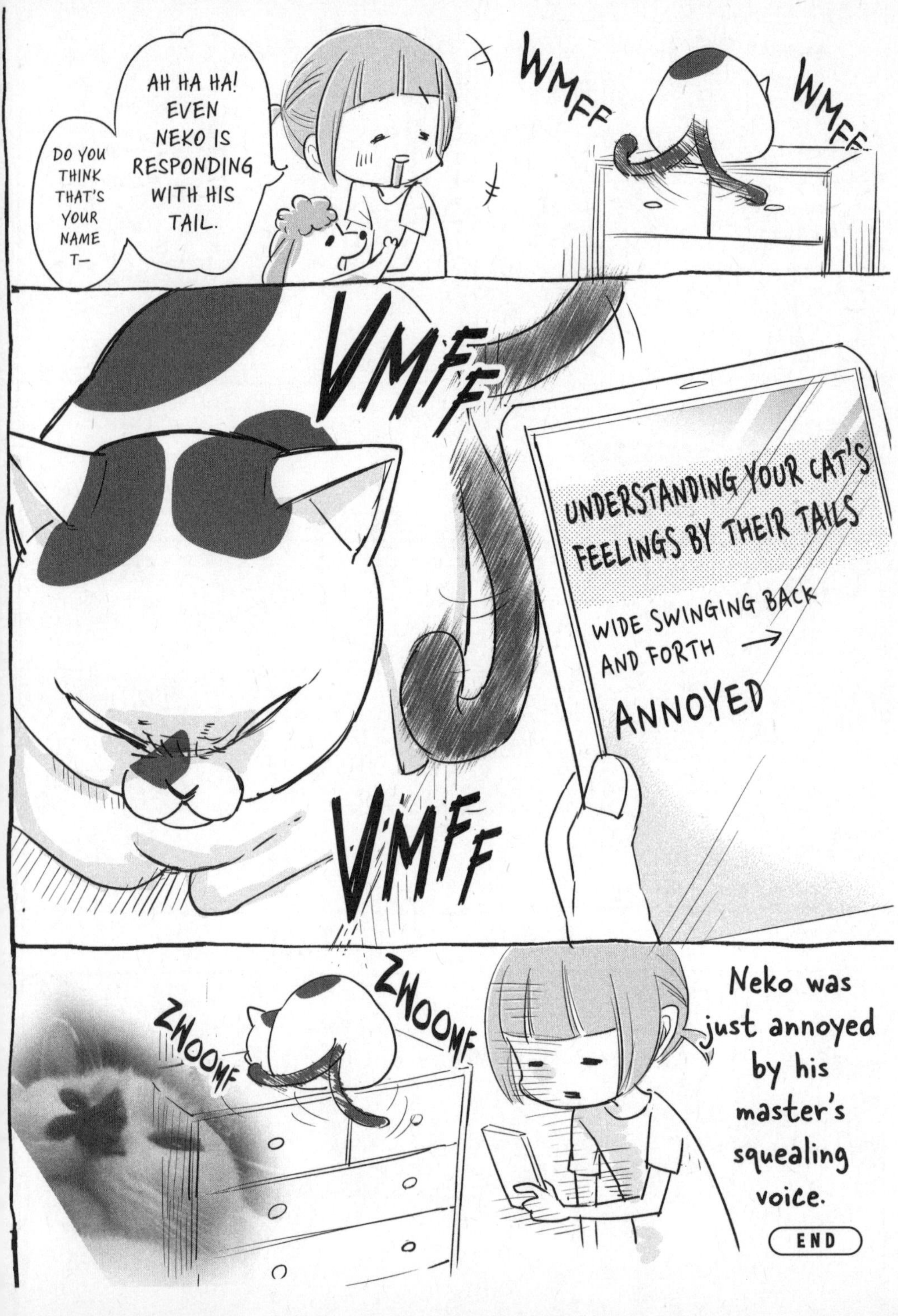
WMFF
WMFF
AH HA HA! EVEN NEKO IS RESPONDING WITH HIS TAIL.
DO YOU THINK THAT'S YOUR NAME T—
UNDERSTANDING YOUR CAT'S FEELINGS BY THEIR TAILS
WIDE SWINGING BACK AND FORTH →
ANNOYED
VMFF
VMFF
Neko was just annoyed by his master's squealing voice.
END
ZWOOMF
ZWOOMF

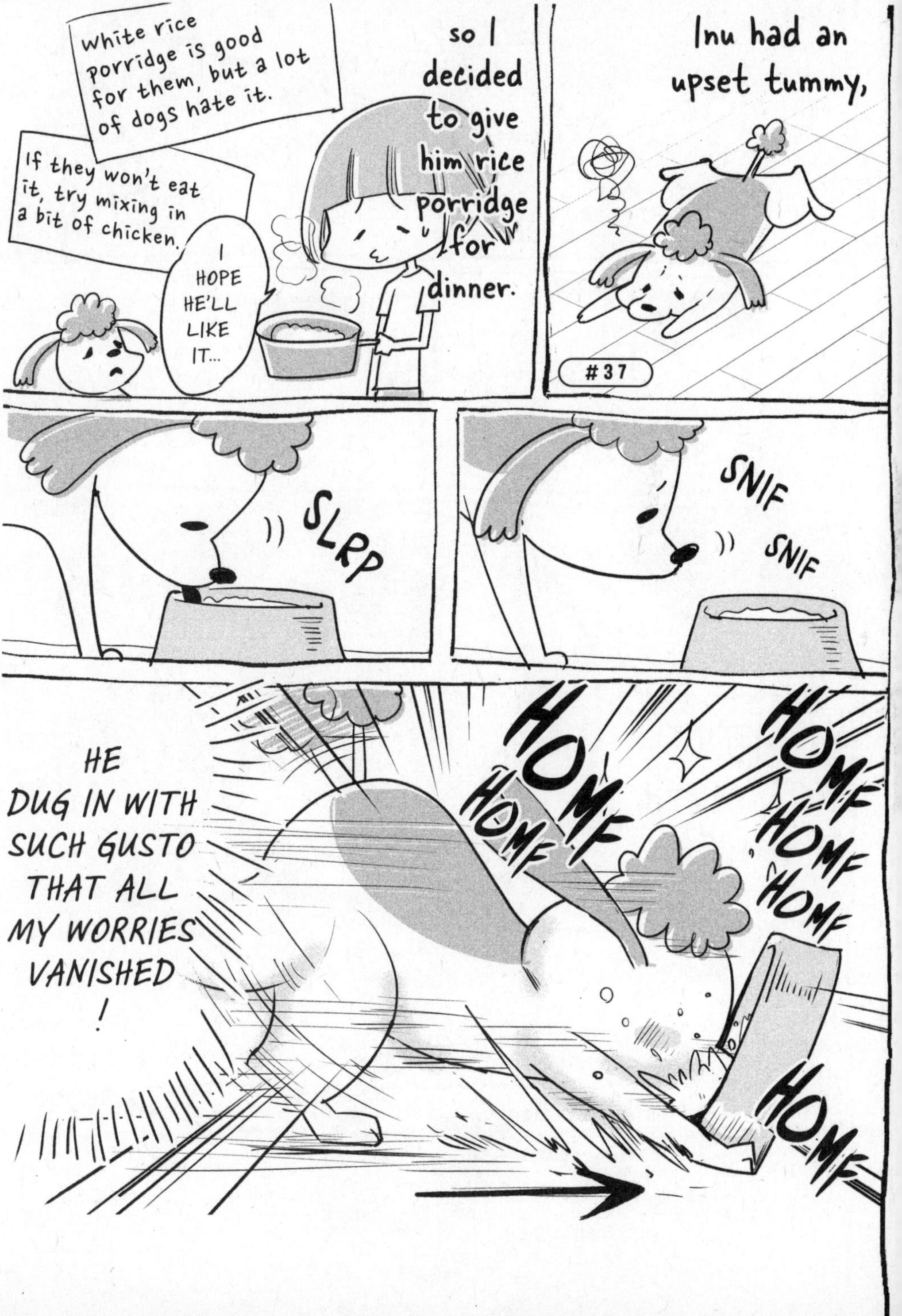
Inu had an upset tummy,
#37
so I decided to give him rice porridge for dinner.
I HOPE HE'LL LIKE IT...
White rice porridge is good for them, but a lot of dogs hate it.
If they won't eat it, try mixing in a bit of chicken.
SNIF
SNIF
SLRP
HOMF HOMF HOMF HOMF
HOMF HOMF
HOMF
HE DUG IN WITH SUCH GUSTO THAT ALL MY WORRIES VANISHED!

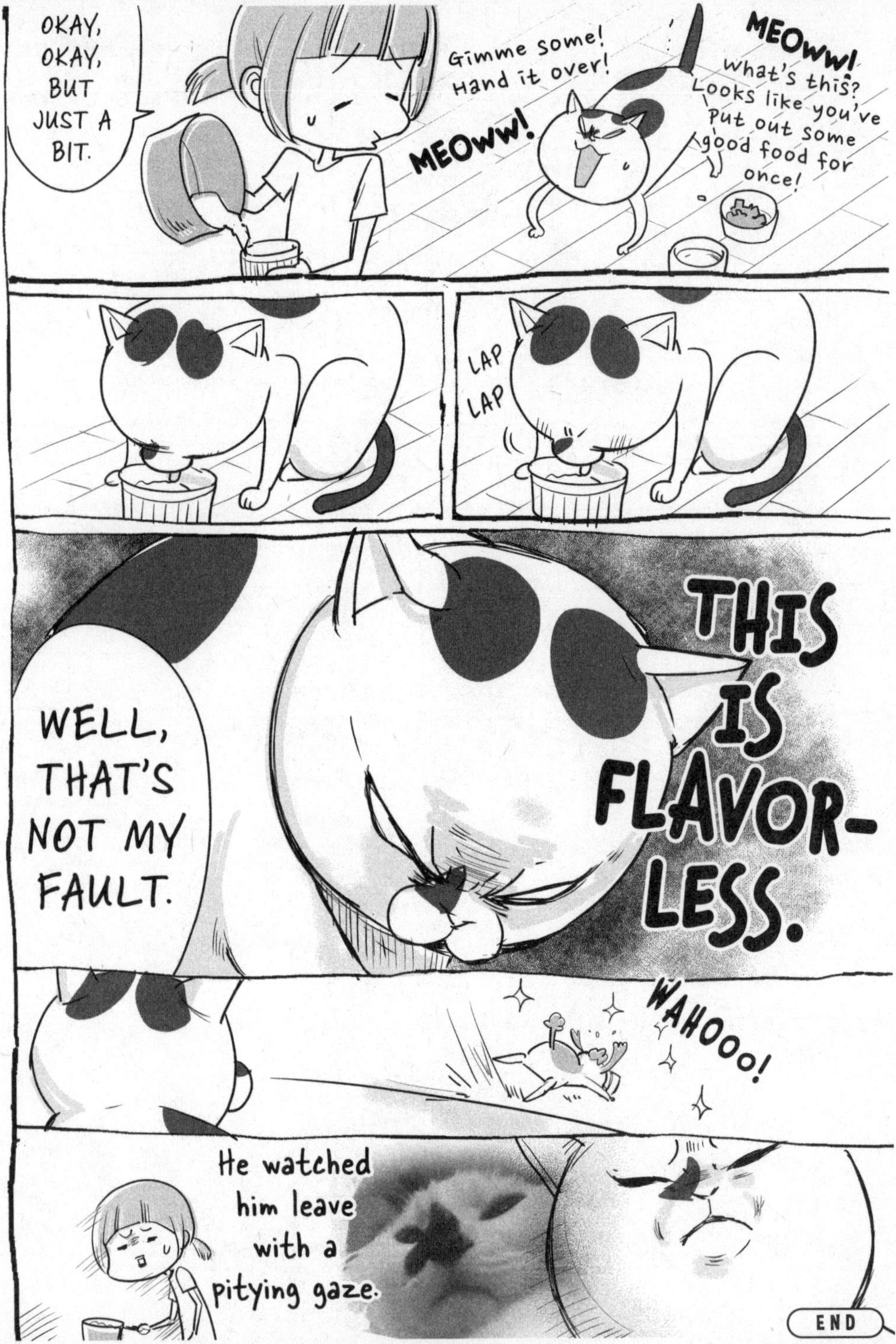
MEOWW!
What's this? Looks like you've put out some good food for once!
Gimme some! Hand it over!
MEOWW!
OKAY, OKAY, BUT JUST A BIT.
LAP LAP
THIS IS FLAVOR-LESS.
WELL, THAT'S NOT MY FAULT.
WAHOOO!
He watched him leave with a pitying gaze.
END

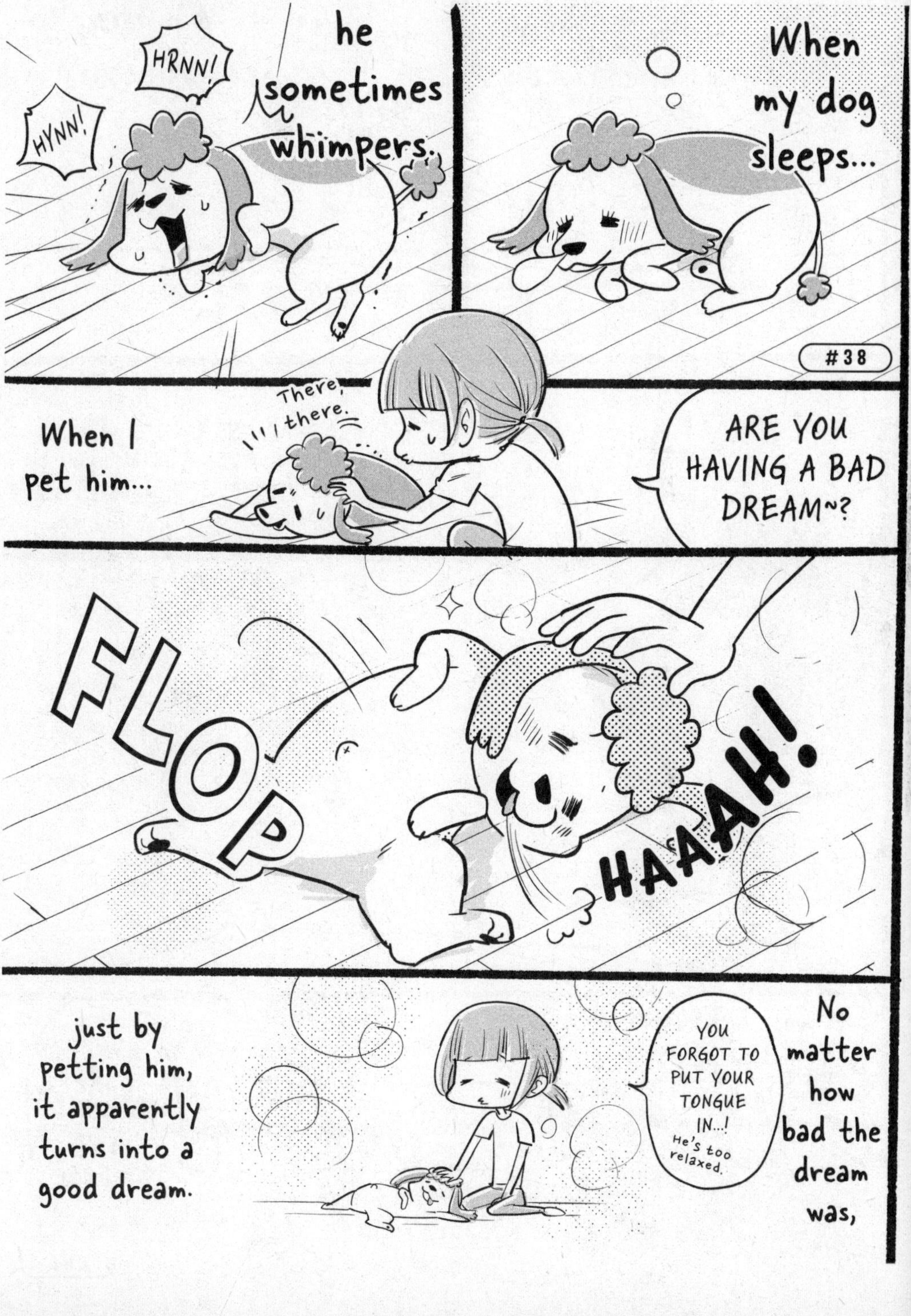
#38
When my dog sleeps...
he sometimes whimpers.
HRNN!
HYNN!
ARE YOU HAVING A BAD DREAM~?
When I pet him...
There, there.
FLOP
HAAAH!
No matter how bad the dream was,
YOU FORGOT TO PUT YOUR TONGUE IN...!
He's too relaxed.
just by petting him, it apparently turns into a good dream.

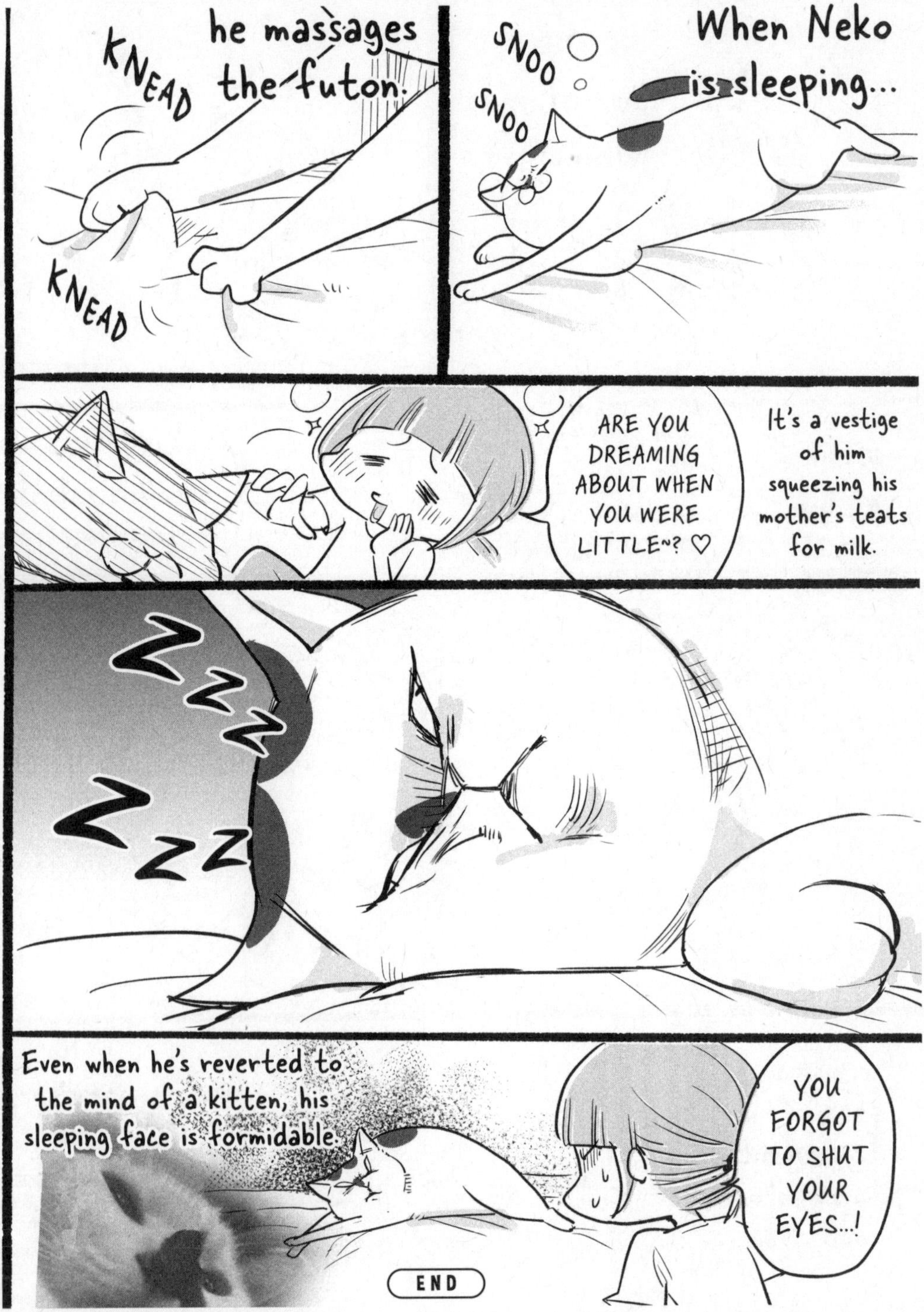
When Neko is sleeping...
SNOO SNOO
he massages the futon.
KNEAD
KNEAD
It's a vestige of him squeezing his mother's teats for milk.
ARE YOU DREAMING ABOUT WHEN YOU WERE LITTLE~? ♡
ZZZ
ZZZ
YOU FORGOT TO SHUT YOUR EYES...!
Even when he's reverted to the mind of a kitten, his sleeping face is formidable.
END

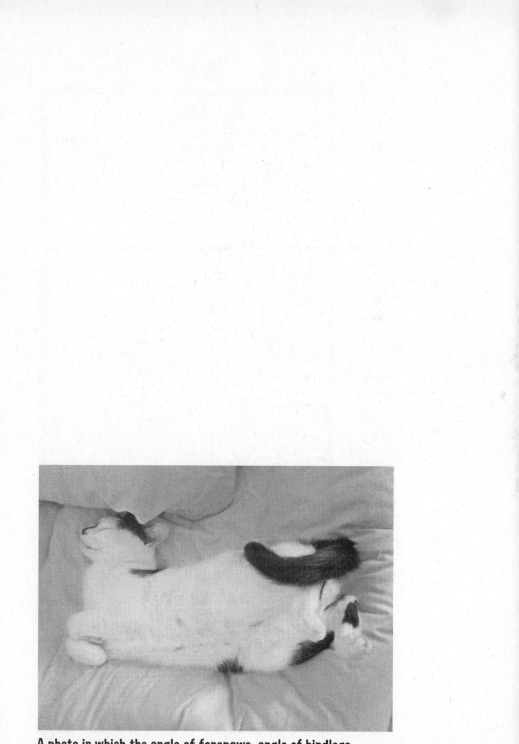

A photo in which the angle of forepaws, angle of hindlegs, and facial expression are all perfect.

Newly-Drawn 4-Panel Strip

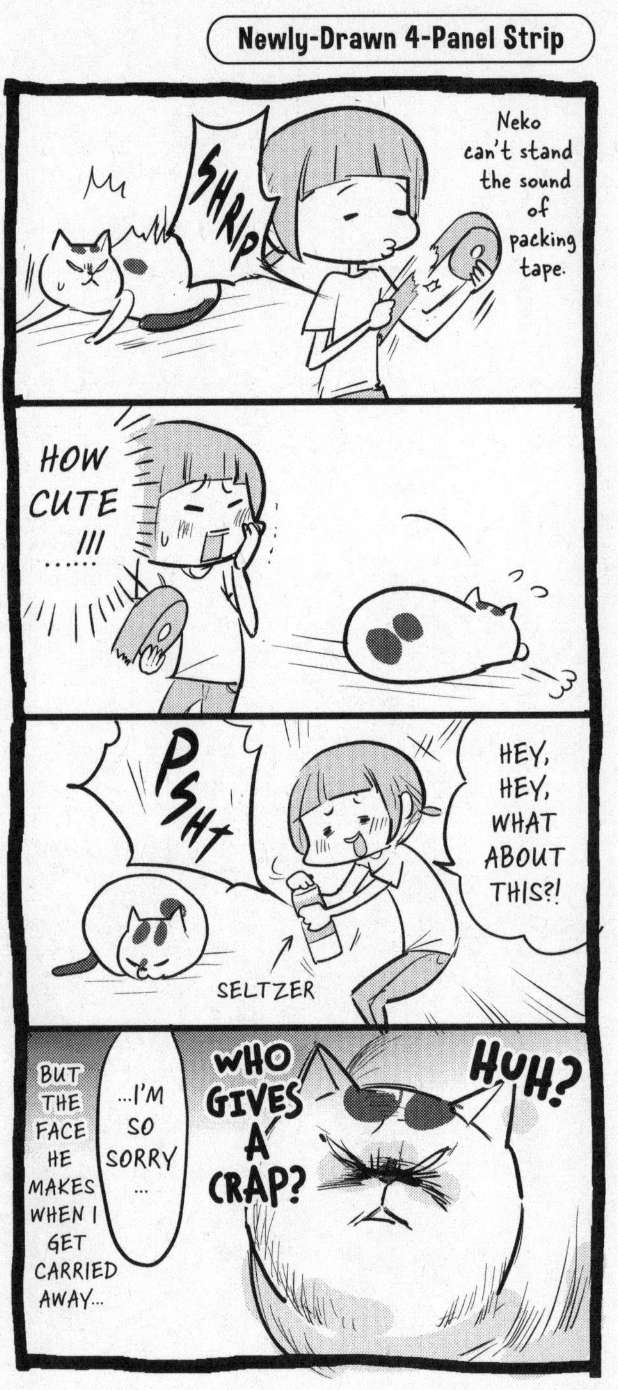
Neko can't stand the sound of packing tape.
SHRIP
HOW CUTE!!!
......
HEY, HEY, WHAT ABOUT THIS?!
PSHT
SELTZER
HUH?
WHO GIVES A CRAP?
...I'M SO SORRY...
BUT THE FACE HE MAKES WHEN I GET CARRIED AWAY...

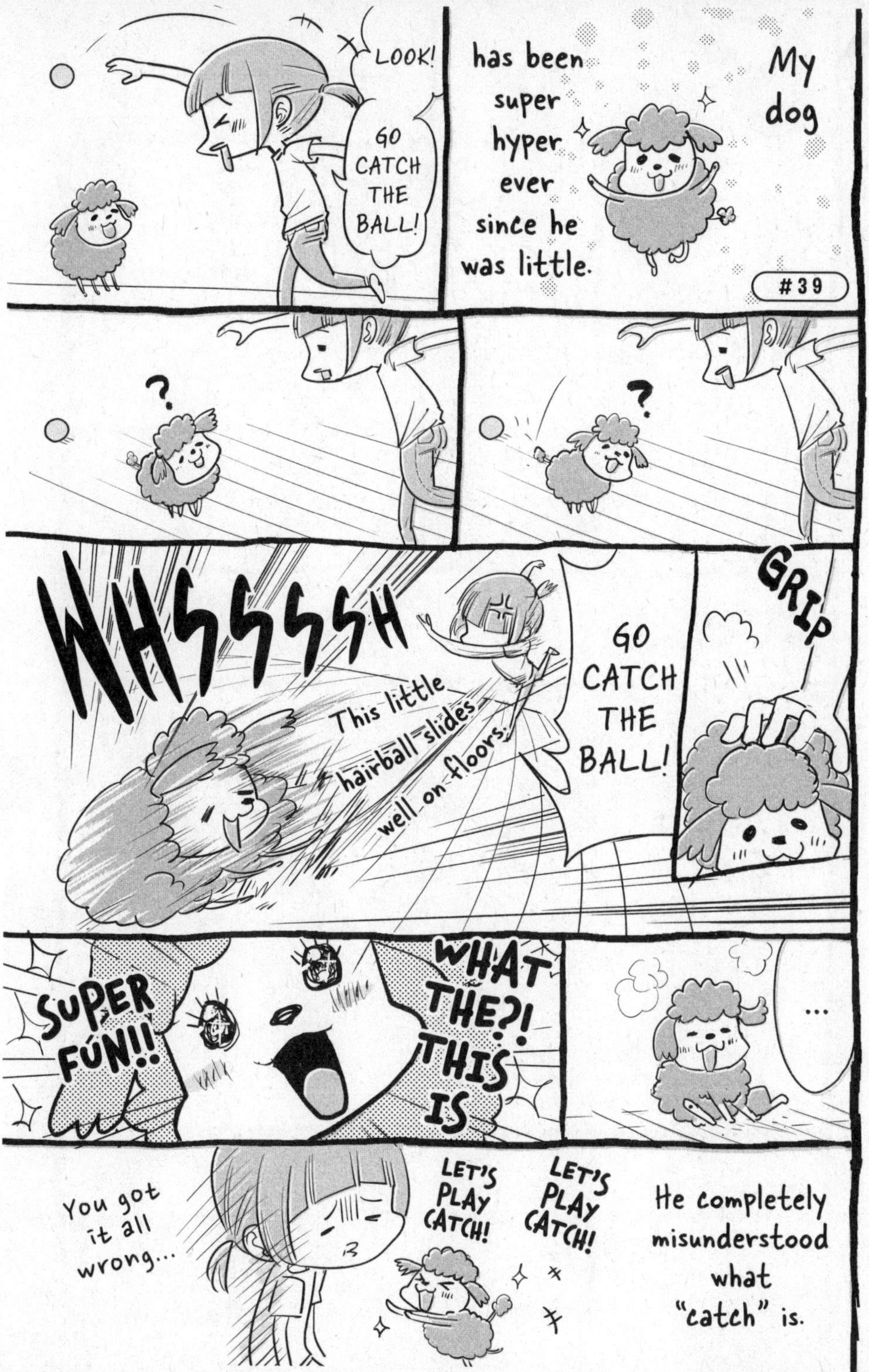
#39
My dog has been super hyper ever since he was little.
LOOK!
GO CATCH THE BALL!
?
?
GRIP
GO CATCH THE BALL!
WHSSSSH
This little hairball slides well on floors.
...
WHAT THE?! THIS IS
SUPER FUN!!
He completely misunderstood what "catch" is.
LET'S PLAY CATCH!
LET'S PLAY CATCH!
You got it all wrong...

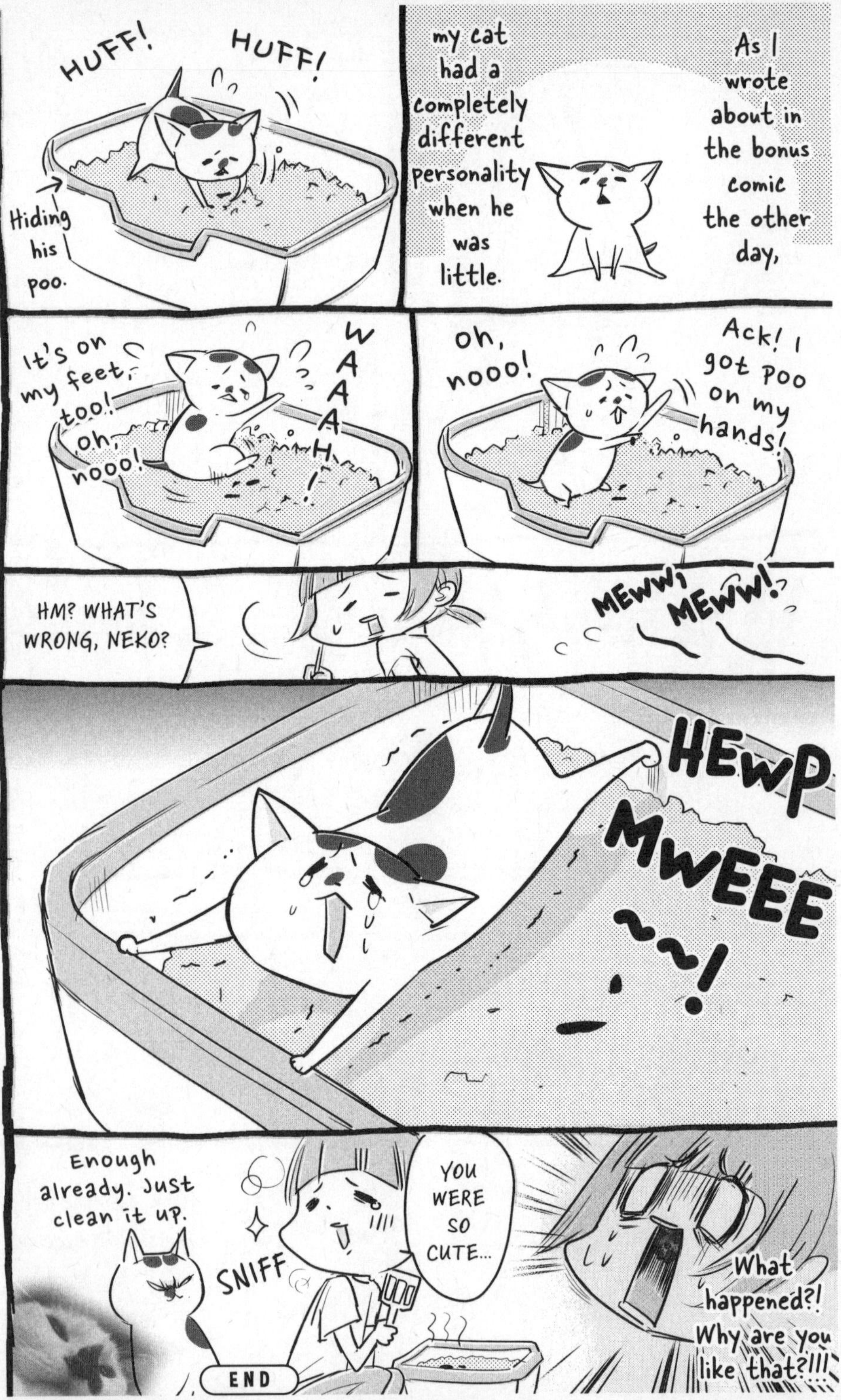
As I wrote about in the bonus comic the other day,
my cat had a completely different personality when he was little.
HUFF! HUFF!
Hiding his poo.
Ack! I got poo on my hands!
Oh, nooo!
WAAAH!
It's on my feet, too! Oh, nooo!
MEWW, MEWW!
HM? WHAT'S WRONG, NEKO?
HEWP MWEEE ~~!
What happened?! Why are you like that?!!!
YOU WERE SO CUTE...
SNIFF
Enough already. Just clean it up.
END

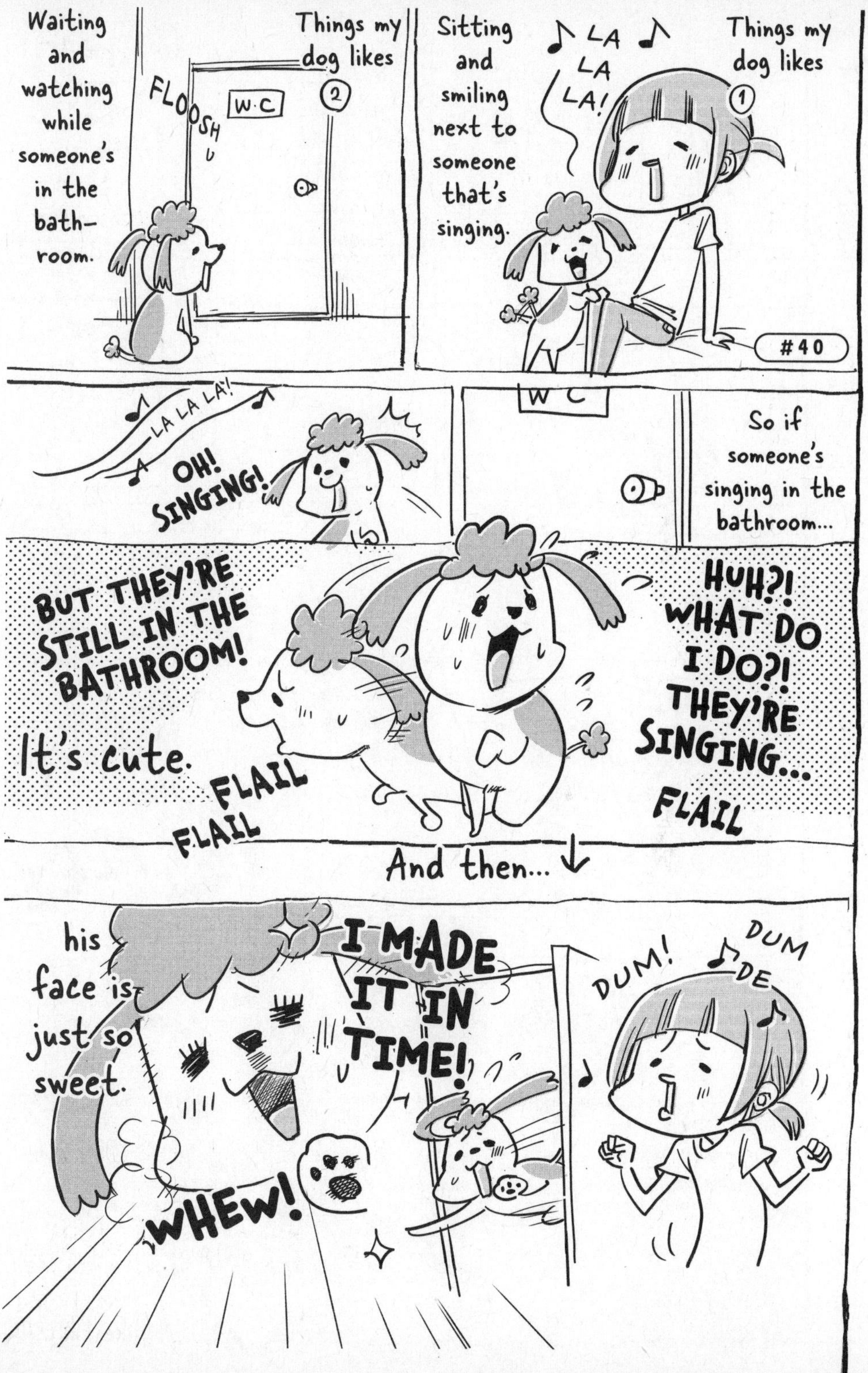
#40
Things my dog likes ①
LA LA LA!
Sitting and smiling next to someone that's singing.
Things my dog likes ②
W.C
FLOOSH
Waiting and watching while someone's in the bathroom.
So if someone's singing in the bathroom...
W C
LA LA LA!
OH! SINGING!
HUH?! WHAT DO I DO?! THEY'RE SINGING...
FLAIL
BUT THEY'RE STILL IN THE BATHROOM!
It's cute.
FLAIL
FLAIL
And then...
DUM DE
DUM!
I MADE IT IN TIME!
his face is just so sweet.
WHEW!

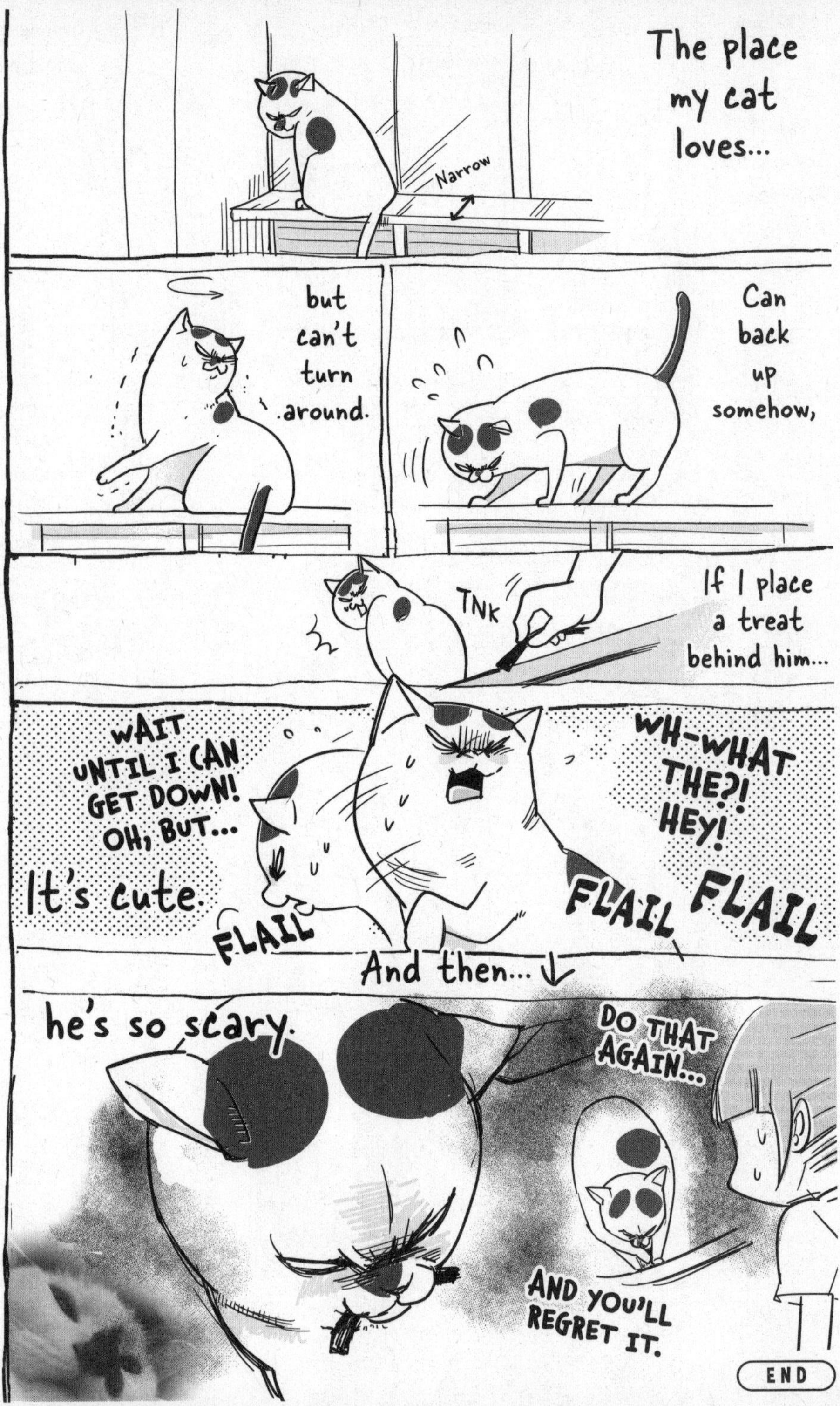
The place my cat loves...
Narrow
Can back up somehow,
but can't turn around.
If I place a treat behind him...
TNK
WH-WHAT THE?! HEY!
FLAIL
FLAIL
WAIT UNTIL I CAN GET DOWN! OH, BUT...
It's cute.
FLAIL
And then...↓
DO THAT AGAIN...
AND YOU'LL REGRET IT.
he's so scary.
END

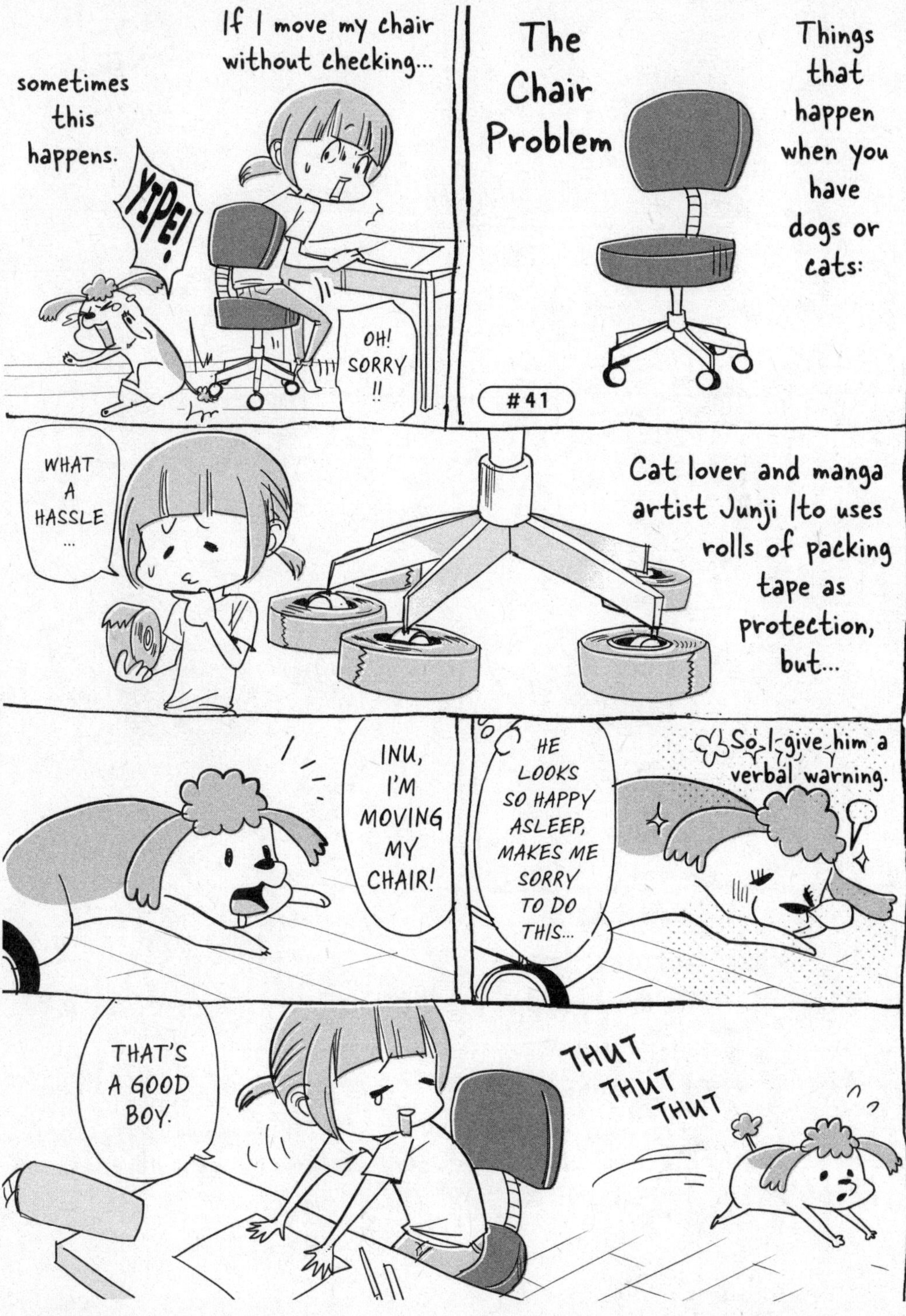
The Chair Problem
Things that happen when you have dogs or cats:
#41
If I move my chair without checking...
sometimes this happens.
YIPE!
OH! SORRY !!
Cat lover and manga artist Junji Ito uses rolls of packing tape as protection, but...
WHAT A HASSLE ...
So I give him a verbal warning.
HE LOOKS SO HAPPY ASLEEP, MAKES ME SORRY TO DO THIS...
INU, I'M MOVING MY CHAIR!
THUT THUT THUT
THAT'S A GOOD BOY.

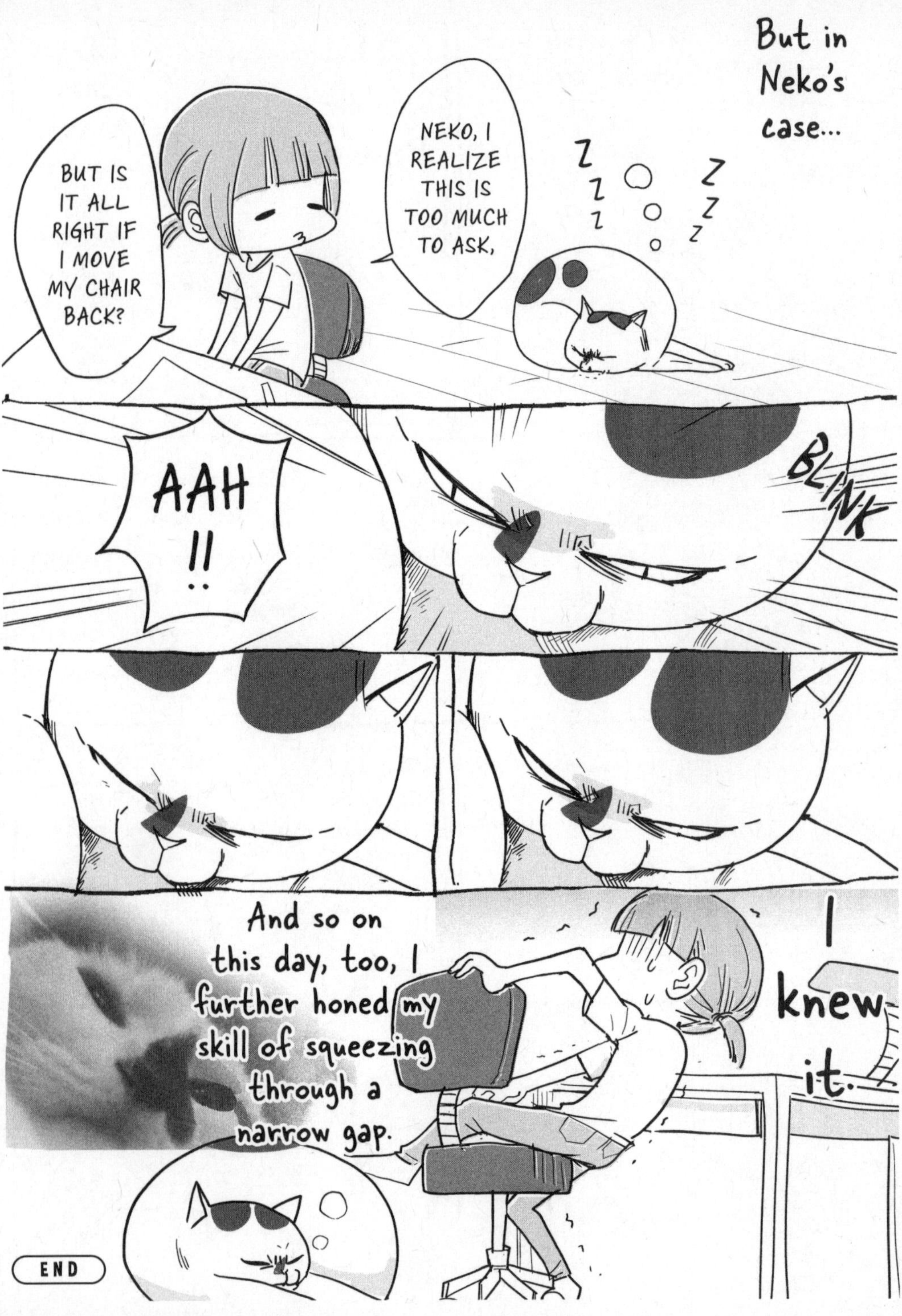

But in Neko's case...
Z Z Z Z Z Z
NEKO, I REALIZE THIS IS TOO MUCH TO ASK,
BUT IS IT ALL RIGHT IF I MOVE MY CHAIR BACK?
BLINK
AAH!!
I knew it.
And so on this day, too, I further honed my skill of squeezing through a narrow gap.
END

A look that pretends Inu isn't even there.

Newly-Drawn 4-Panel Strip

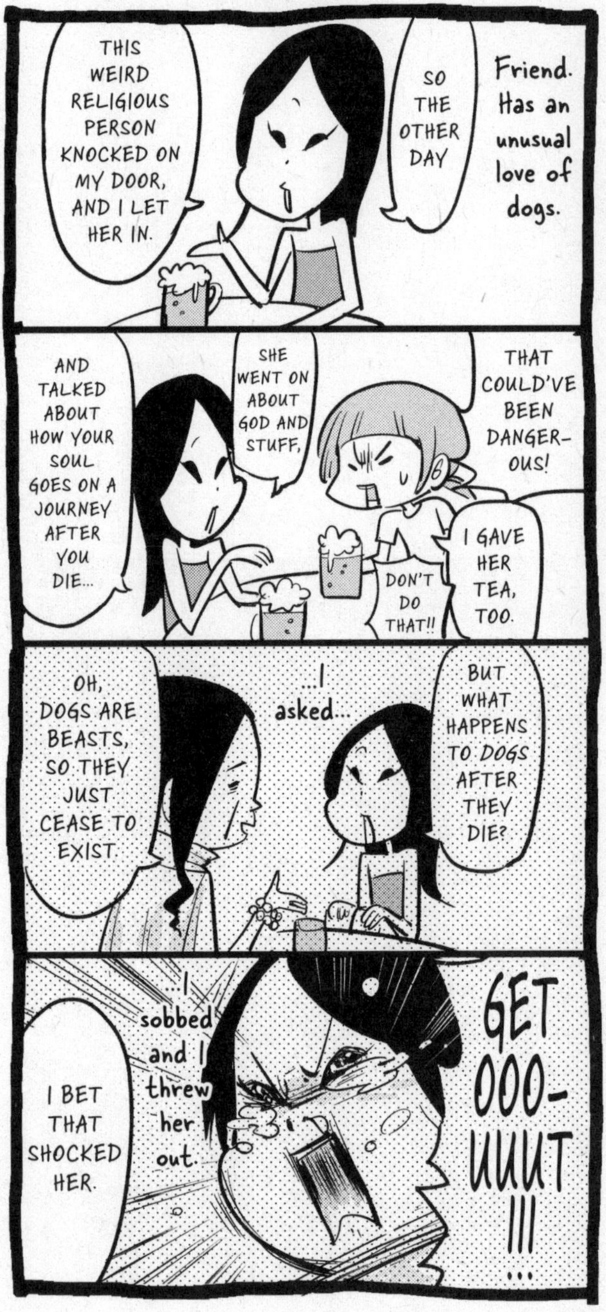

Friend. Has an unusual love of dogs.
SO THE OTHER DAY
THIS WEIRD RELIGIOUS PERSON KNOCKED ON MY DOOR, AND I LET HER IN.
THAT COULD'VE BEEN DANGER-OUS!
SHE WENT ON ABOUT GOD AND STUFF,
AND TALKED ABOUT HOW YOUR SOUL GOES ON A JOURNEY AFTER YOU DIE...
I GAVE HER TEA, TOO.
DON'T DO THAT!!
BUT WHAT HAPPENS TO DOGS AFTER THEY DIE?
...I asked...
OH, DOGS ARE BEASTS, SO THEY JUST CEASE TO EXIST.
GET OOO-UUUT!!!...
...I sobbed and I threw her out.
I BET THAT SHOCKED HER.

New Comic Siblings (1)

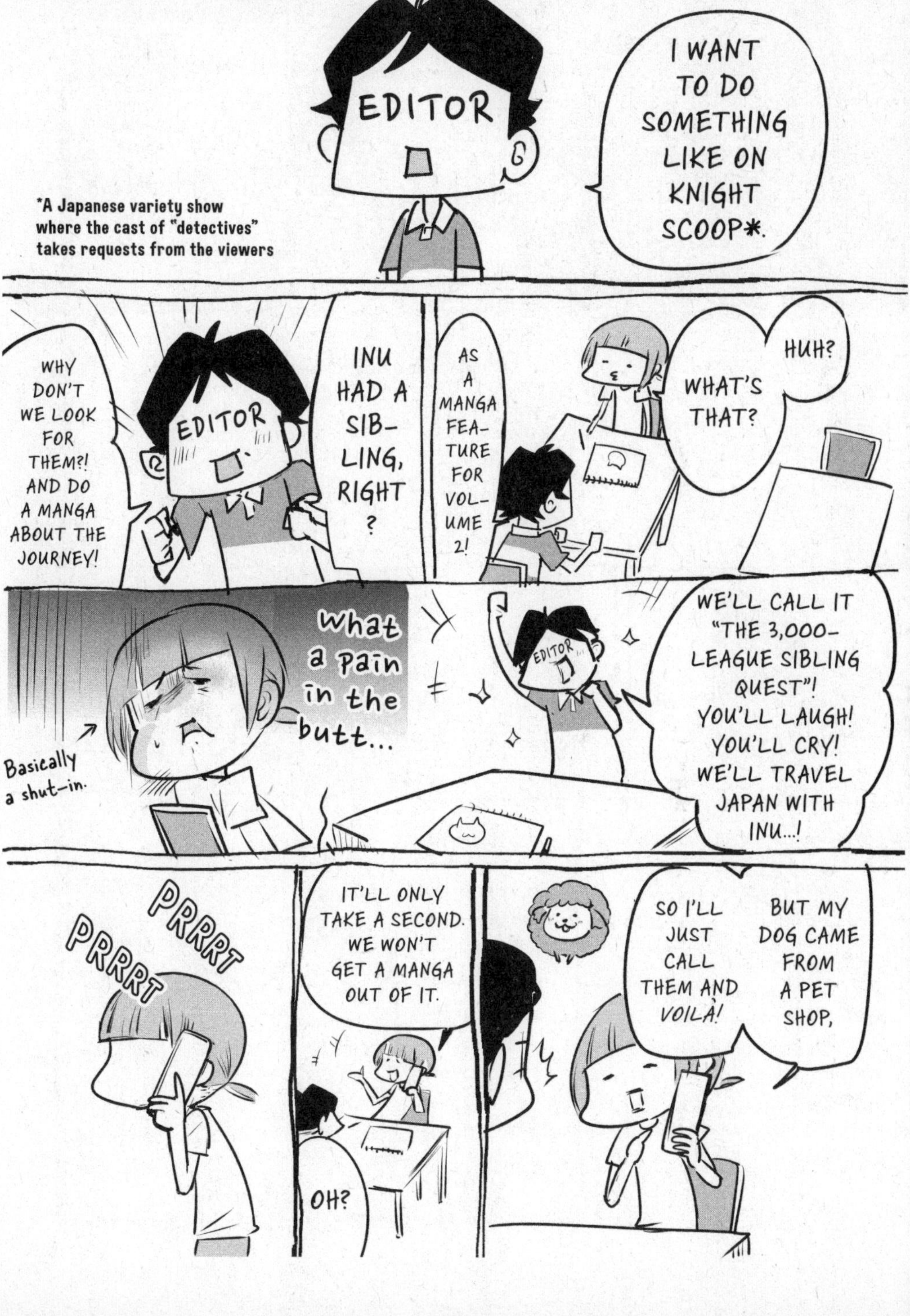
EDITOR
I WANT TO DO SOMETHING LIKE ON KNIGHT SCOOP*.
*A Japanese variety show where the cast of "detectives" takes requests from the viewers
HUH?
WHAT'S THAT?
AS A MANGA FEATURE FOR VOLUME 2!
INU HAD A SIBLING, RIGHT?
EDITOR
WHY DON'T WE LOOK FOR THEM?! AND DO A MANGA ABOUT THE JOURNEY!
WE'LL CALL IT "THE 3,000-LEAGUE SIBLING QUEST"! YOU'LL LAUGH! YOU'LL CRY! WE'LL TRAVEL JAPAN WITH INU...!
EDITOR
what a pain in the butt...
Basically a shut-in.
BUT MY DOG CAME FROM A PET SHOP,
SO I'LL JUST CALL THEM AND VOILÀ!
IT'LL ONLY TAKE A SECOND. WE WON'T GET A MANGA OUT OF IT.
OH?
PRRRT
PRRRT

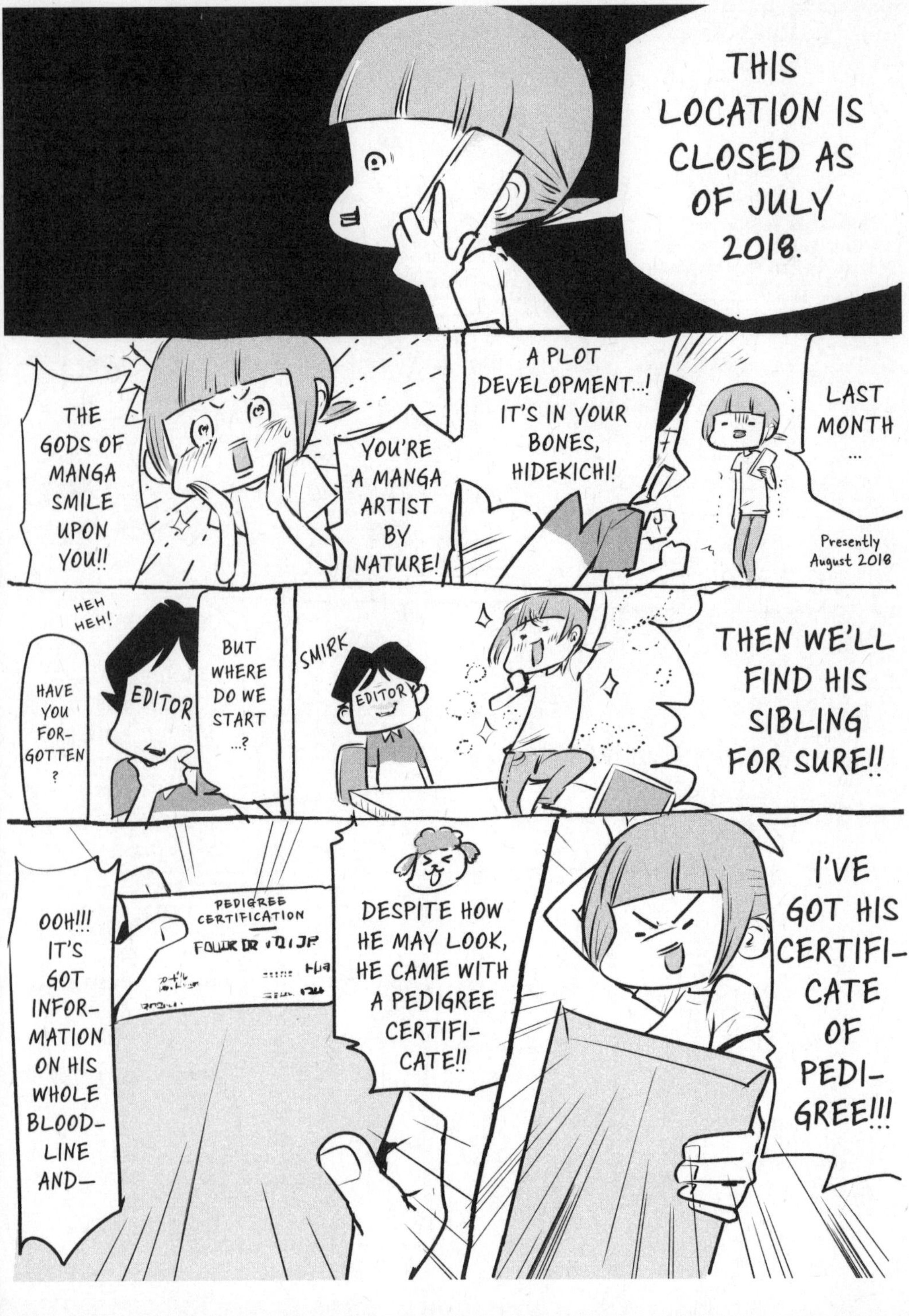
THIS LOCATION IS CLOSED AS OF JULY 2018.
LAST MONTH ...
Presently August 2018
A PLOT DEVELOPMENT...! IT'S IN YOUR BONES, HIDEKICHI!
YOU'RE A MANGA ARTIST BY NATURE!
THE GODS OF MANGA SMILE UPON YOU!!
THEN WE'LL FIND HIS SIBLING FOR SURE!!
SMIRK
EDITOR
BUT WHERE DO WE START ...?
HEH HEH!
EDITOR
HAVE YOU FOR-GOTTEN ?
I'VE GOT HIS CERTIFI-CATE OF PEDI-GREE!!!
DESPITE HOW HE MAY LOOK, HE CAME WITH A PEDIGREE CERTIFI-CATE!!
PEDIGREE CERTIFICATION
OOH!!! IT'S GOT INFOR-MATION ON HIS WHOLE BLOOD-LINE AND—

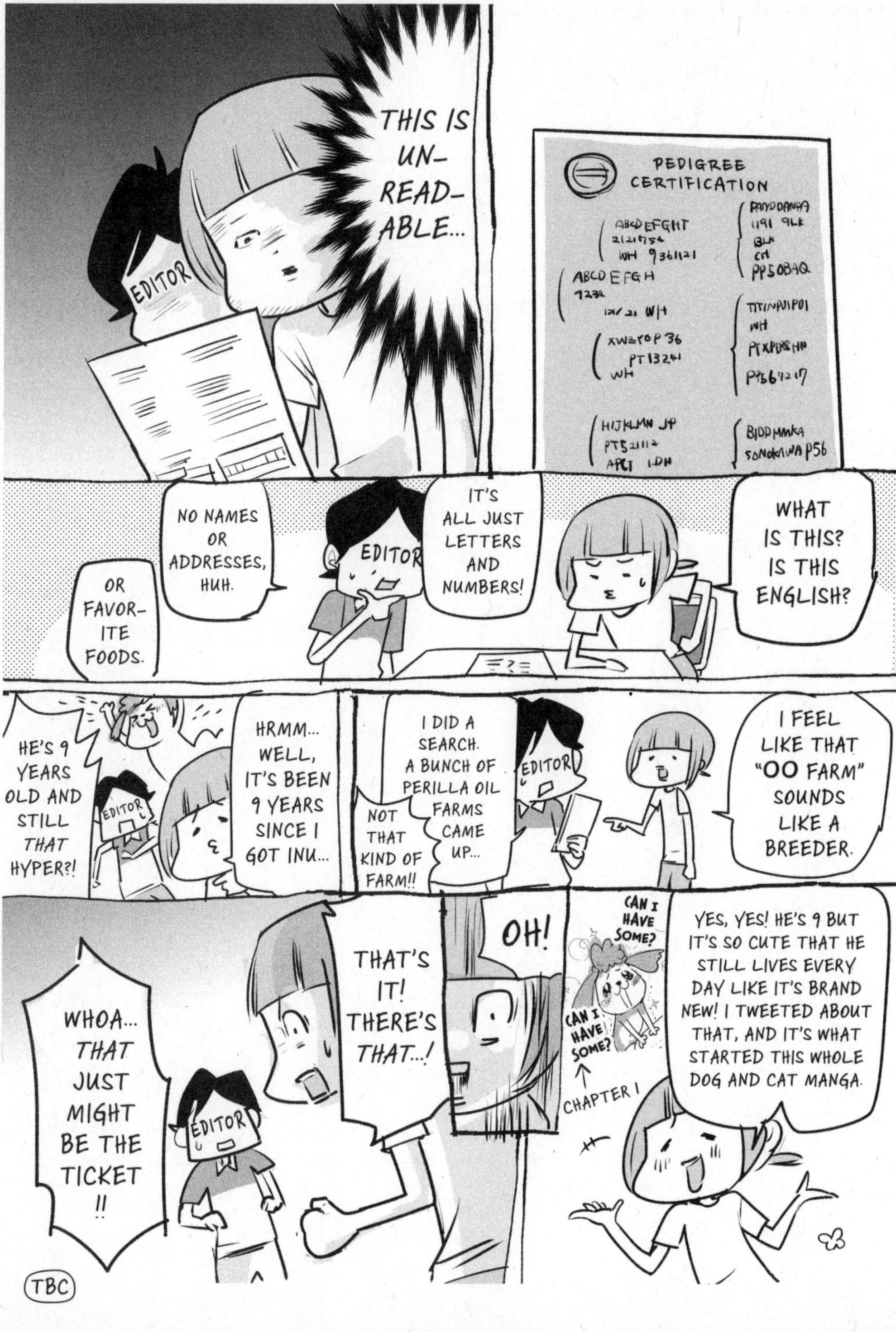
PEDIGREE CERTIFICATION
THIS IS UN-READ-ABLE...
EDITOR
WHAT IS THIS? IS THIS ENGLISH?
IT'S ALL JUST LETTERS AND NUMBERS!
EDITOR
NO NAMES OR ADDRESSES, HUH.
OR FAVOR-ITE FOODS.
I FEEL LIKE THAT "OO FARM" SOUNDS LIKE A BREEDER.
EDITOR
I DID A SEARCH. A BUNCH OF PERILLA OIL FARMS CAME UP...
NOT THAT KIND OF FARM!!
HRMM... WELL, IT'S BEEN 9 YEARS SINCE I GOT INU...
HE'S 9 YEARS OLD AND STILL THAT HYPER?!
EDITOR
YES, YES! HE'S 9 BUT IT'S SO CUTE THAT HE STILL LIVES EVERY DAY LIKE IT'S BRAND NEW! I TWEETED ABOUT THAT, AND IT'S WHAT STARTED THIS WHOLE DOG AND CAT MANGA.
CAN I HAVE SOME?
CAN I HAVE SOME?
CHAPTER 1
OH!
THAT'S IT! THERE'S THAT...!
WHOA... THAT JUST MIGHT BE THE TICKET!!
EDITOR
TBC

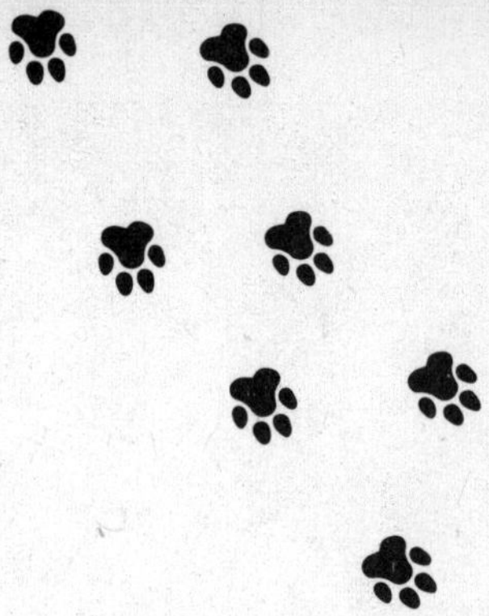

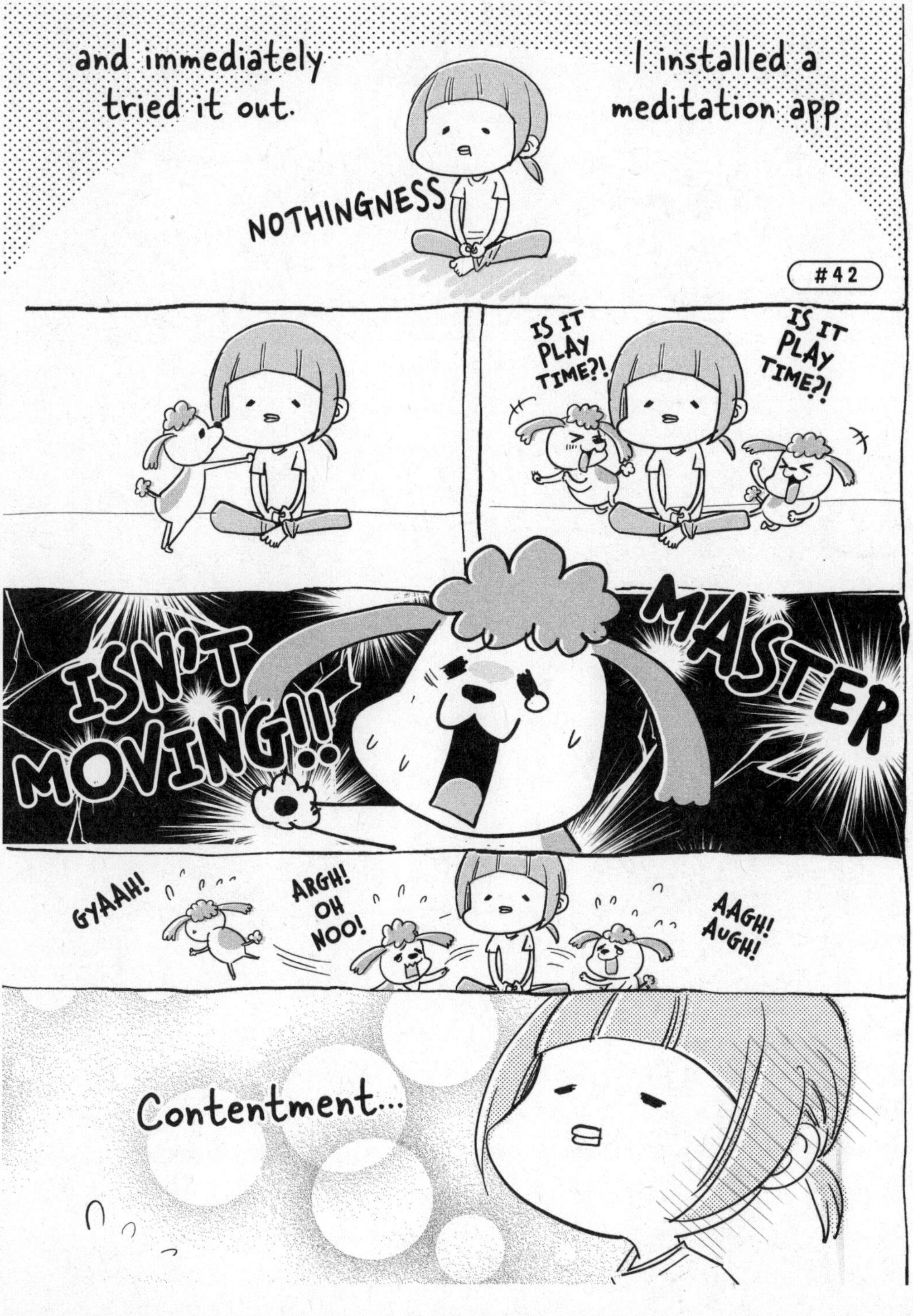
I installed a meditation app
and immediately tried it out.
NOTHINGNESS
#42
IS IT PLAY TIME?!
IS IT PLAY TIME?!
MASTER ISN'T MOVING!!
AAGH! AUGH!
ARGH! OH NOO!
GYAAH!
Contentment...

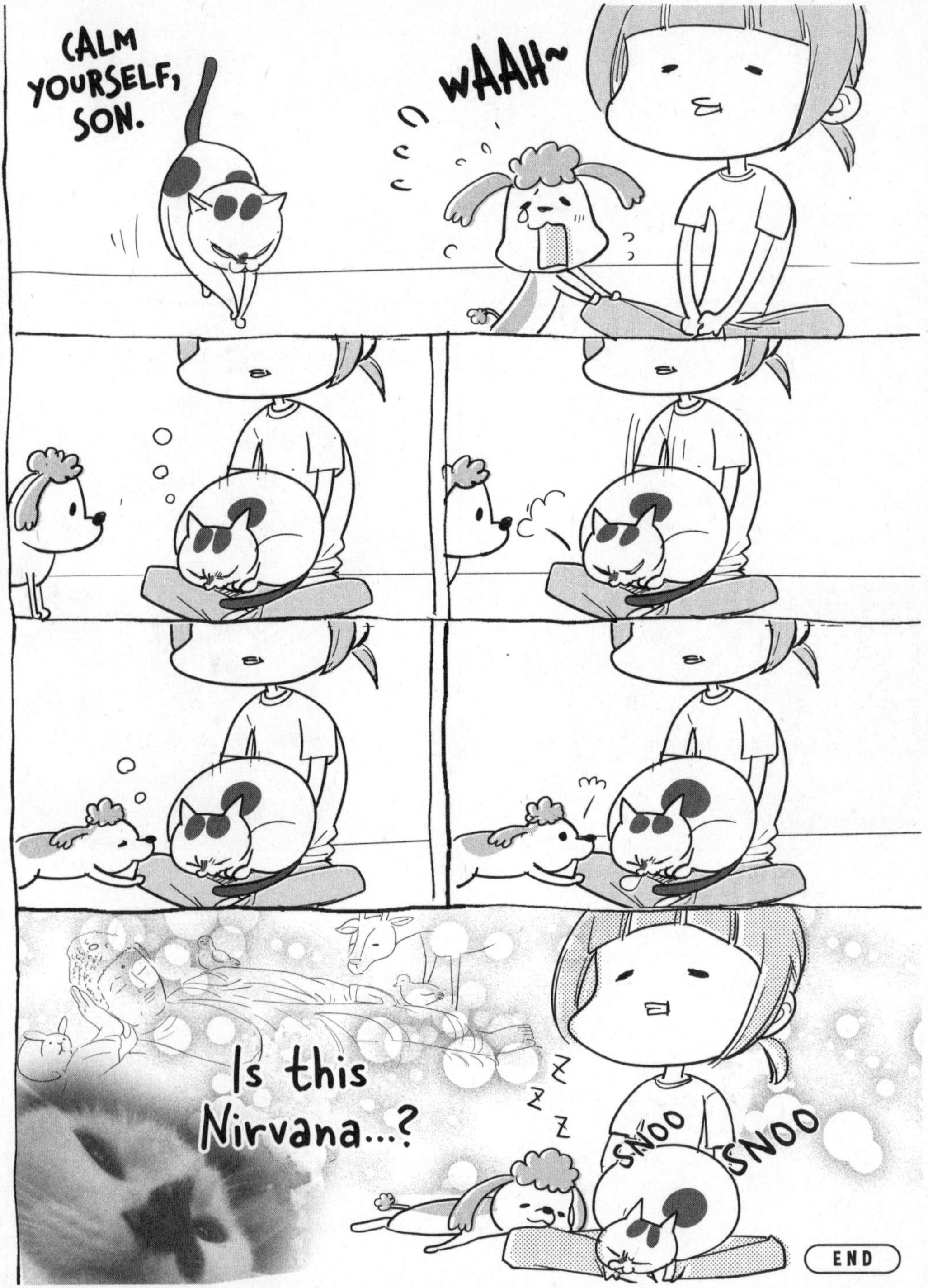
wAAH~
CALM YOURSELF, SON.
Z Z Z
SNOO SNOO
Is this Nirvana...?
END

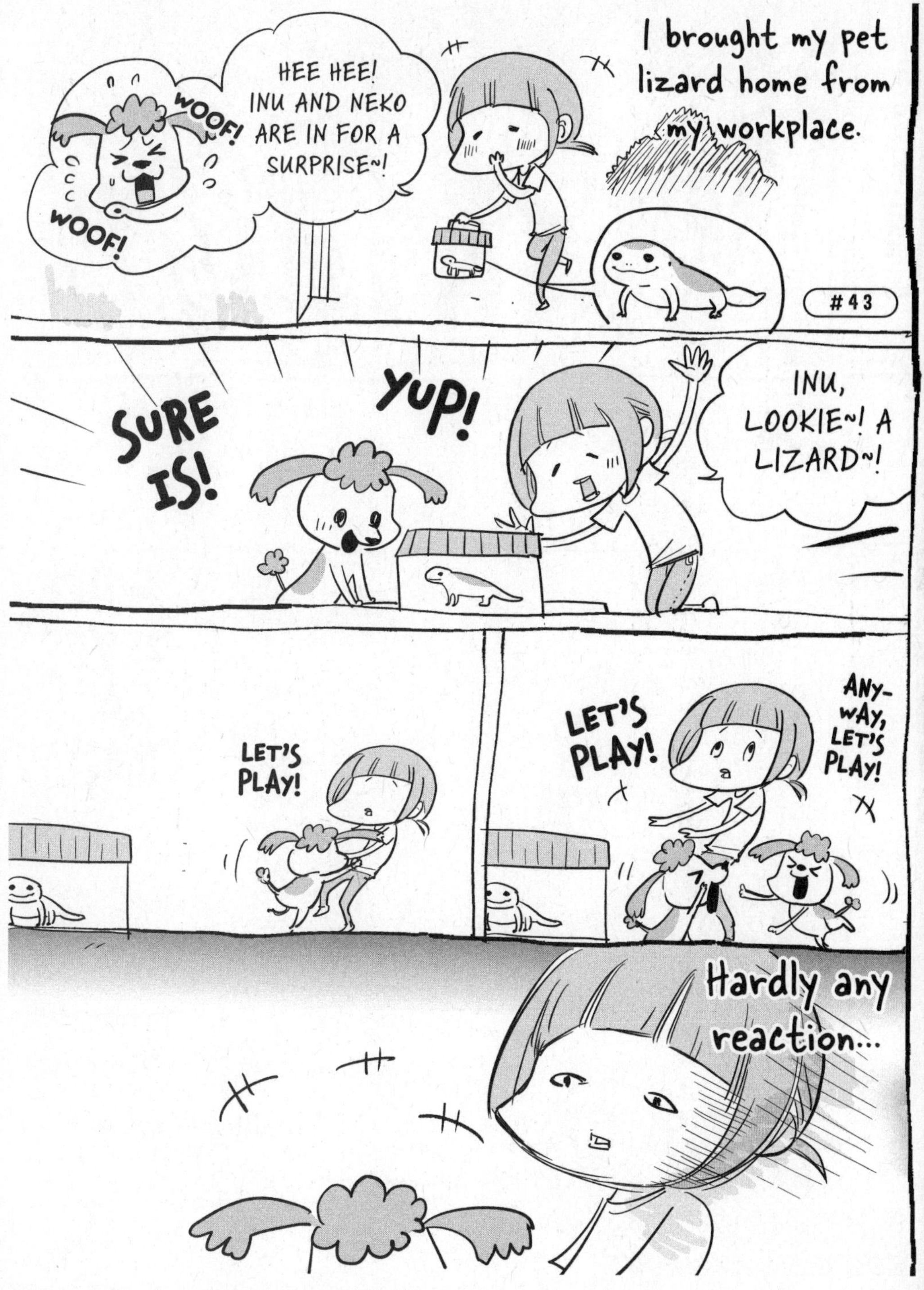
I brought my pet lizard home from my workplace.
#43
HEE HEE! INU AND NEKO ARE IN FOR A SURPRISE~!
WOOF!
WOOF!
INU, LOOKIE~! A LIZARD~!
YUP!
SURE IS!
ANY-WAY, LET'S PLAY!
LET'S PLAY!
LET'S PLAY!
Hardly any reaction...

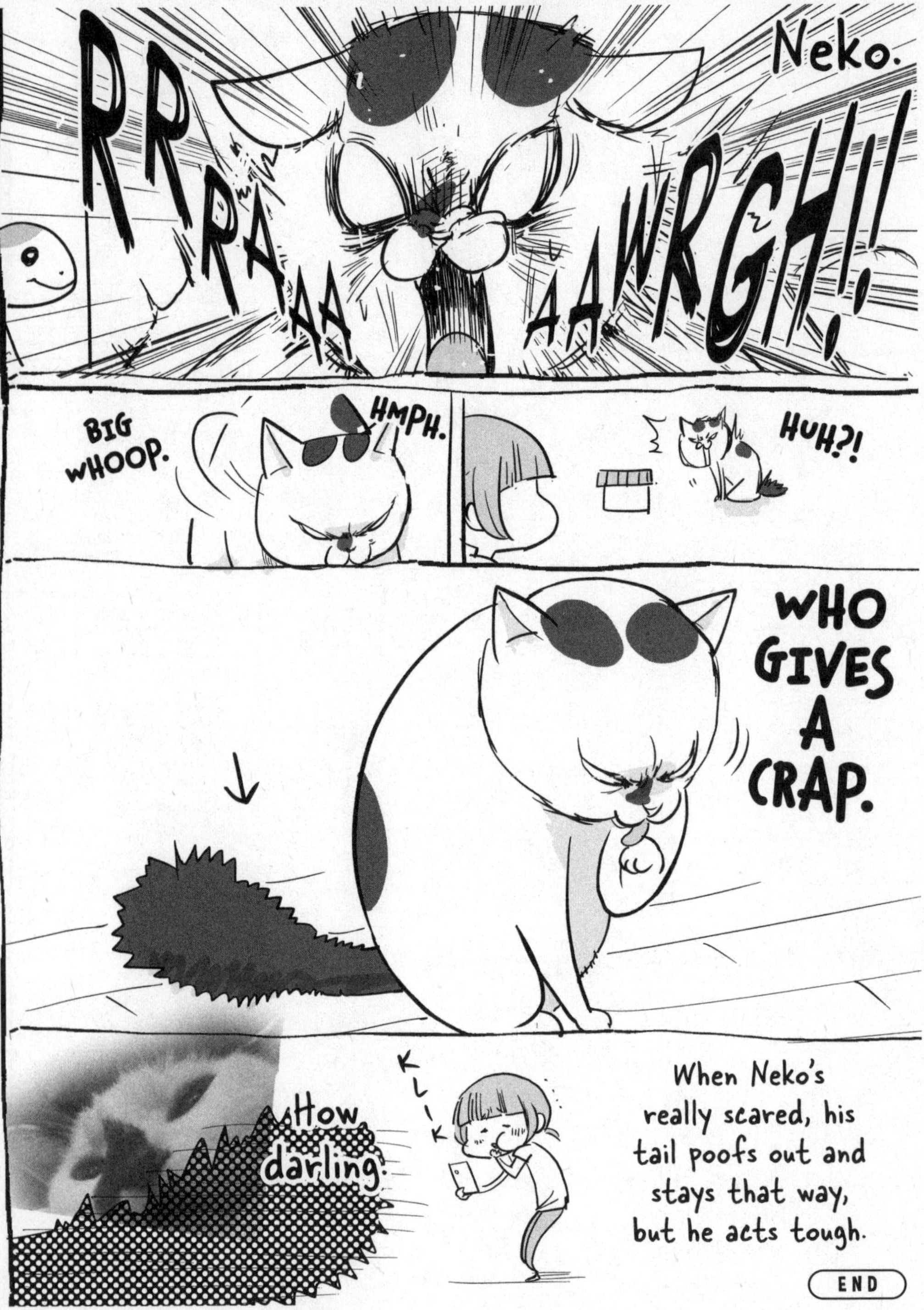
Neko.
RRRAAAAAAWRGH!!
HUH?!
HMPH.
BIG WHOOP.
WHO GIVES A CRAP.
When Neko's really scared, his tail poofs out and stays that way, but he acts tough.
END
KLIK
How darling.

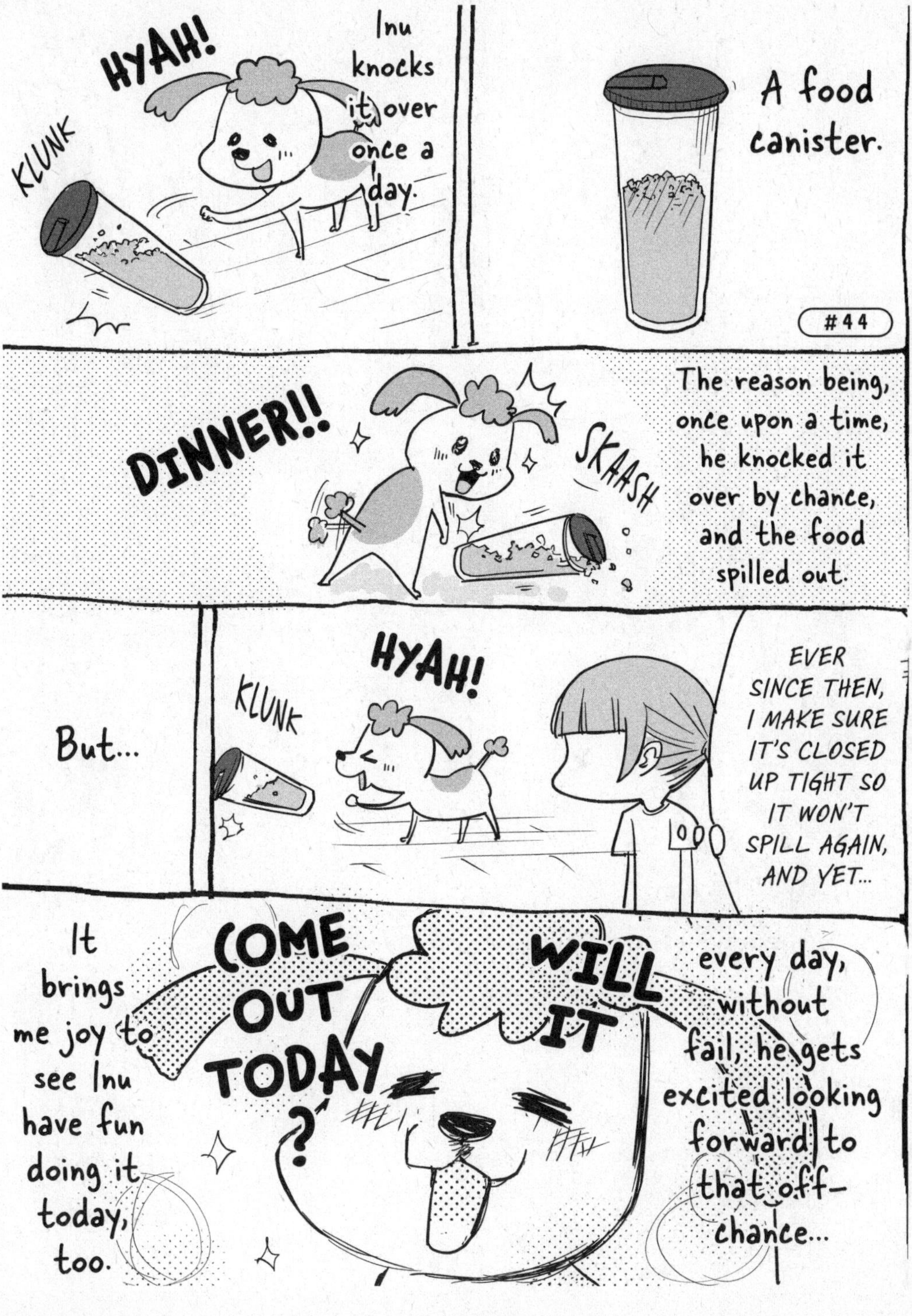
A food canister.
#44
Inu knocks it over once a day.
HYAH!
KLUNK
The reason being, once upon a time, he knocked it over by chance, and the food spilled out.
SKAASH
DINNER!!
EVER SINCE THEN, I MAKE SURE IT'S CLOSED UP TIGHT SO IT WON'T SPILL AGAIN, AND YET...
HYAH!
KLUNK
But...
every day, without fail, he gets excited looking forward to that off-chance...
WILL IT
COME OUT TODAY
?
It brings me joy to see Inu have fun doing it today, too.

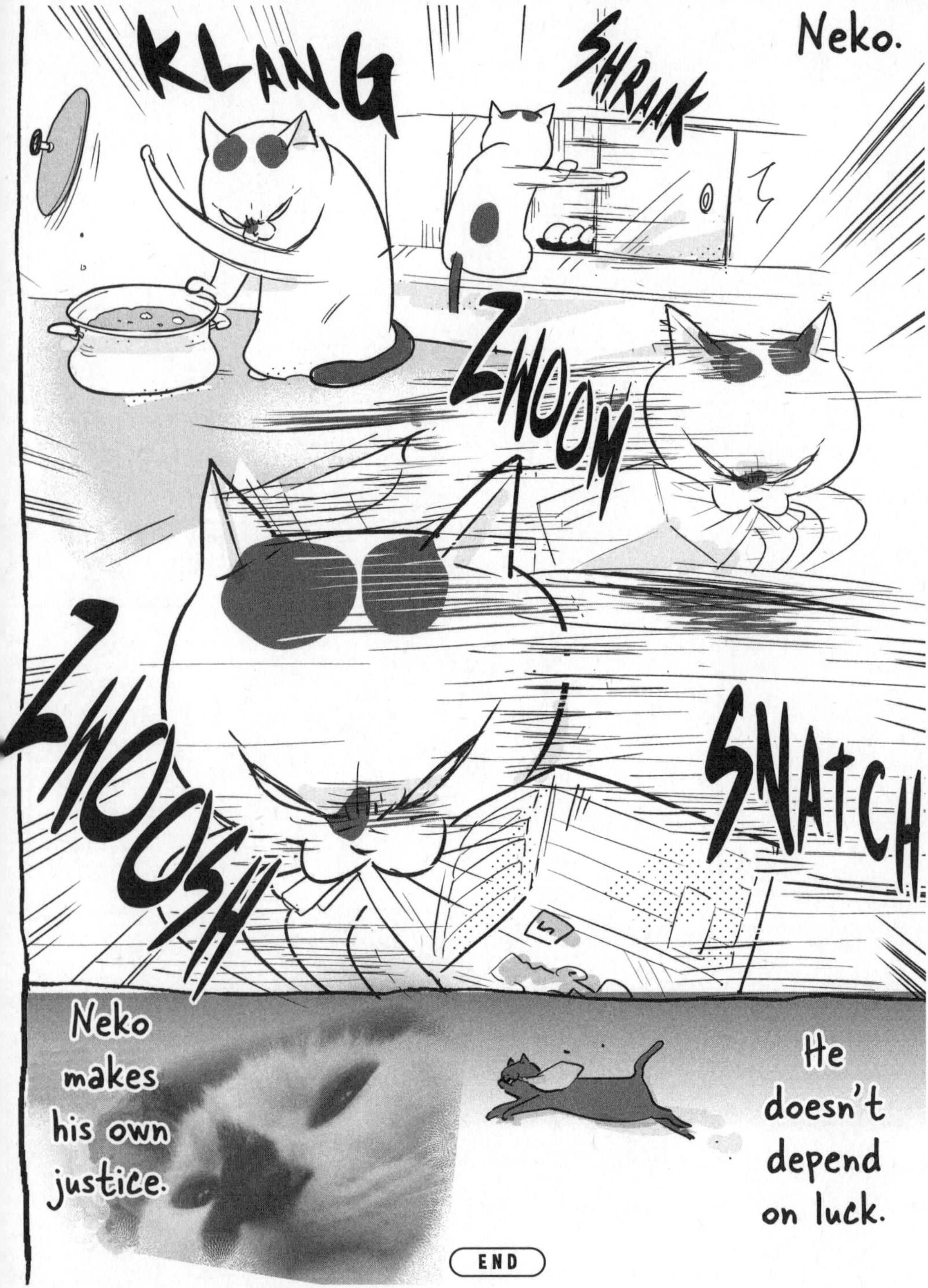
Neko.
SHRAAK
KLANG
ZWOOM
SNATCH
ZWOOSH
He doesn't depend on luck.
Neko makes his own justice.
END

Beaming with joy for a present I got at a signing.

Newly-Drawn 4-Panel Strip

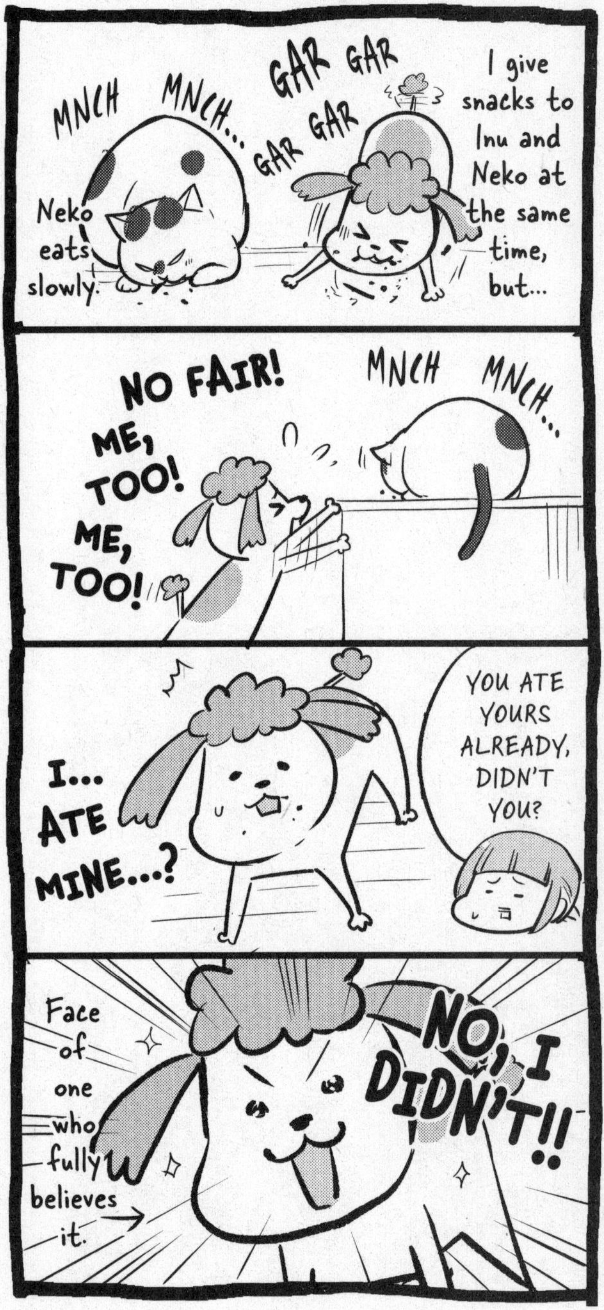

I give snacks to Inu and Neko at the same time, but...
GAR GAR
GAR GAR
MNCH MNCH...
Neko eats slowly.
MNCH MNCH...
NO FAIR!
ME, TOO!
ME, TOO!
YOU ATE YOURS ALREADY, DIDN'T YOU?
I... ATE MINE...?
NO, I DIDN'T!!
Face of one who fully believes it.

#45

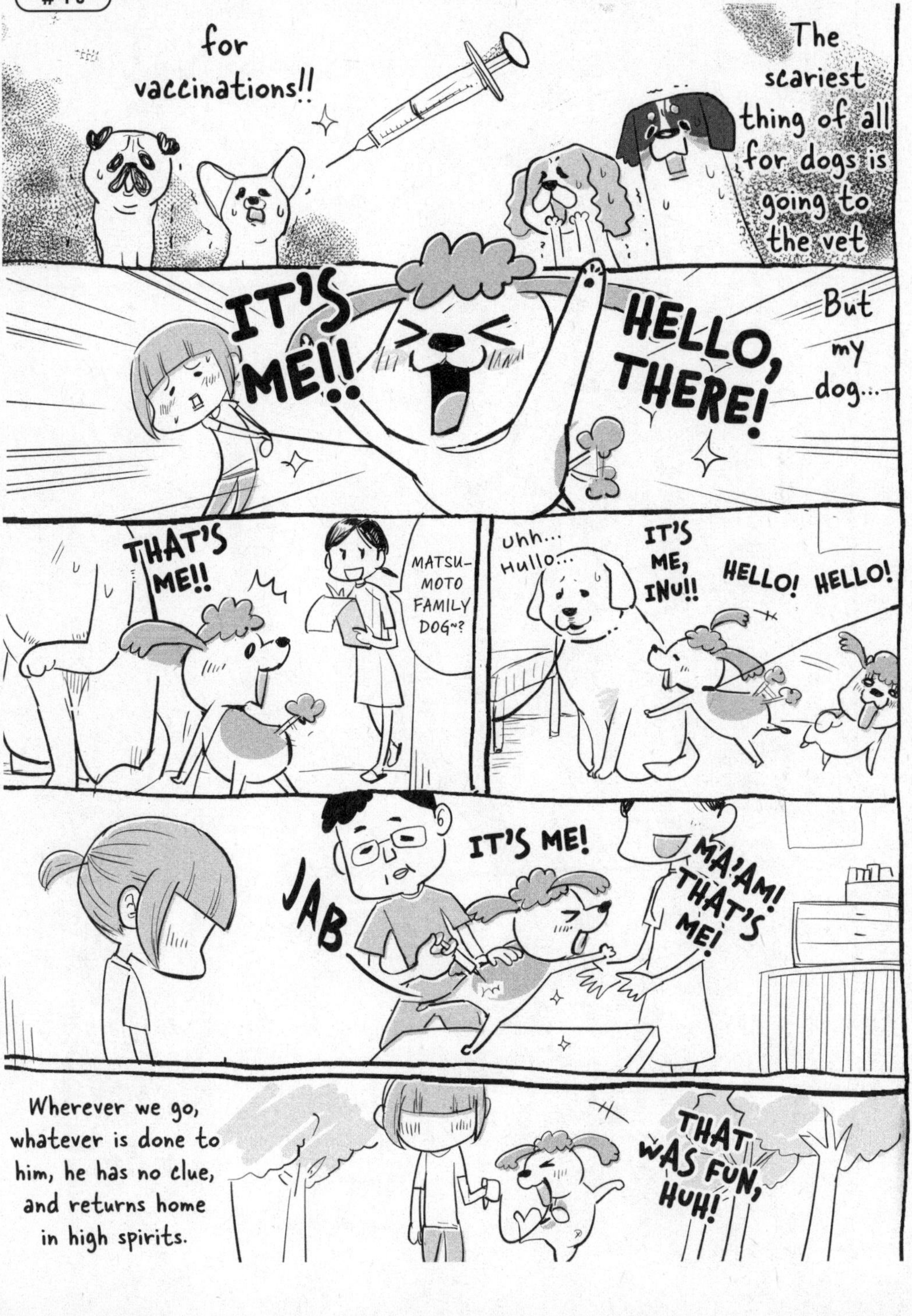
The scariest thing of all for dogs is going to the vet
for vaccinations!!
But my dog...
HELLO, THERE!
IT'S ME!!
MATSU-MOTO FAMILY DOG~?
THAT'S ME!!
IT'S ME, INU!!
uhh... Hullo...
HELLO! HELLO!
MA'AM! THAT'S ME!
IT'S ME!
JAB
THAT WAS FUN, HUH!
Wherever we go, whatever is done to him, he has no clue, and returns home in high spirits.

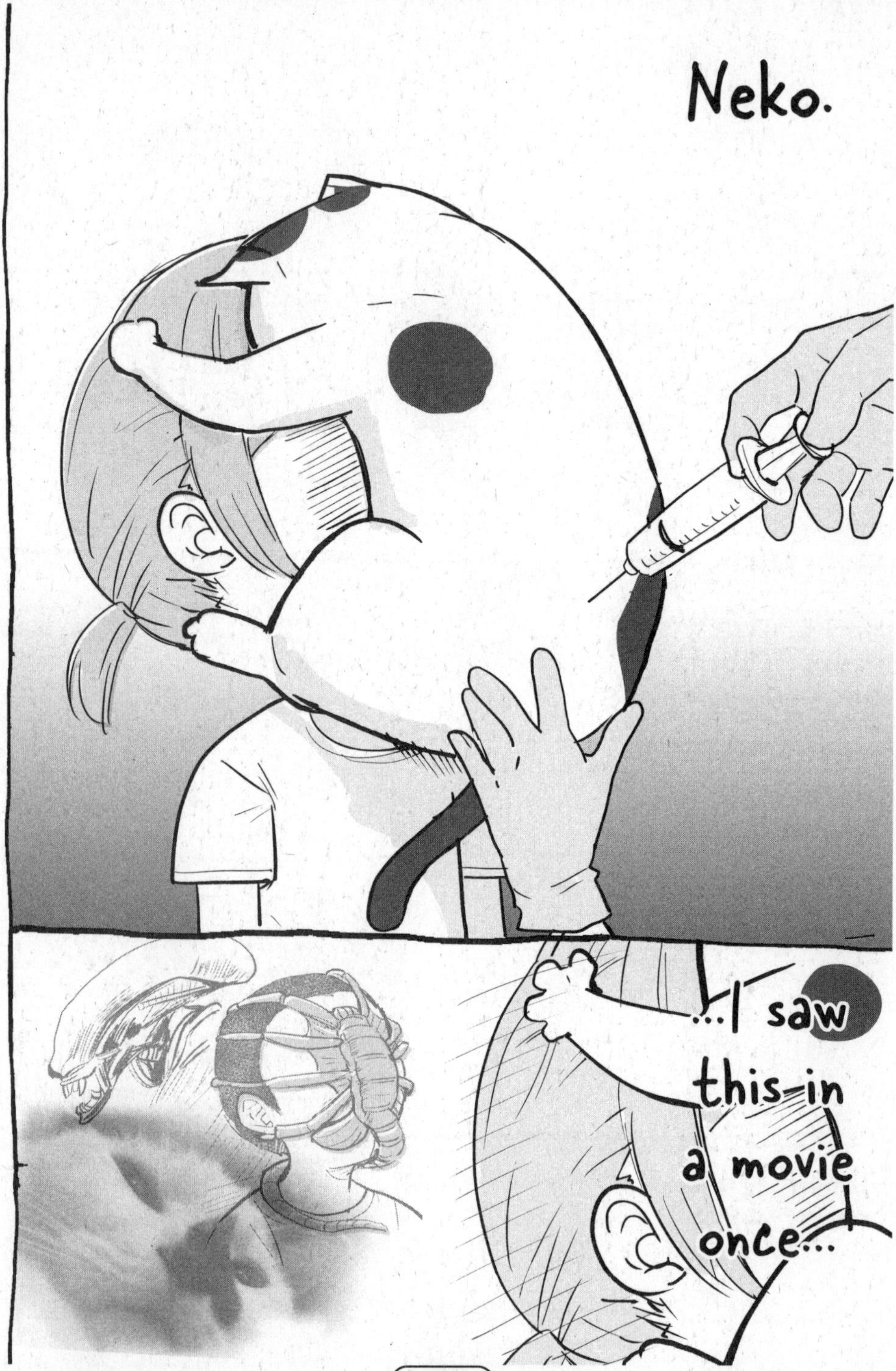
Neko.
...I saw this in a movie once...

END

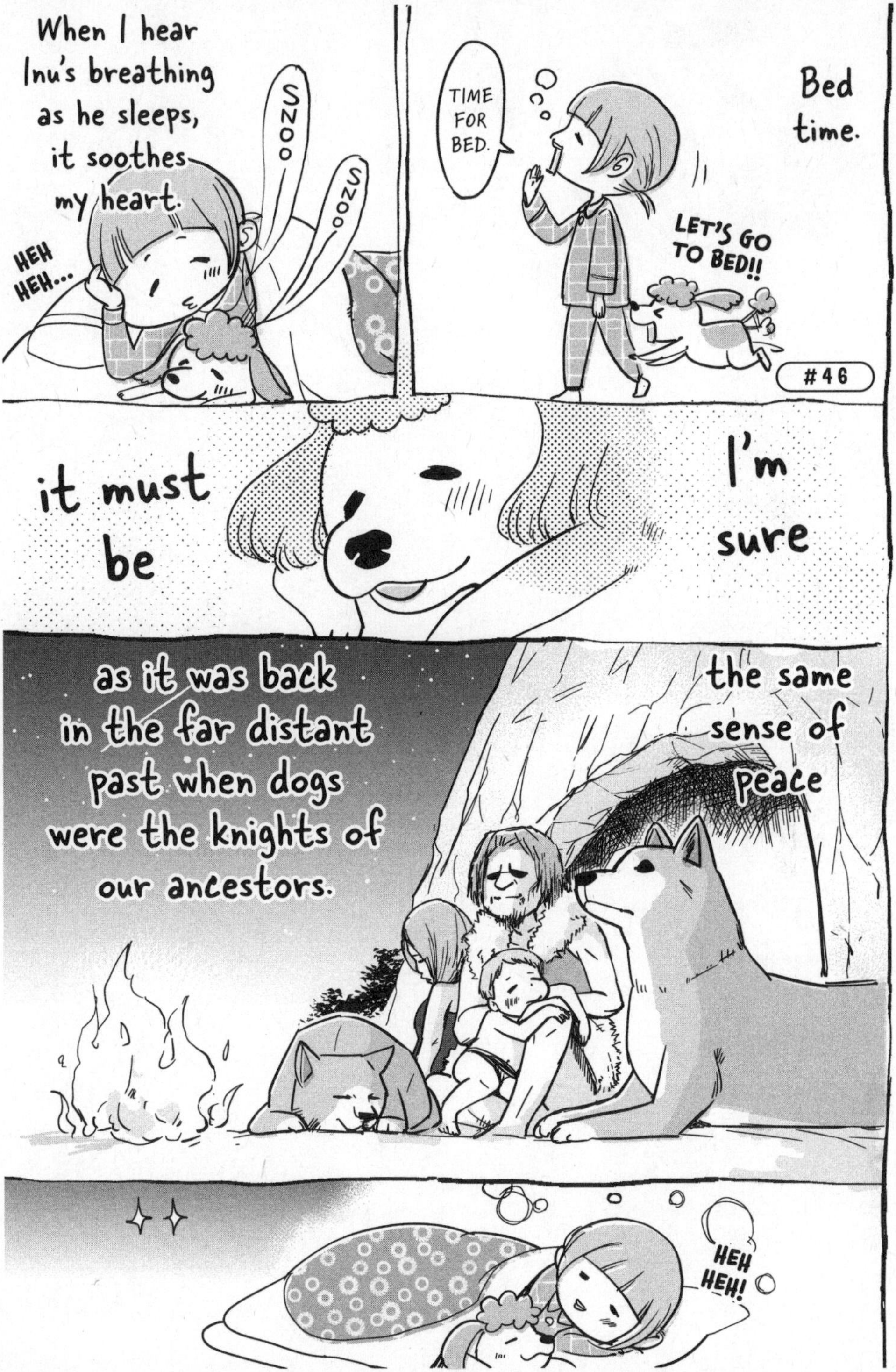
Bed time.
TIME FOR BED.
LET'S GO TO BED!!
#46
When I hear Inu's breathing as he sleeps, it soothes my heart.
SNOO
SNOO
HEH HEH...
I'm sure
it must be
the same sense of peace
as it was back in the far distant past when dogs were the knights of our ancestors.
HEH HEH!

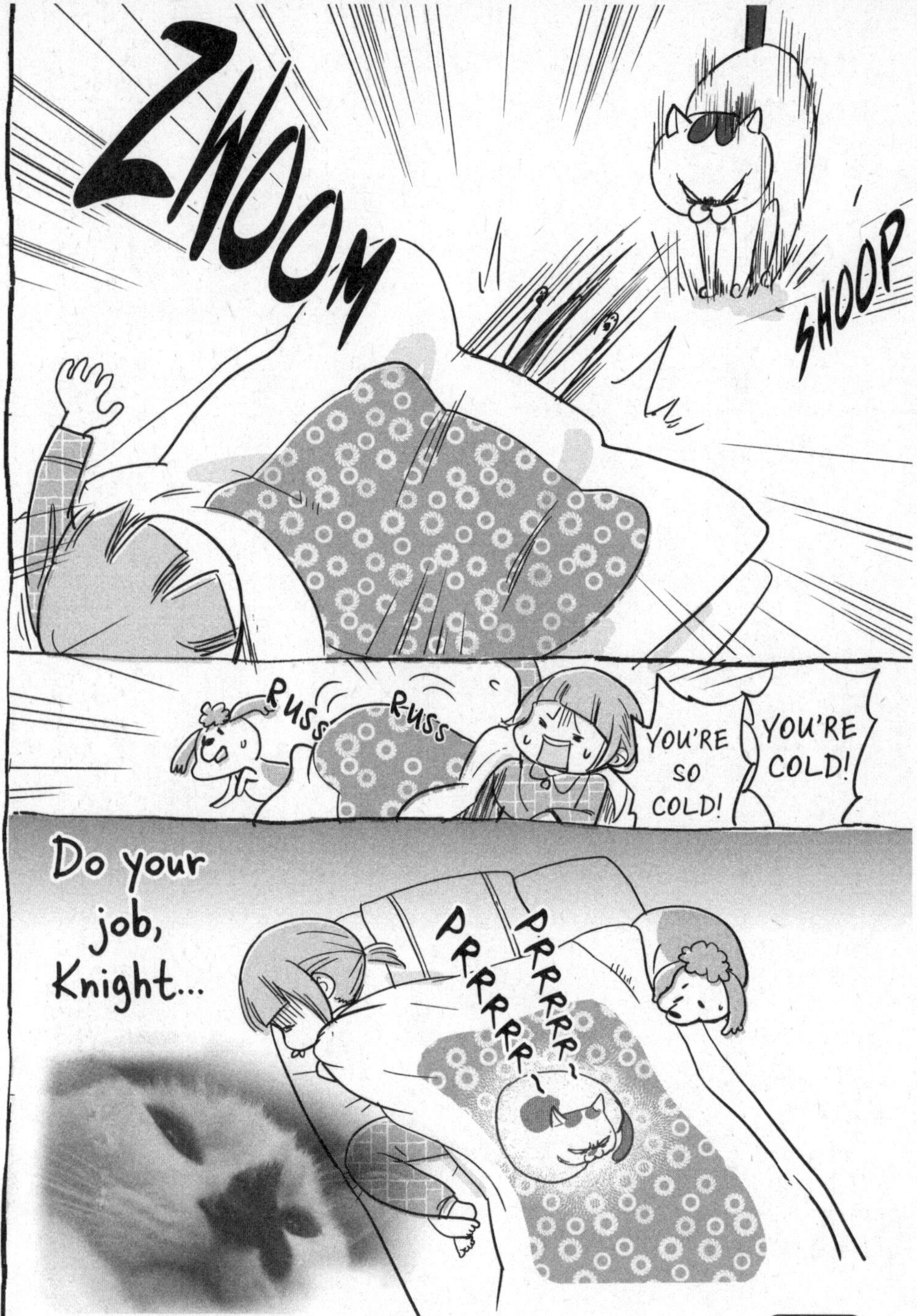
SHOOP
ZWOOM
YOU'RE COLD!
YOU'RE SO COLD!
RUSS
RUSS
PRRRRRR
PRRRRRR
Do your job, Knight...

END

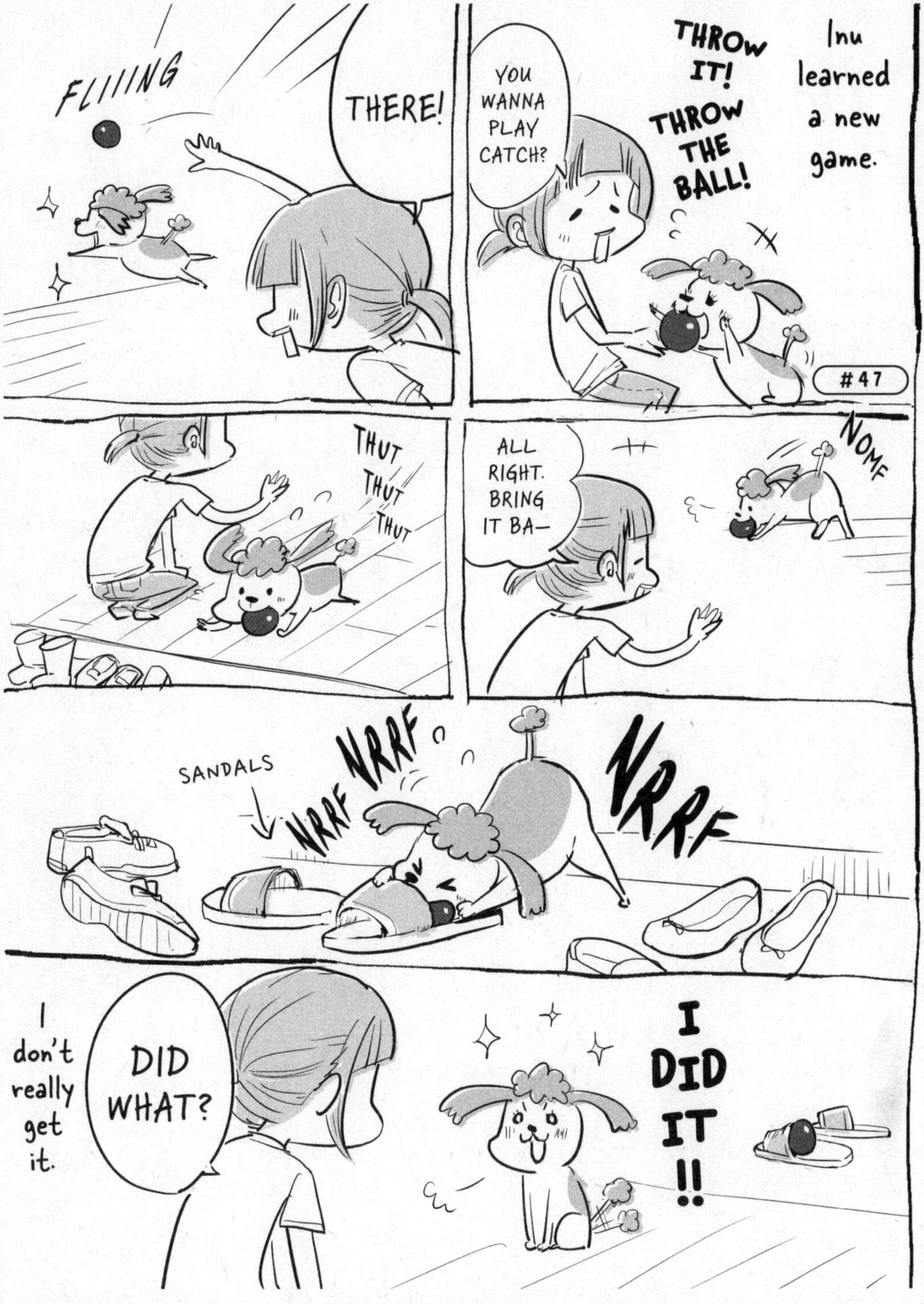
Inu learned a new game.
THROW IT! THROW THE BALL!
YOU WANNA PLAY CATCH?
#47
THERE!
FLIIING
NOMF
ALL RIGHT. BRING IT BA—
THUT THUT THUT
NRRF
NRRF
NRRF
SANDALS
I DID IT!!
DID WHAT?
I don't really get it.

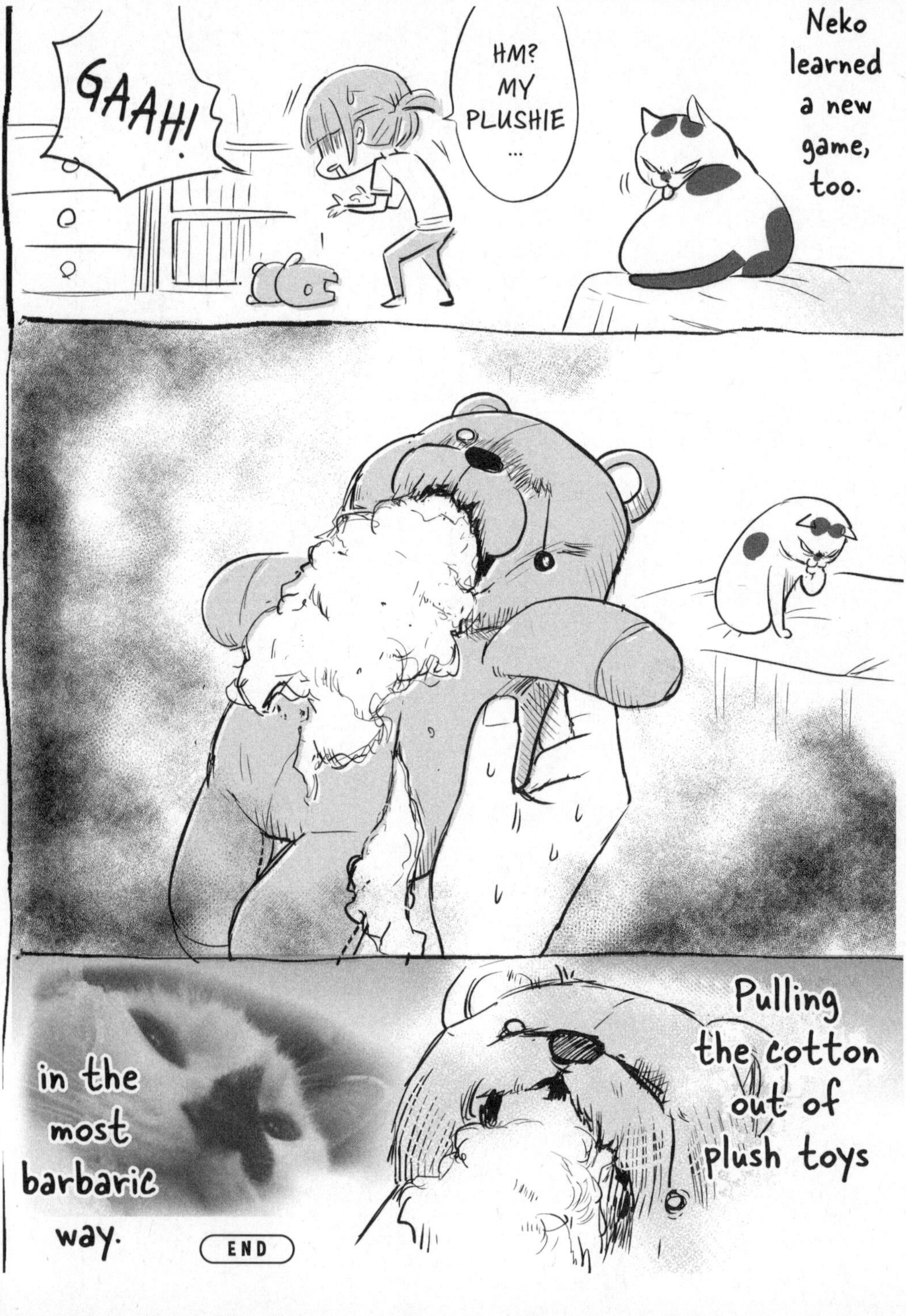
Neko learned a new game, too.
HM? MY PLUSHIE ...
GAAH!
Pulling the cotton out of plush toys
in the most barbaric way.
END

A picture of Inu-kun when he was little, with his sibling.

Newly-Drawn 4-Panel Strip

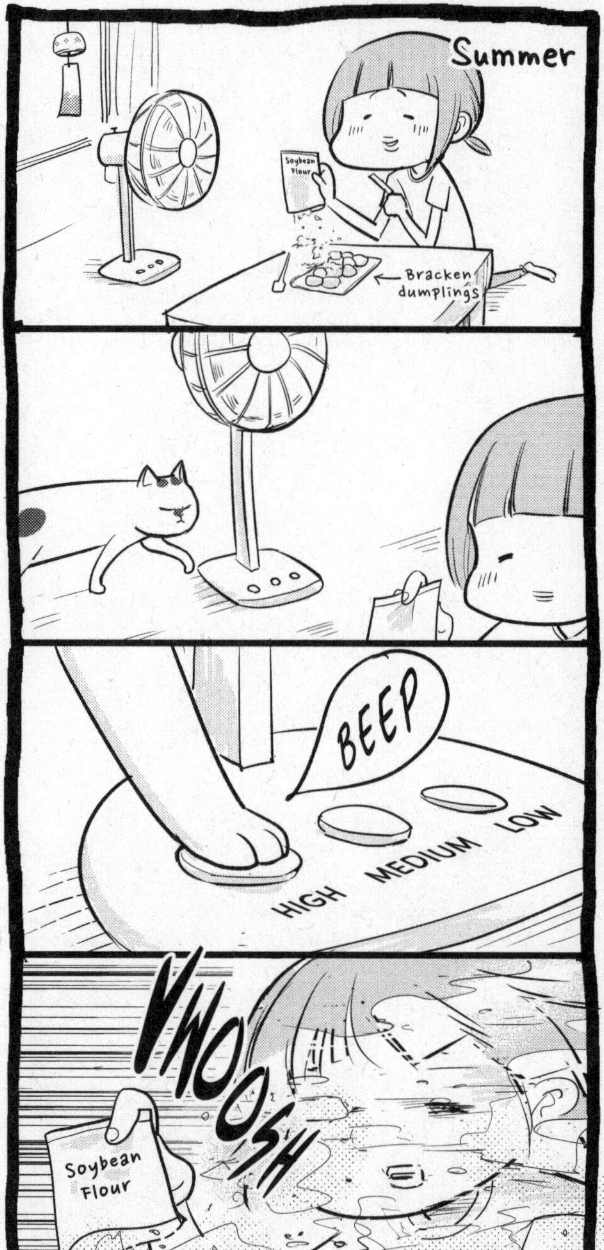
Summer
Soybean Flour
Bracken dumplings
BEEP
HIGH MEDIUM LOW
VWOOSH
Soybean Flour

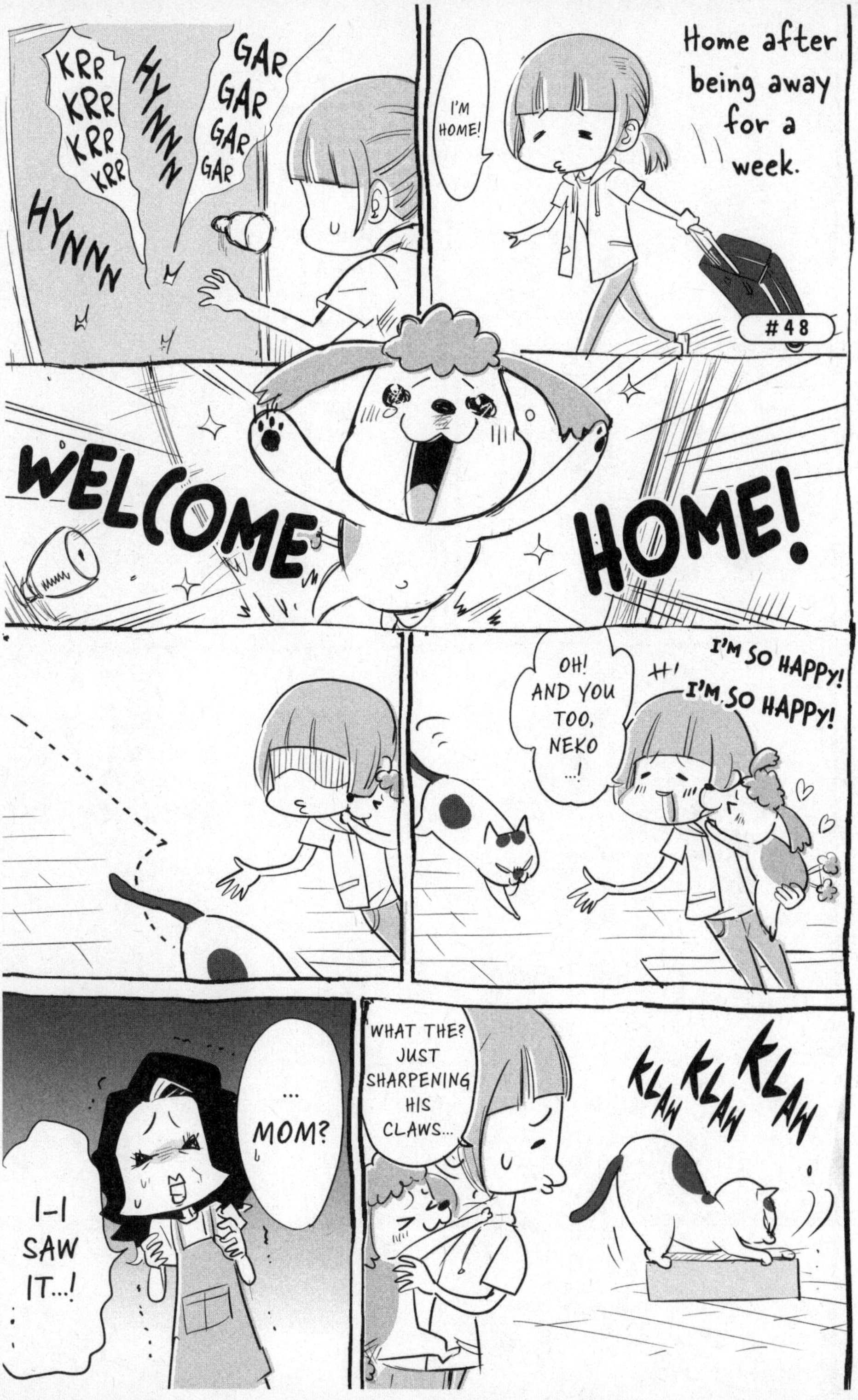
Home after being away for a week.
I'M HOME!
#48
GAR GAR GAR GAR
HYNNN
KRR KRR KRR KRR
HYNNNN
WELCOME HOME!
I'M SO HAPPY! I'M SO HAPPY!
OH! AND YOU TOO, NEKO ...!
KLAW KLAW KLAW
WHAT THE? JUST SHARPENING HIS CLAWS...
... MOM?
I-I SAW IT...!

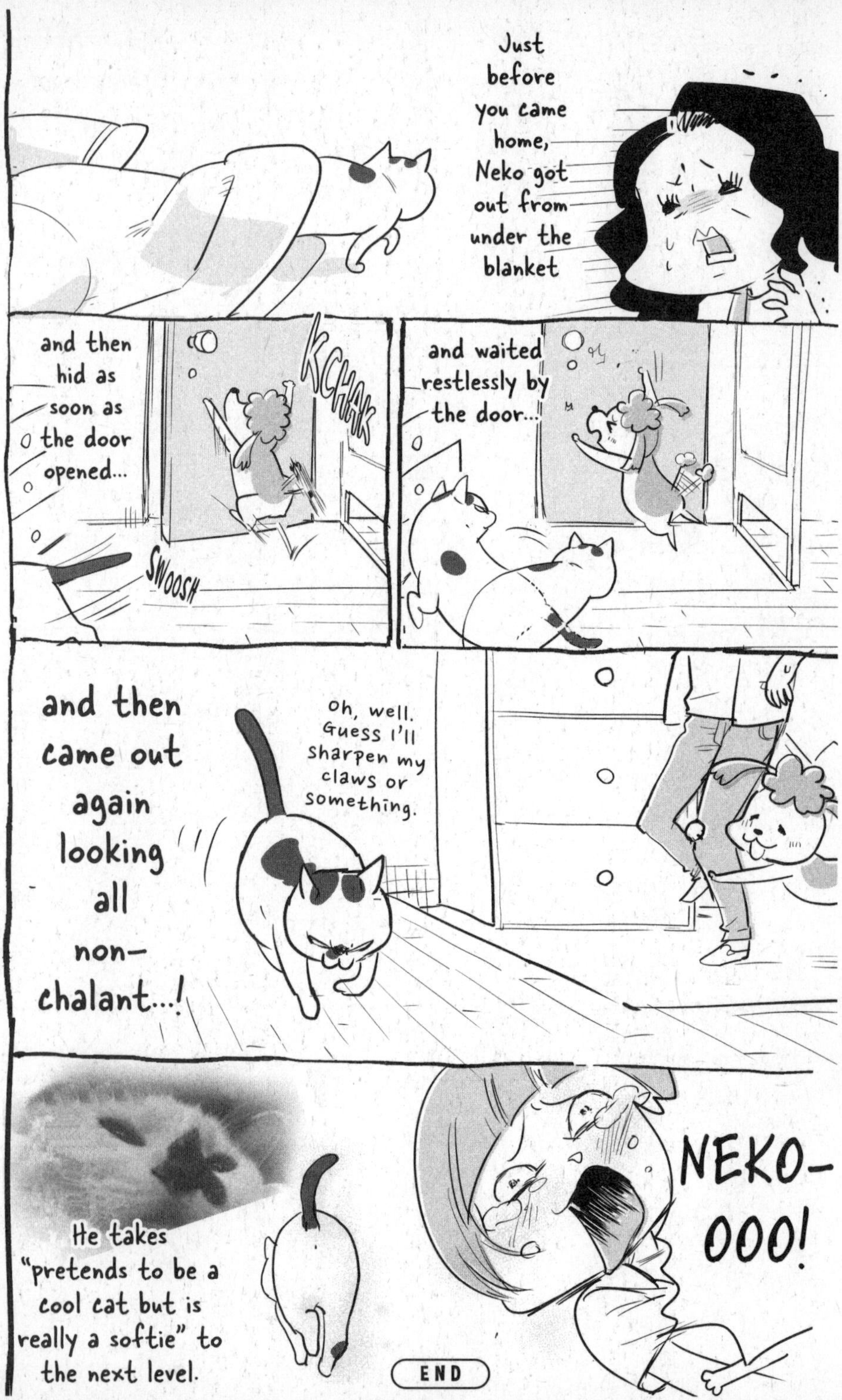
Just before you came home, Neko got out from under the blanket
and waited restlessly by the door...
and then hid as soon as the door opened...
KCHAK
SWOOSH
Oh, well. Guess I'll sharpen my claws or something.
and then came out again looking all non-chalant...!
NEKO-OOO!
He takes "pretends to be a cool cat but is really a softie" to the next level.
END

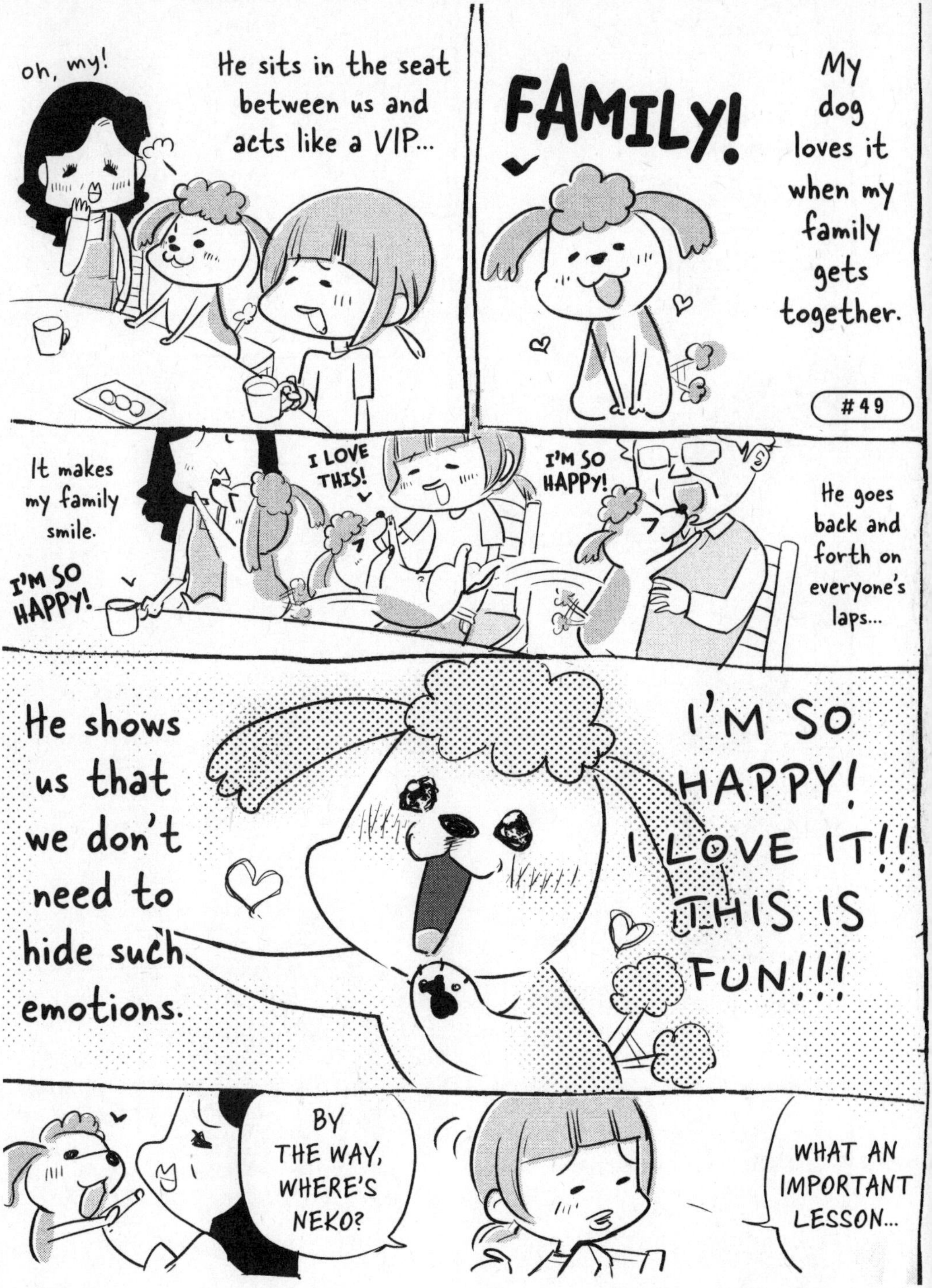
My dog loves it when my family gets together.
FAMILY!
#49
He sits in the seat between us and acts like a VIP...
oh, my!
He goes back and forth on everyone's laps...
I'M SO HAPPY!
I LOVE THIS!
It makes my family smile.
I'M SO HAPPY!
I'M SO HAPPY! I LOVE IT!! THIS IS FUN!!!
He shows us that we don't need to hide such emotions.
WHAT AN IMPORTANT LESSON...
BY THE WAY, WHERE'S NEKO?

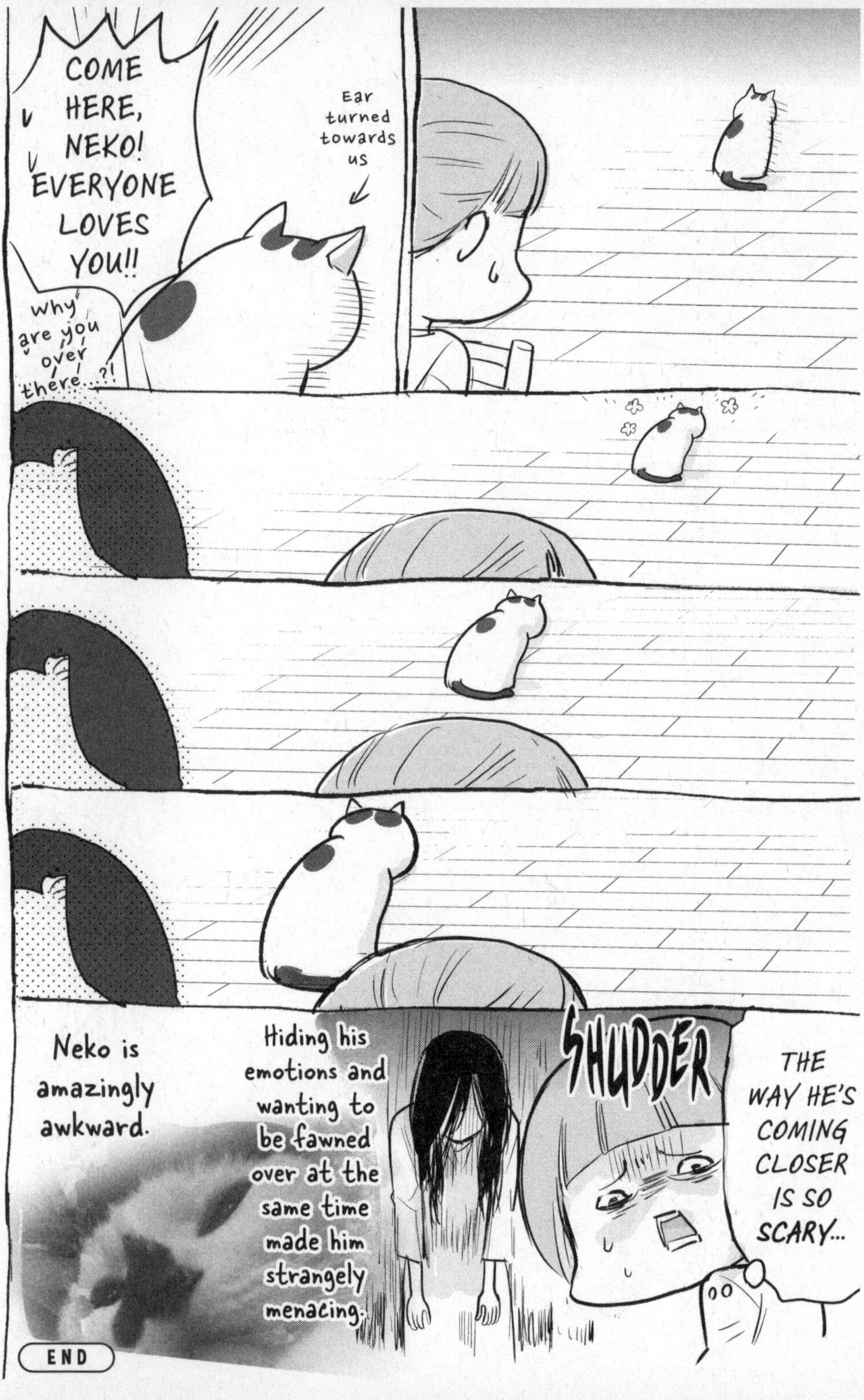
COME HERE, NEKO! EVERYONE LOVES YOU!!
Ear turned towards us
why are you over there...?!
SHUDDER
THE WAY HE'S COMING CLOSER IS SO SCARY...
Hiding his emotions and wanting to be fawned over at the same time made him strangely menacing.
Neko is amazingly awkward.
END

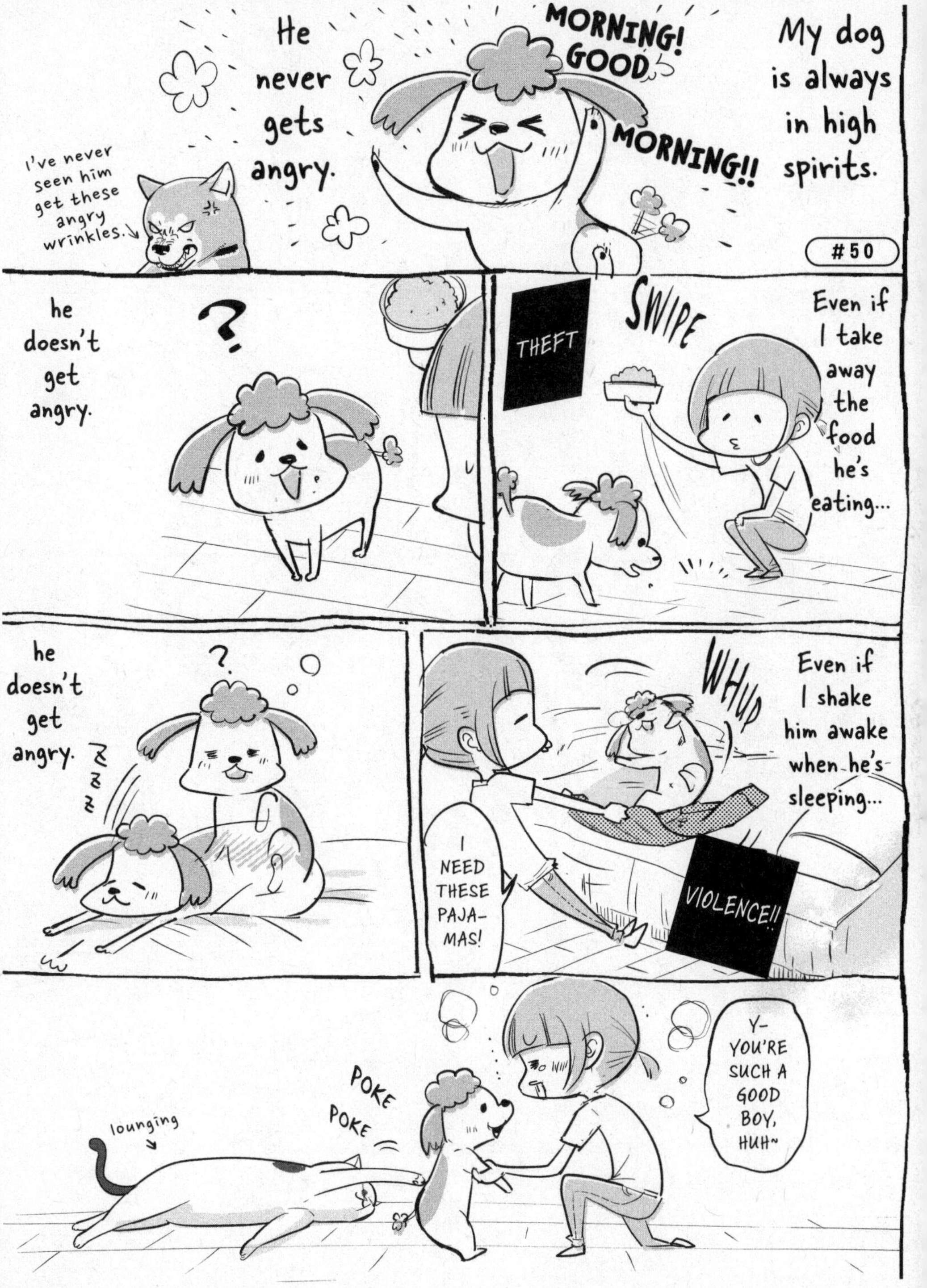
My dog is always in high spirits.
GOOD MORNING!
MORNING!!
He never gets angry.
I've never seen him get these angry wrinkles.
#50
Even if I take away the food he's eating...
SWIPE
THEFT
he doesn't get angry.
Even if I shake him awake when he's sleeping...
WHUD
VIOLENCE!!
I NEED THESE PAJAMAS!
he doesn't get angry.
Z Z Z
Y-YOU'RE SUCH A GOOD BOY, HUH~
POKE
POKE
lounging

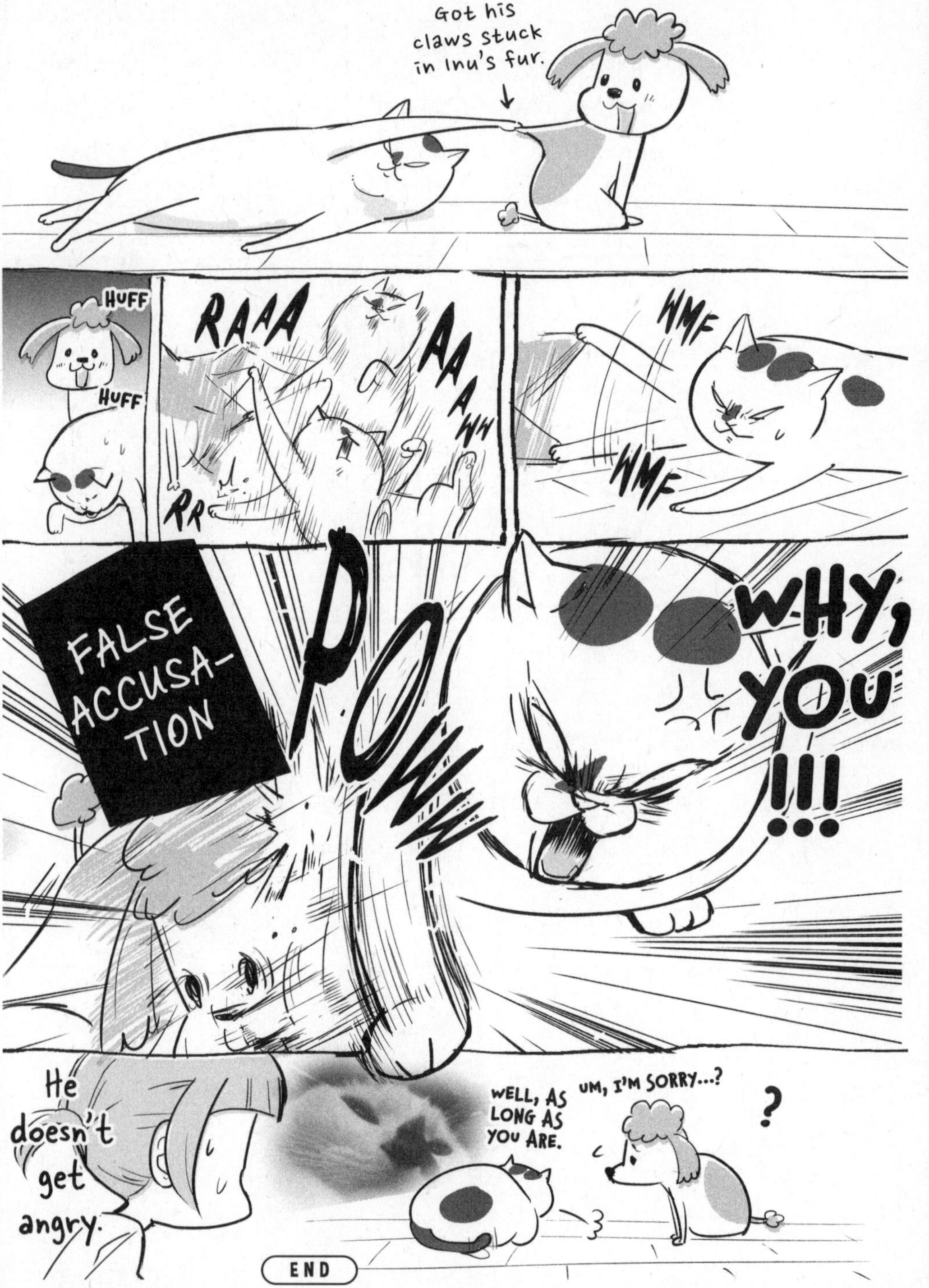
Got his claws stuck in Inu's fur.
WMF
WMF
RAAA
AAAAWW
RR
HUFF
HUFF
WHY, YOU!!!
POWW
FALSE ACCUSA-TION
?
UM, I'M SORRY...?
WELL, AS LONG AS YOU ARE.
He doesn't get angry.
END

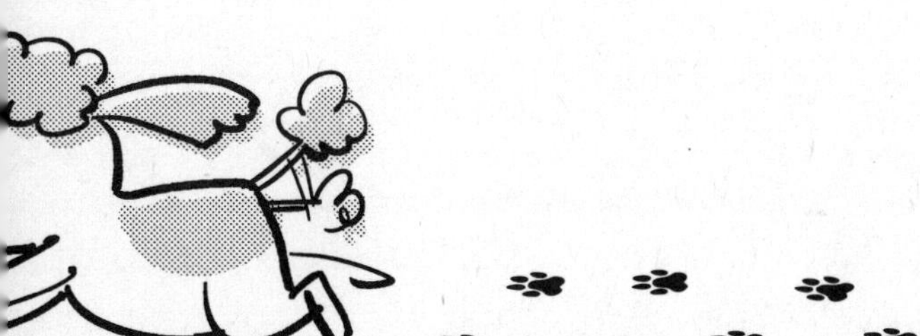

Bonus

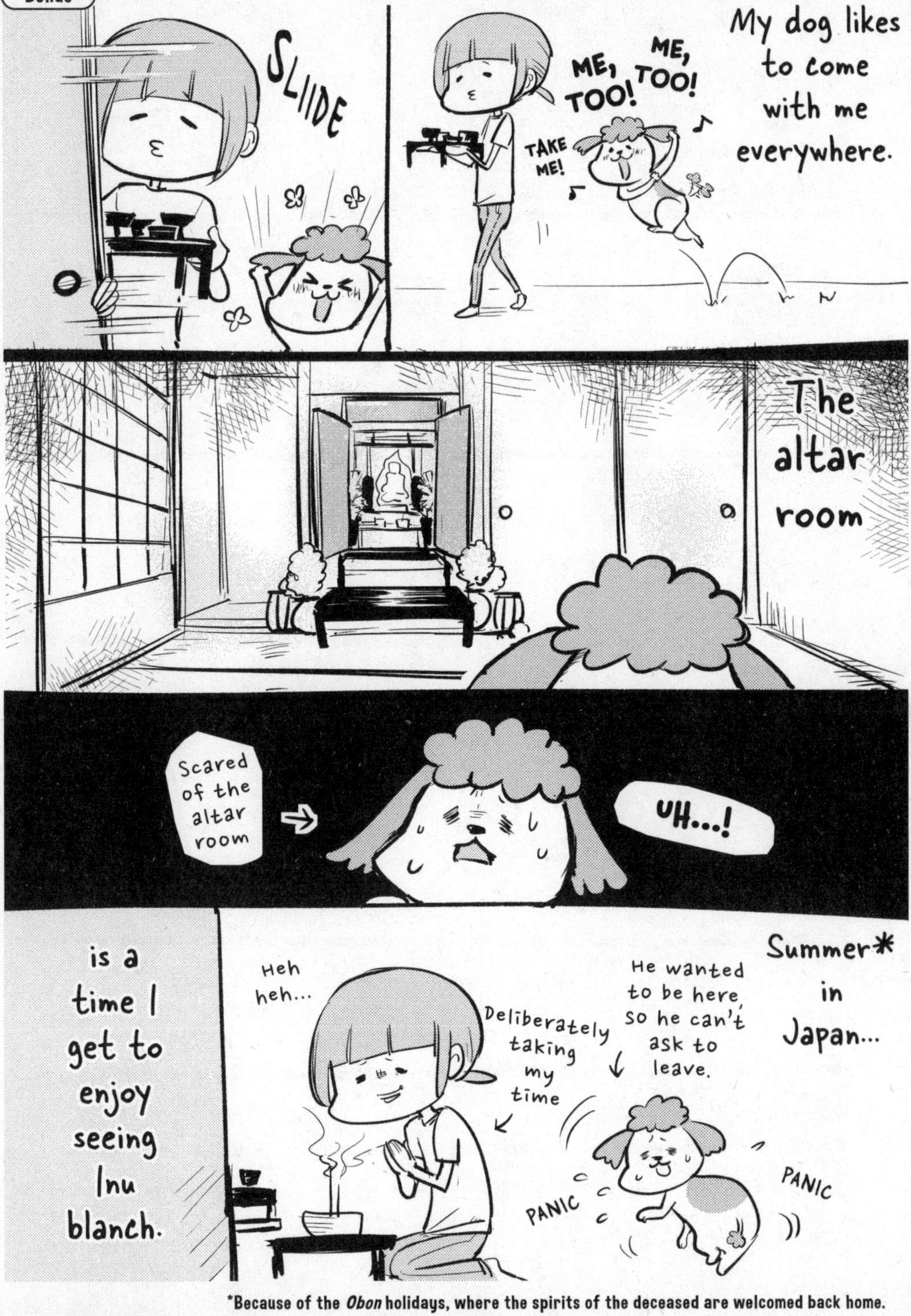
My dog likes to come with me everywhere.
ME, TOO!
ME, TOO!
TAKE ME!
SLIIDE
The altar room
UH...!
Scared of the altar room
Summer* in Japan...
He wanted to be here, so he can't ask to leave.
Deliberately taking my time
Heh heh...
PANIC
PANIC
is a time I get to enjoy seeing Inu blanch.

*Because of the *Obon* holidays, where the spirits of the deceased are welcomed back home.

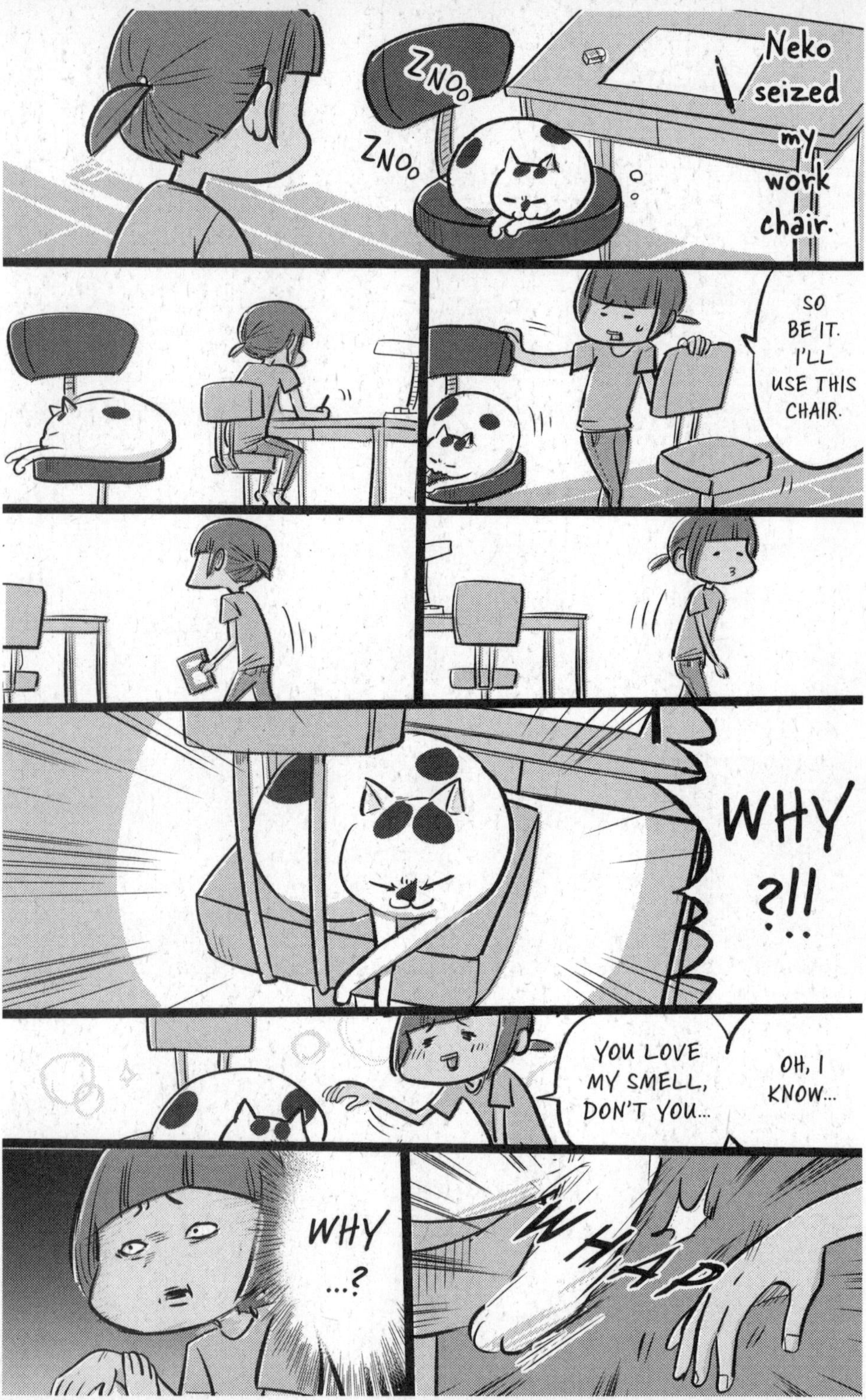
Neko seized my work chair.
ZNOo
ZNOo
SO BE IT. I'LL USE THIS CHAIR.
WHY ?!! ...
OH, I KNOW...
YOU LOVE MY SMELL, DON'T YOU...
WHAP
WHY ...?

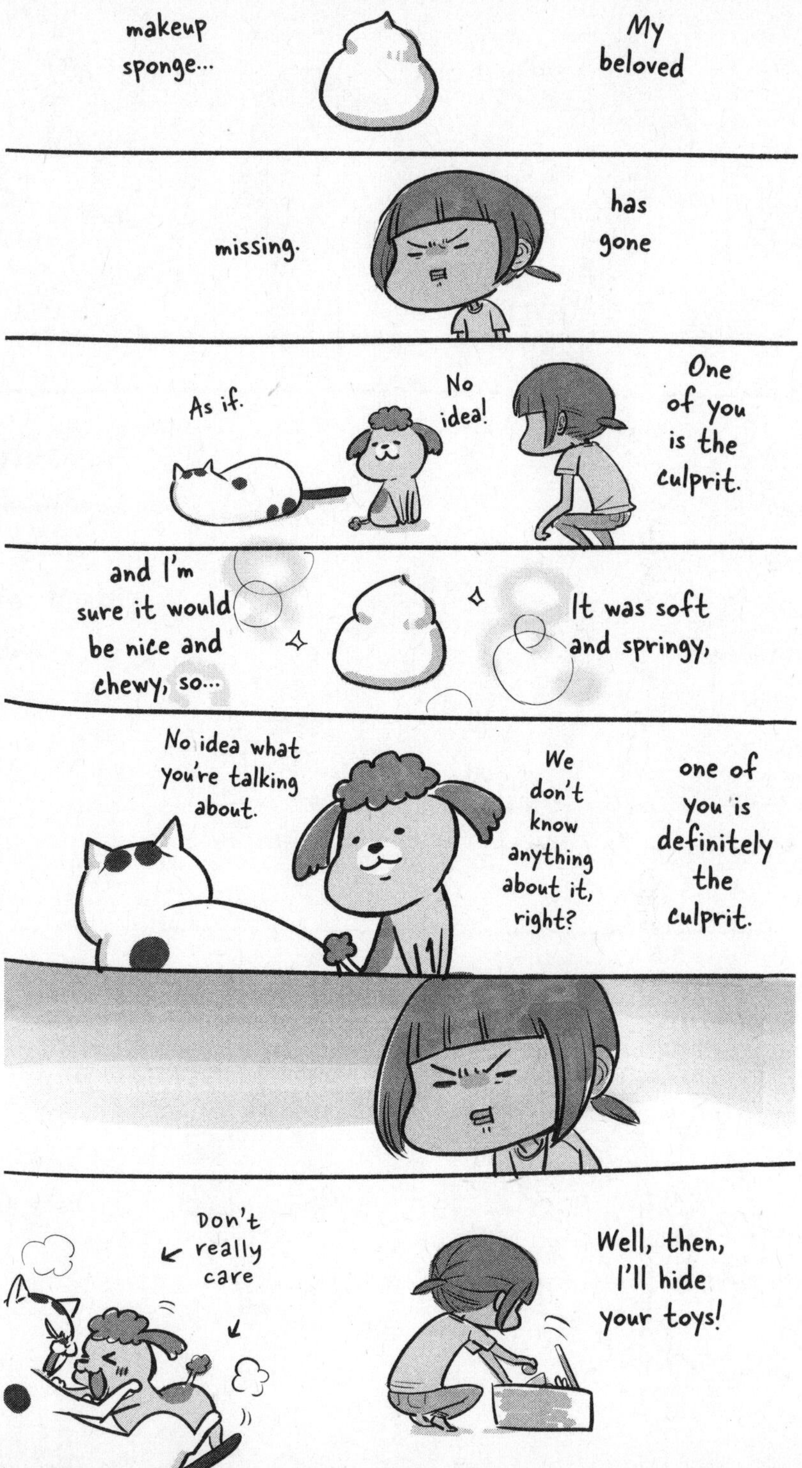
My beloved
makeup sponge...
has gone
missing.
One of you is the culprit.
No idea!
As if.
It was soft and springy,
and I'm sure it would be nice and chewy, so...
one of you is definitely the culprit.
We don't know anything about it, right?
No idea what you're talking about.
Well, then, I'll hide your toys!
Don't really care

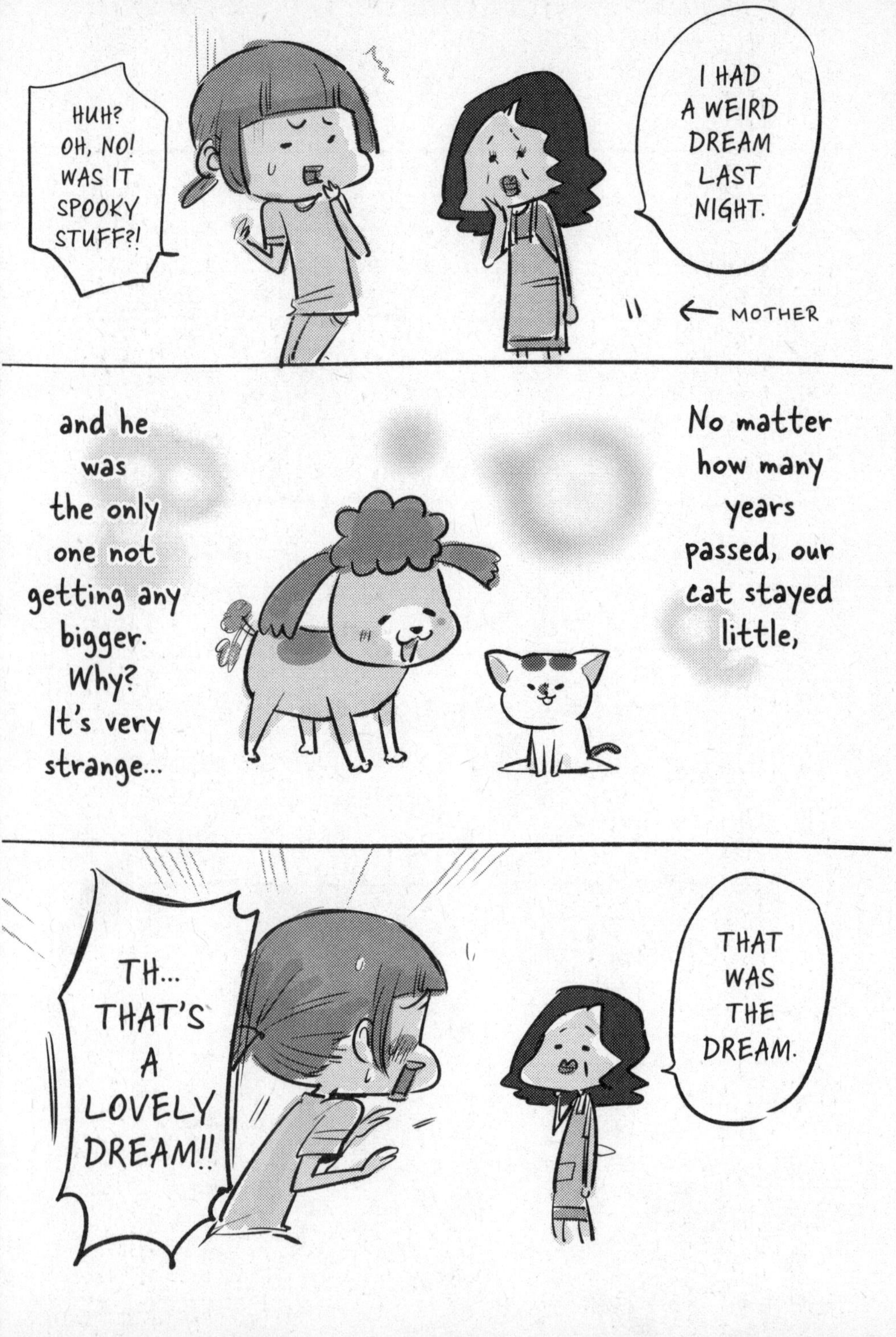
I HAD A WEIRD DREAM LAST NIGHT.
MOTHER
HUH? OH, NO! WAS IT SPOOKY STUFF?!
No matter how many years passed, our cat stayed little,
and he was the only one not getting any bigger. Why? It's very strange...
THAT WAS THE DREAM.
TH... THAT'S A LOVELY DREAM!!

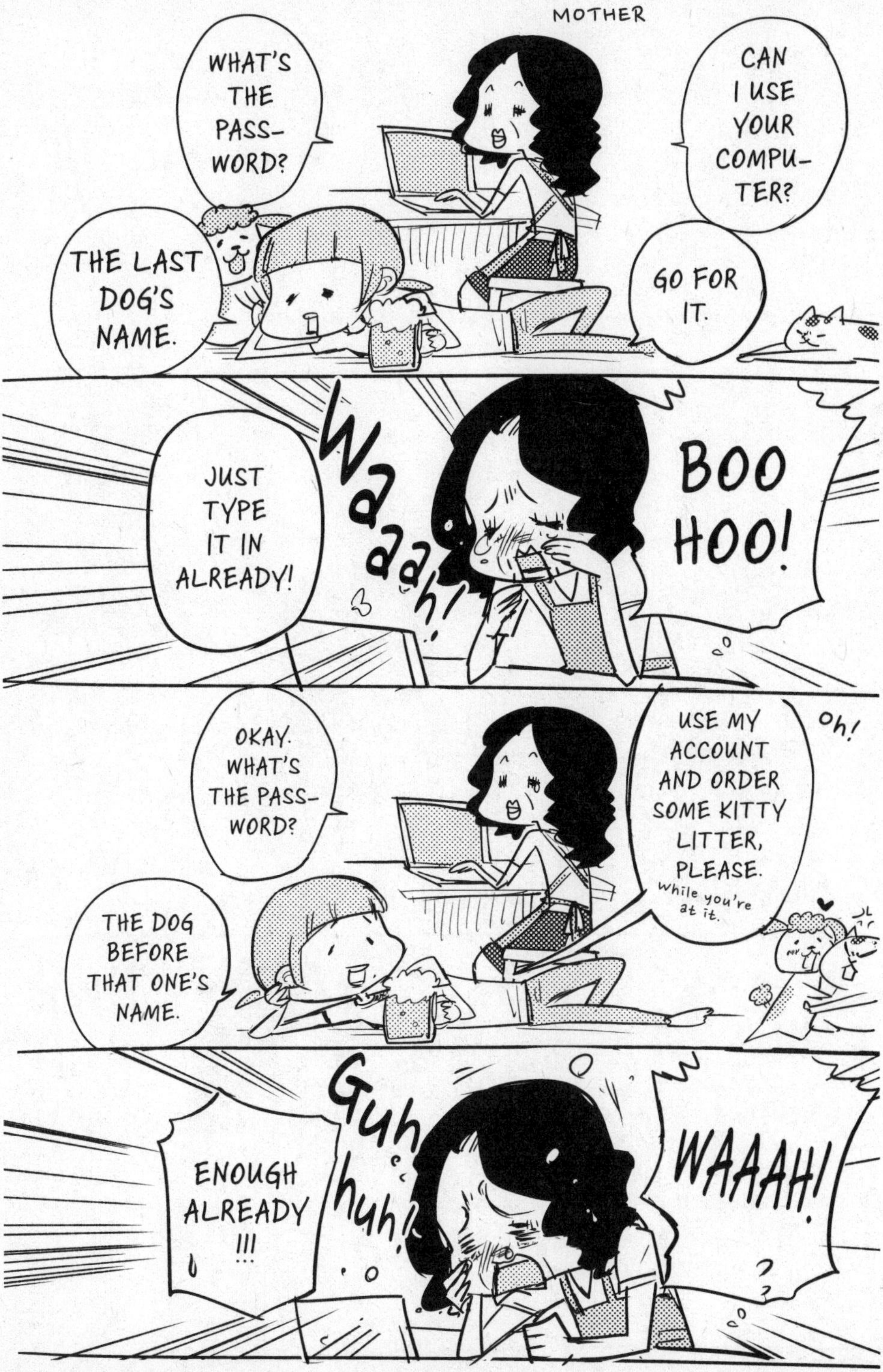
MOTHER
CAN I USE YOUR COMPUTER?
WHAT'S THE PASSWORD?
GO FOR IT.
THE LAST DOG'S NAME.
BOO HOO!
Waaah!
JUST TYPE IT IN ALREADY!
oh!
USE MY ACCOUNT AND ORDER SOME KITTY LITTER, PLEASE.
while you're at it.
OKAY. WHAT'S THE PASSWORD?
THE DOG BEFORE THAT ONE'S NAME.
WAAAH!
Guh huh!
ENOUGH ALREADY!!!

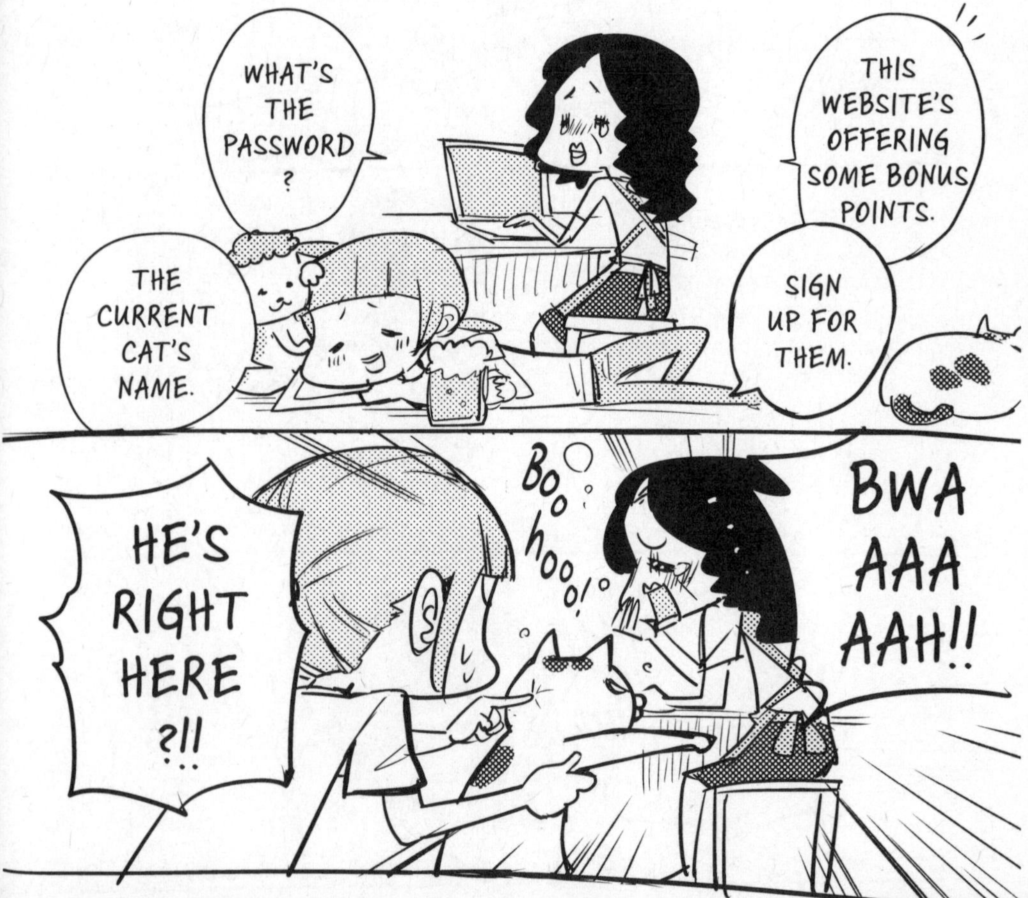
THIS WEBSITE'S OFFERING SOME BONUS POINTS.
SIGN UP FOR THEM.
WHAT'S THE PASSWORD ?
THE CURRENT CAT'S NAME.
BWA AAA AAH!!
Boo hooo!
HE'S RIGHT HERE ?!!

Definitely beckoning... and bewitching.

Newly-Drawn 4-Panel Strip

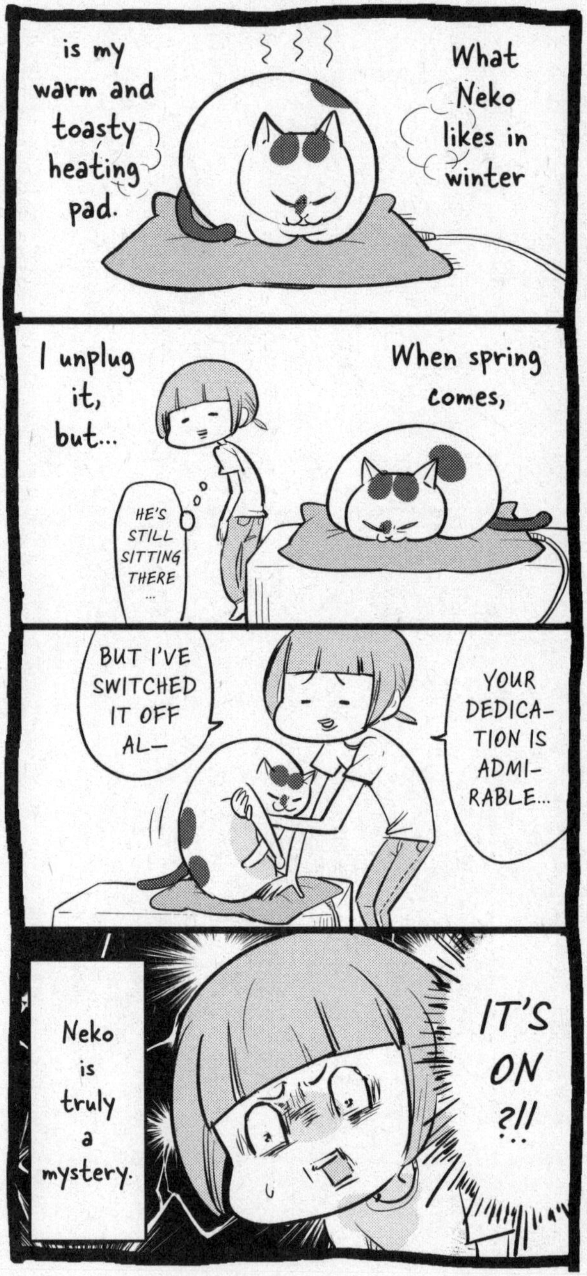
What Neko likes in winter
is my warm and toasty heating pad.
When spring comes,
I unplug it, but...
HE'S STILL SITTING THERE...
YOUR DEDICATION IS ADMIRABLE...
BUT I'VE SWITCHED IT OFF AL—
IT'S ON ?!!
Neko is truly a mystery.

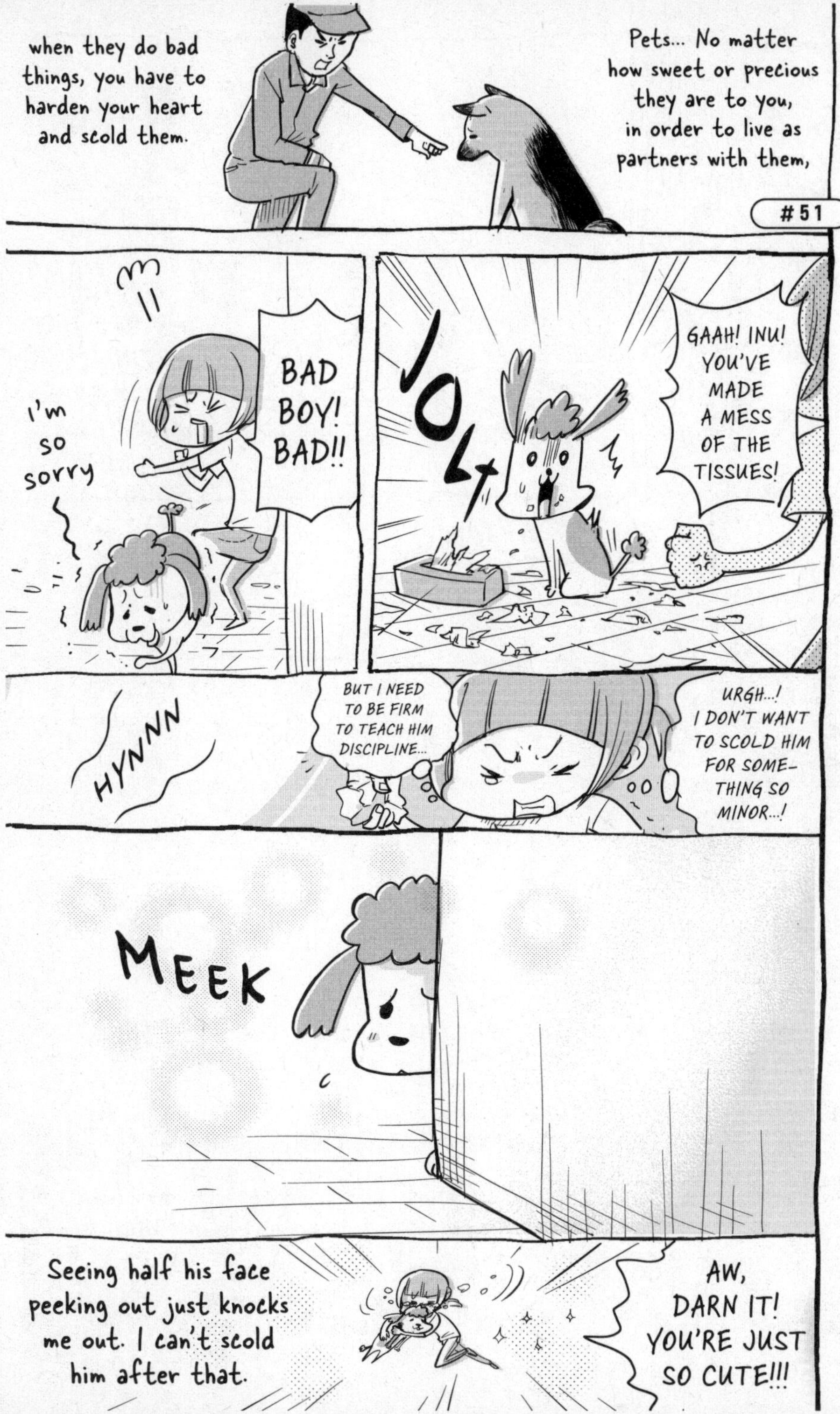
Pets... No matter how sweet or precious they are to you, in order to live as partners with them,
when they do bad things, you have to harden your heart and scold them.
#51
GAAH! INU! YOU'VE MADE A MESS OF THE TISSUES!
JOLT
BAD BOY! BAD!!
I'm so sorry
URGH...! I DON'T WANT TO SCOLD HIM FOR SOMETHING SO MINOR...!
BUT I NEED TO BE FIRM TO TEACH HIM DISCIPLINE...
HYNNN
MEEK
AW, DARN IT! YOU'RE JUST SO CUTE!!!
Seeing half his face peeking out just knocks me out. I can't scold him after that.

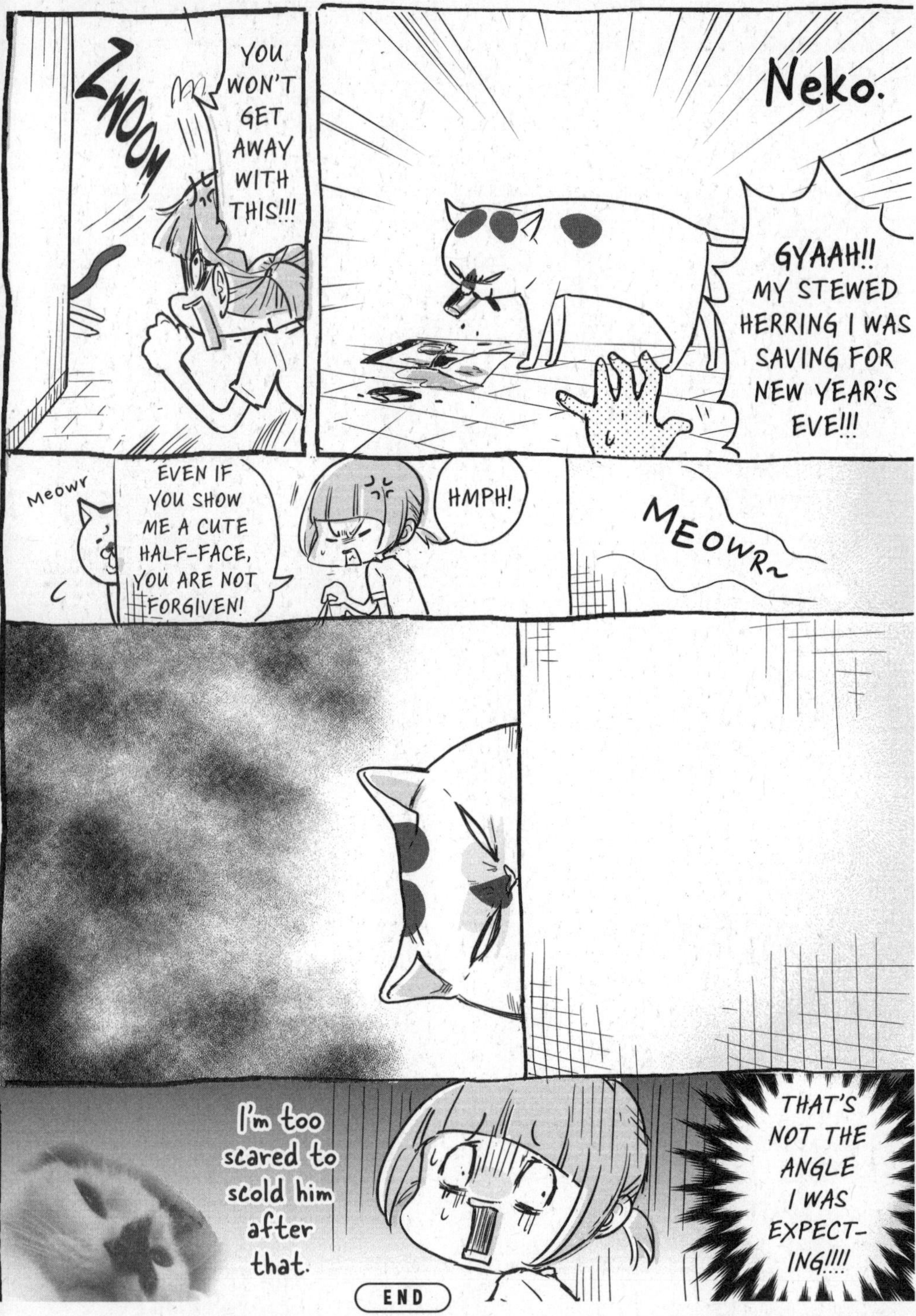
Neko.
GYAAH!! MY STEWED HERRING I WAS SAVING FOR NEW YEAR'S EVE!!!
ZWOOM
YOU WON'T GET AWAY WITH THIS!!!
MEOWR~
HMPH!
EVEN IF YOU SHOW ME A CUTE HALF-FACE, YOU ARE NOT FORGIVEN!
Meowr
THAT'S NOT THE ANGLE I WAS EXPECTING!!!!
I'm too scared to scold him after that.
END

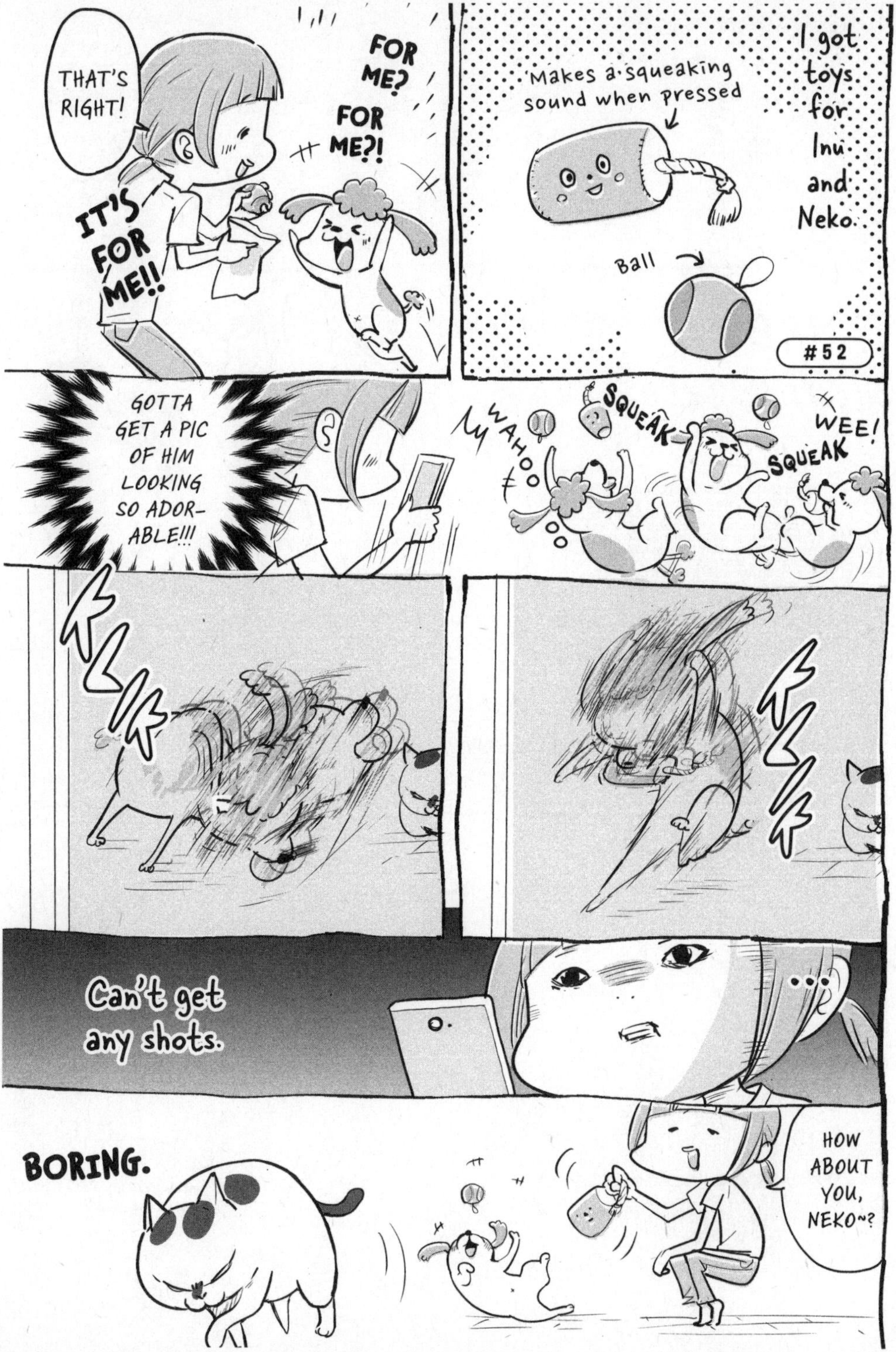
I got toys for Inu and Neko.
Makes a squeaking sound when pressed
Ball
#52
FOR ME?
FOR ME?!
THAT'S RIGHT!
IT'S FOR ME!!
WEE!
SQUEAK
SQUEAK
WAHOO
GOTTA GET A PIC OF HIM LOOKING SO ADORABLE!!!
KLIK
KLIK
...
Can't get any shots.
HOW ABOUT YOU, NEKO~?
BORING.

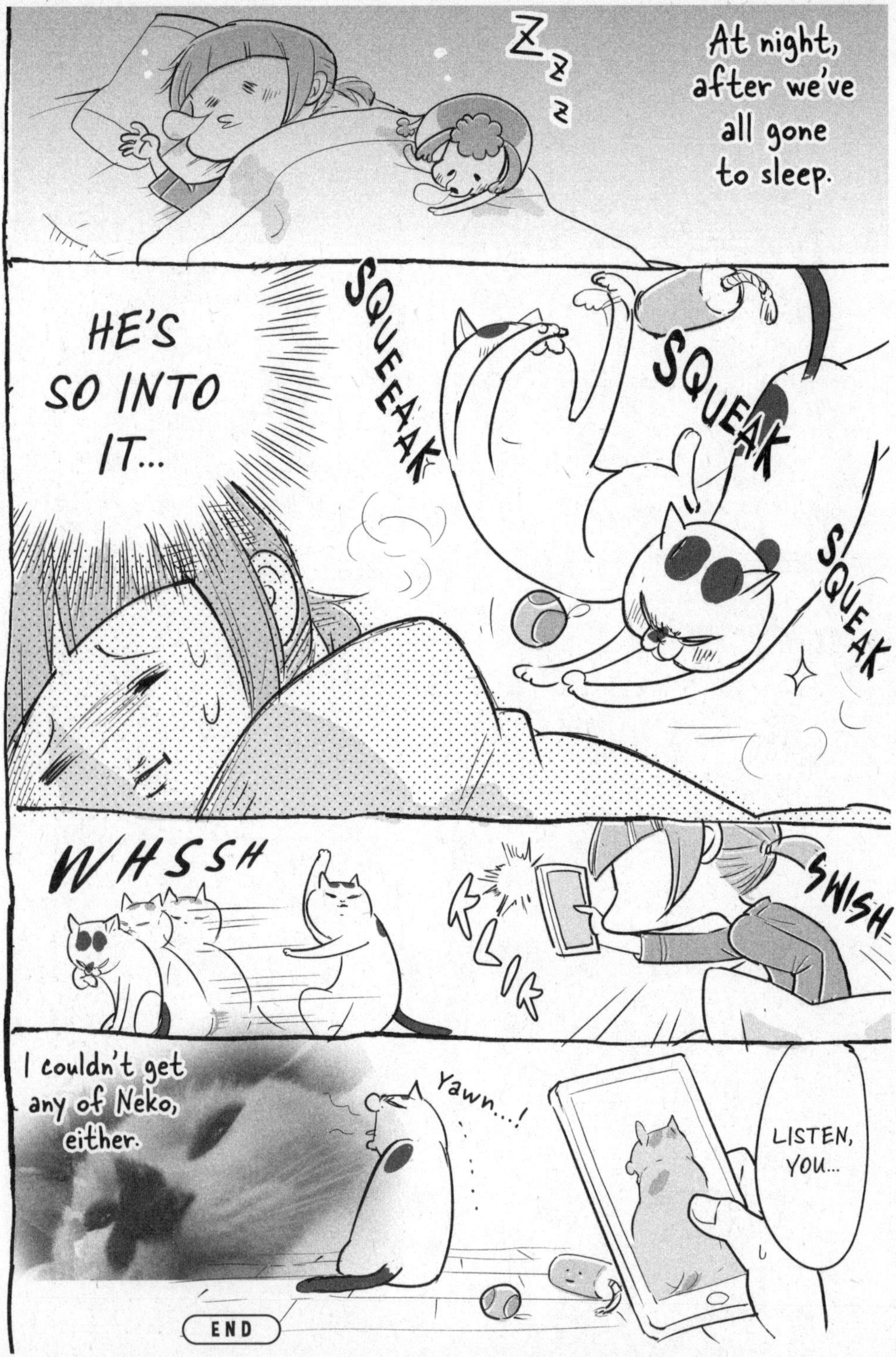
At night, after we've all gone to sleep.
Z z z
SQUEAK
SQUEAK
SQUEEAAK
HE'S SO INTO IT...
SWISH
KLIK
WHSSH
LISTEN, YOU...
Yawn...!
I couldn't get any of Neko, either.
END

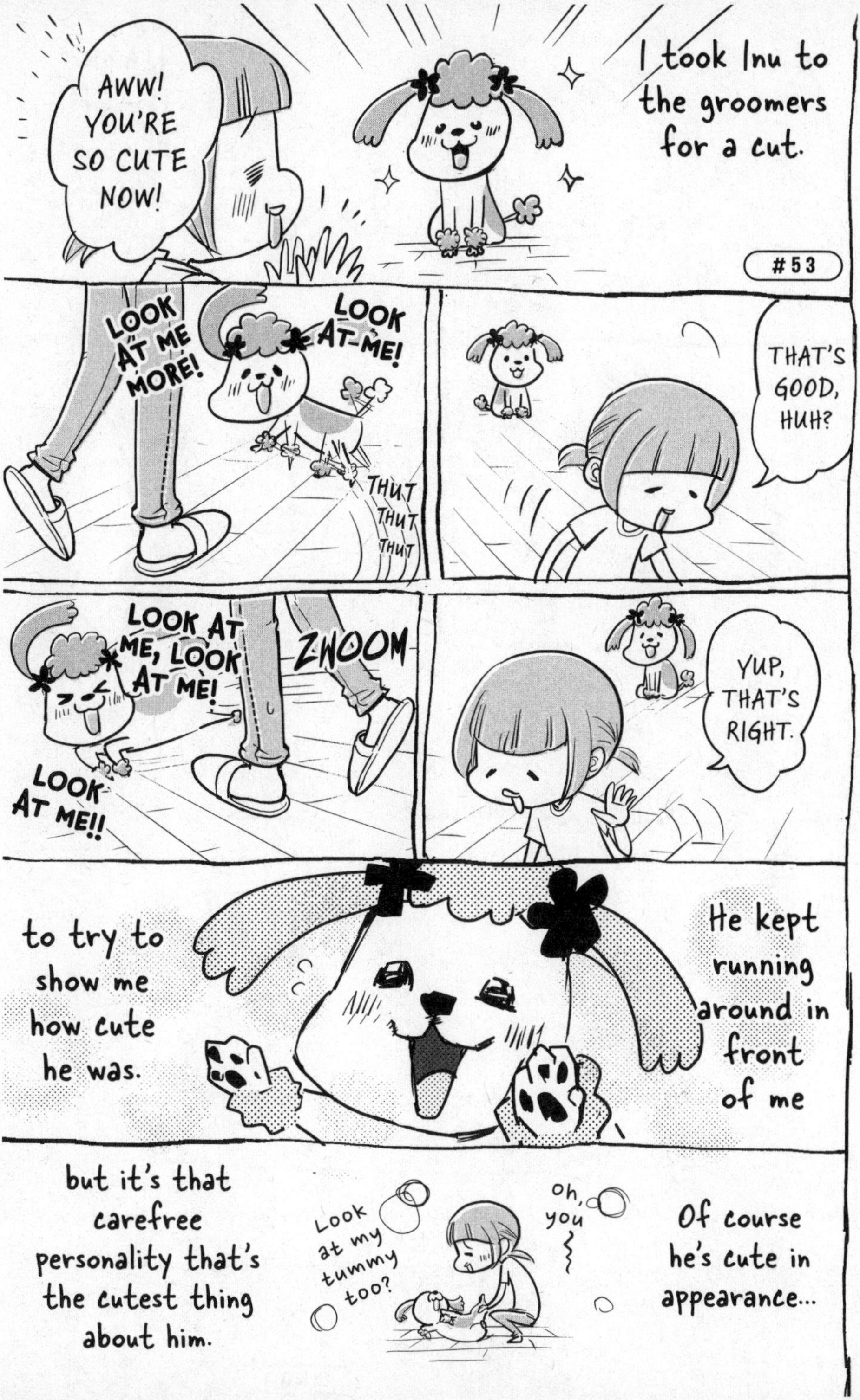
#53
I took Inu to the groomers for a cut.
AWW! YOU'RE SO CUTE NOW!
THAT'S GOOD, HUH?
LOOK AT-ME!
LOOK AT ME MORE!
THUT THUT THUT
YUP, THAT'S RIGHT.
ZWOOM
LOOK AT ME, LOOK AT ME!
LOOK AT ME!!
He kept running around in front of me
to try to show me how cute he was.
Of course he's cute in appearance...
Oh, you~
Look at my tummy too?
but it's that carefree personality that's the cutest thing about him.

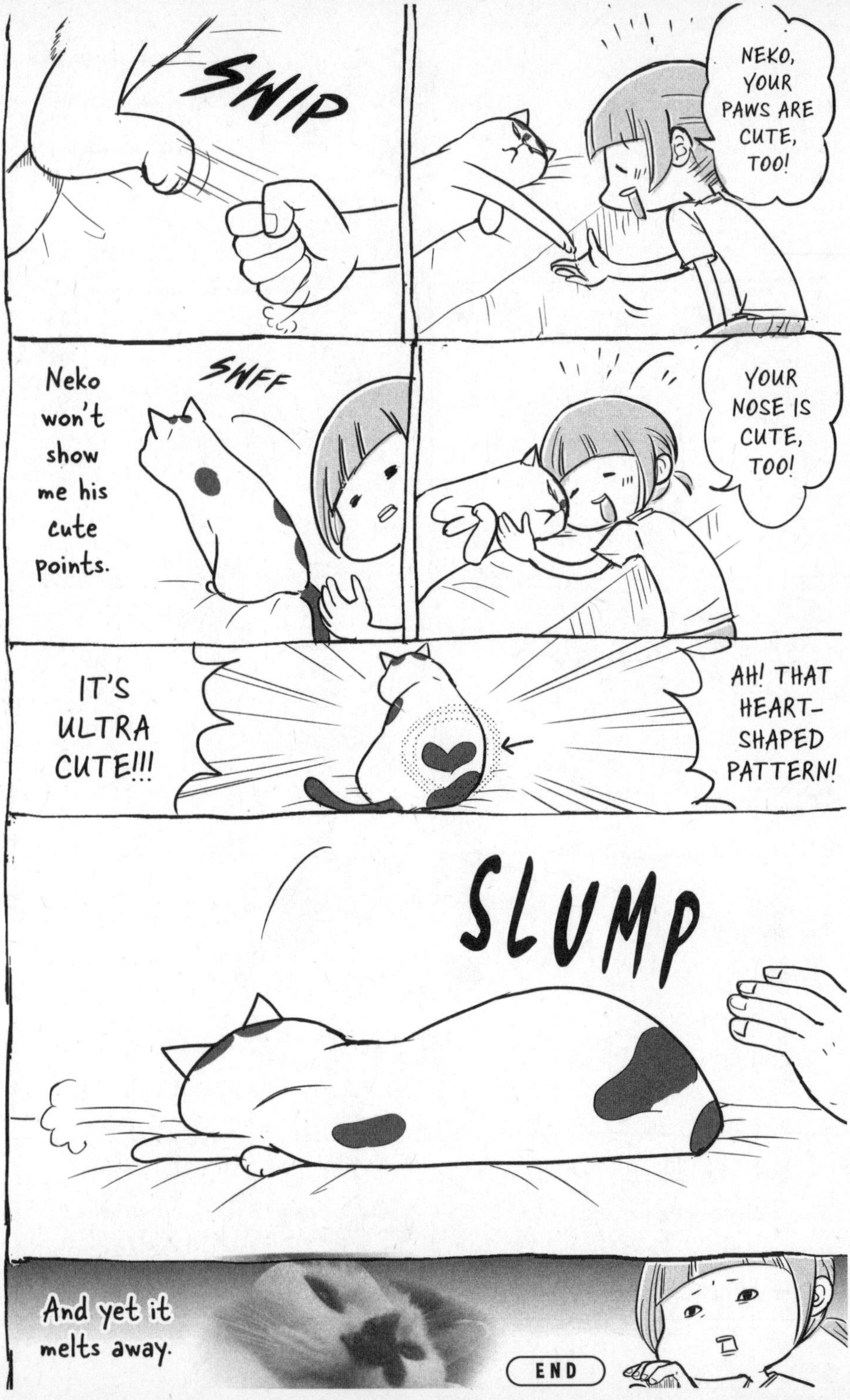
NEKO, YOUR PAWS ARE CUTE, TOO!
SWIP
YOUR NOSE IS CUTE, TOO!
SWFF
Neko won't show me his cute points.
AH! THAT HEART-SHAPED PATTERN!
IT'S ULTRA CUTE!!!
SLUMP
And yet it melts away.
END

I've got snacks (Beans. For *me*.) so they're gazing at me intensely.

Newly-Drawn 4-Panel Strip

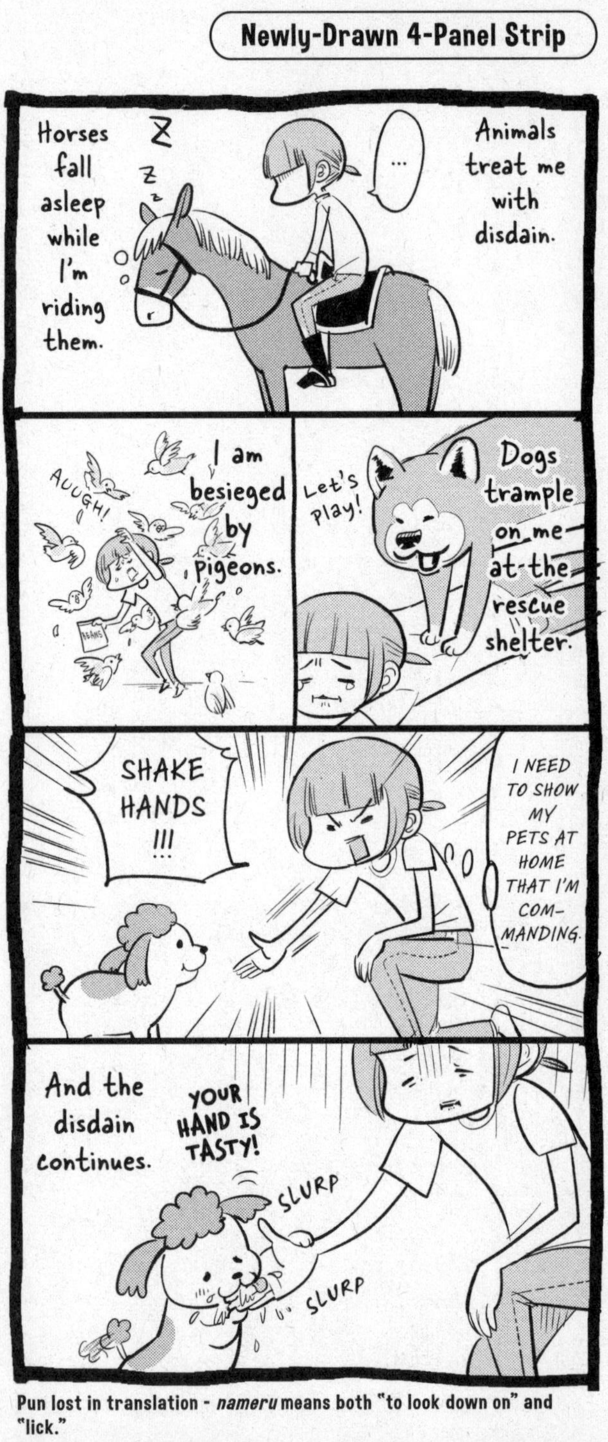
Animals treat me with disdain.
...
Z z z
Horses fall asleep while I'm riding them.
Dogs trample on me at the rescue shelter.
Let's play!
I am besieged by pigeons.
AUUGH!
BEANS
I NEED TO SHOW MY PETS AT HOME THAT I'M COM-MANDING.
SHAKE HANDS !!!
YOUR HAND IS TASTY!
And the disdain continues.
SLURP
SLURP

Pun lost in translation - *nameru* means both "to look down on" and "lick."

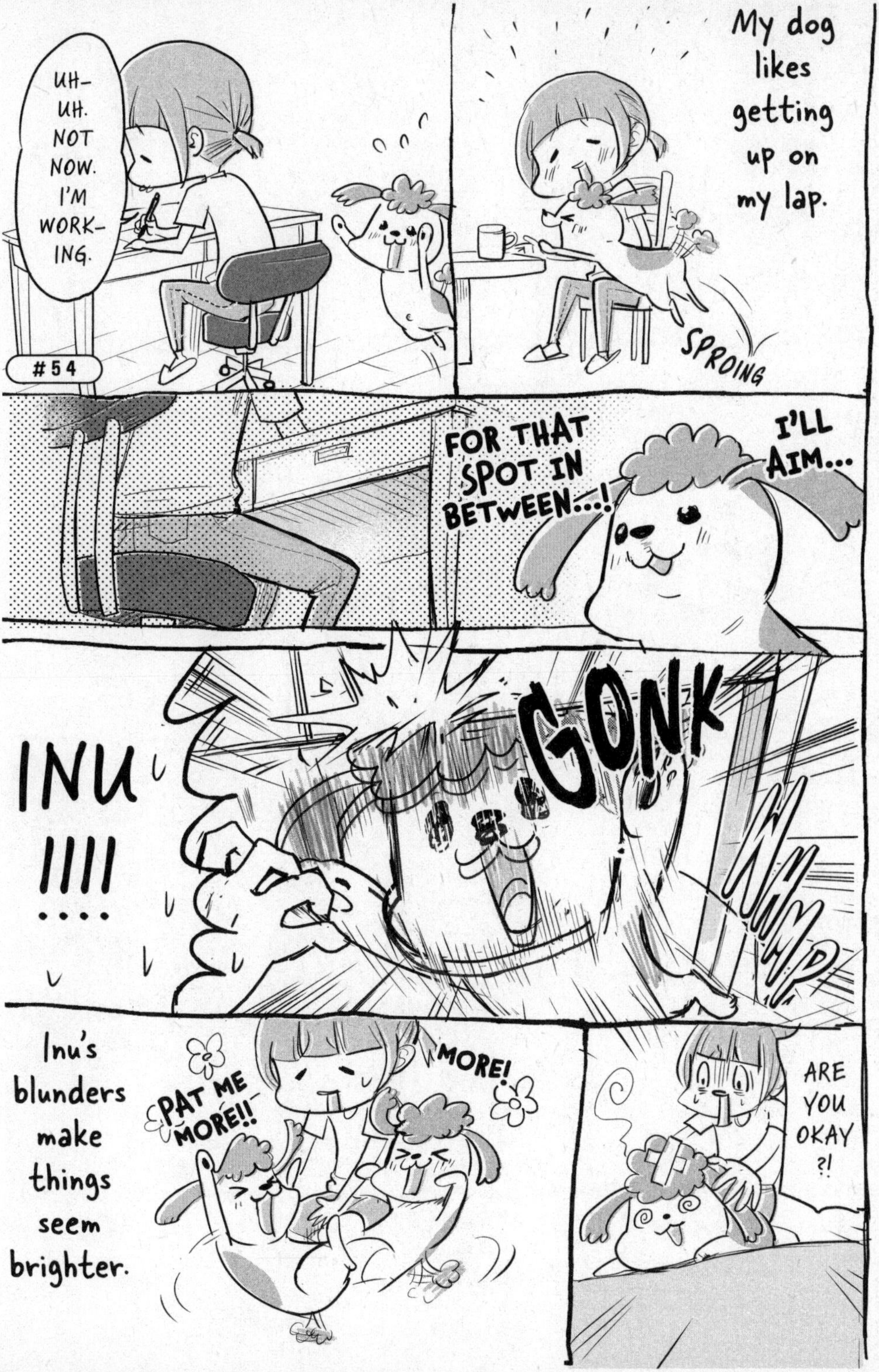
My dog likes getting up on my lap.
SPROING
#54
UH-UH. NOT NOW. I'M WORKING.
I'LL AIM...
FOR THAT SPOT IN BETWEEN...!
GONK
WHUMP
INU!!!!....
ARE YOU OKAY?!
MORE!
PAT ME MORE!!
Inu's blunders make things seem brighter.

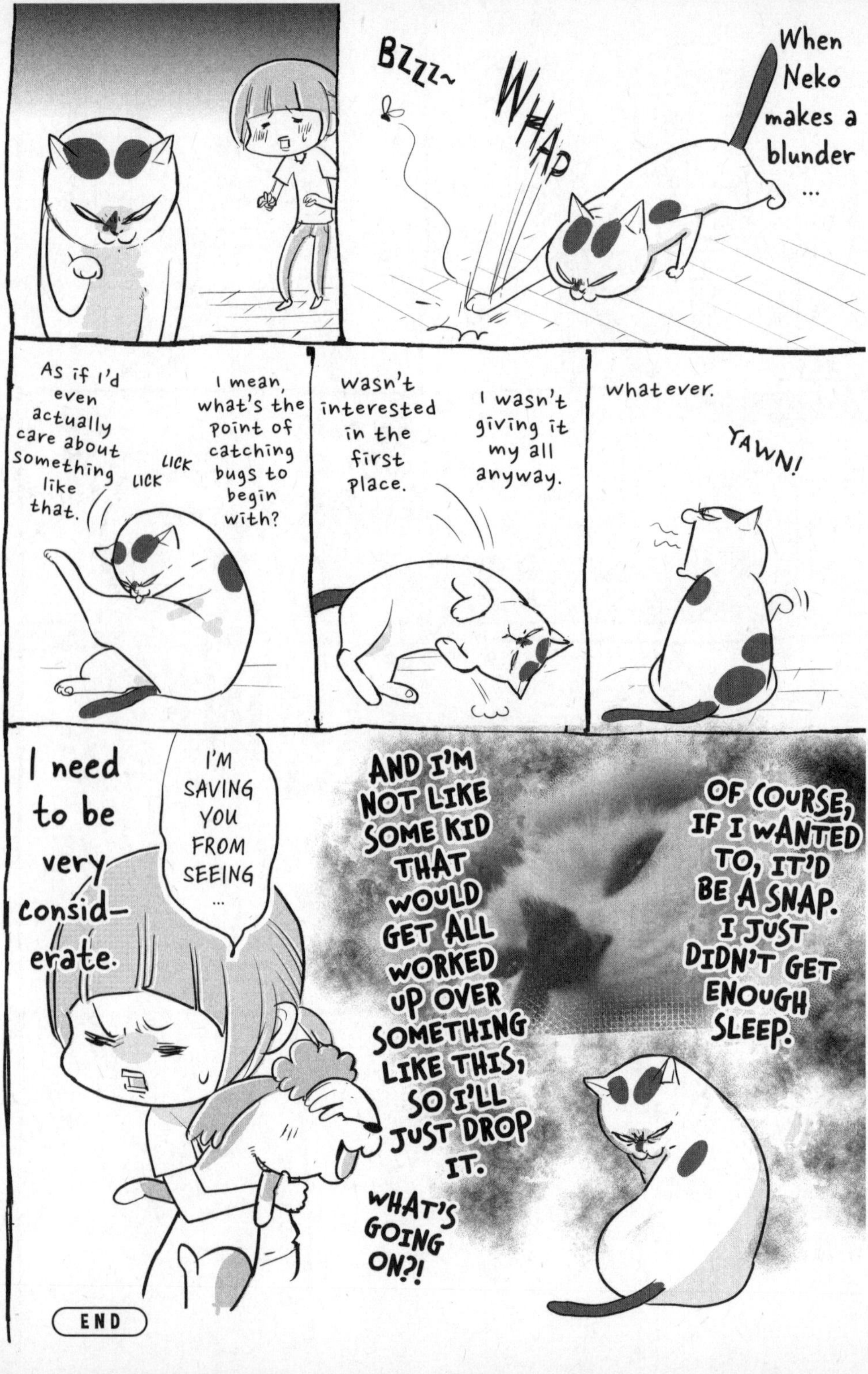
When Neko makes a blunder ...
BZZZ~
WHAP
Whatever.
YAWN!
I wasn't giving it my all anyway.
wasn't interested in the first place.
I mean, what's the point of catching bugs to begin with?
LICK
LICK
As if I'd even actually care about something like that.
OF COURSE, IF I WANTED TO, IT'D BE A SNAP. I JUST DIDN'T GET ENOUGH SLEEP.
AND I'M NOT LIKE SOME KID THAT WOULD GET ALL WORKED UP OVER SOMETHING LIKE THIS, SO I'LL JUST DROP IT.
WHAT'S GOING ON?!
I'M SAVING YOU FROM SEEING ...
I need to be very consid-erate.
END

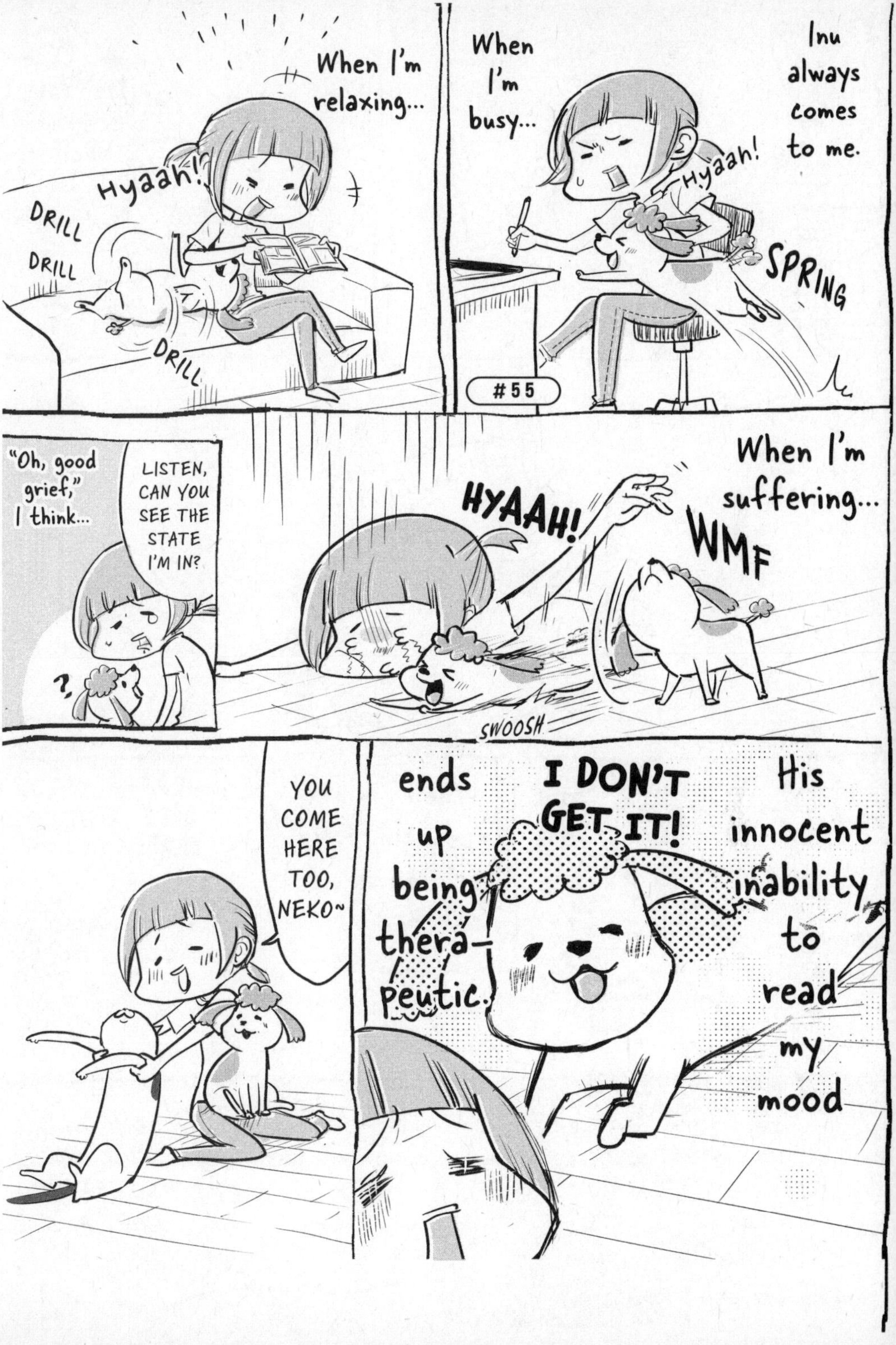
Inu always comes to me.
When I'm busy...
Hyaah!
SPRING
#55
When I'm relaxing...
Hyaah!
DRILL
DRILL
DRILL
When I'm suffering...
WMF
HYAAH!
SWOOSH
LISTEN, CAN YOU SEE THE STATE I'M IN?
"Oh, good grief," I think...
?
His innocent inability to read my mood
I DON'T GET IT!
ends up being thera-peutic.
YOU COME HERE TOO, NEKO~

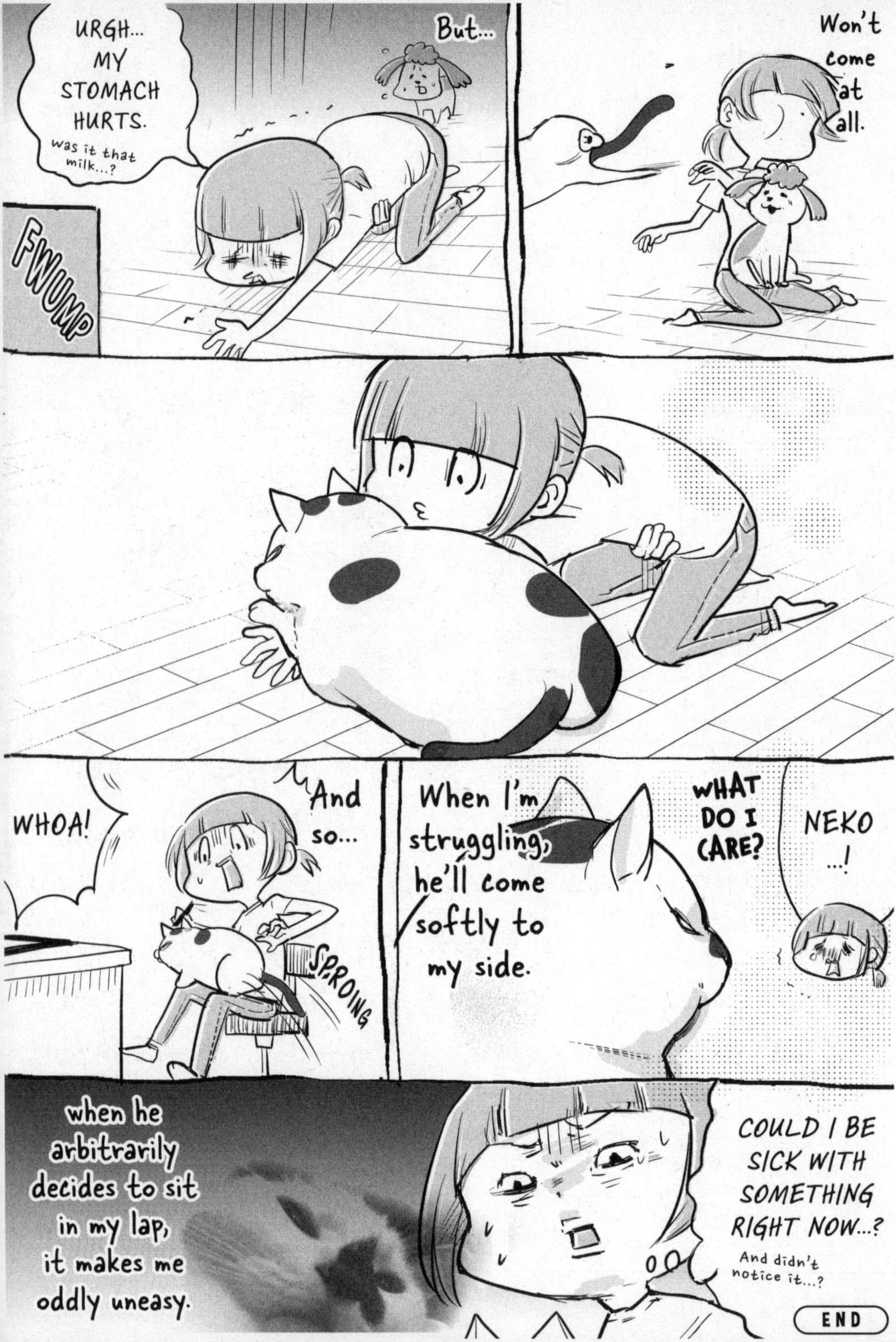
Won't come at all.
But...
URGH... MY STOMACH HURTS.
was it that milk...?
FWUMP
NEKO ...!
WHAT DO I CARE?
When I'm struggling, he'll come softly to my side.
And so...
WHOA!
SPROING
COULD I BE SICK WITH SOMETHING RIGHT NOW...?
And didn't notice it...?
when he arbitrarily decides to sit in my lap, it makes me oddly uneasy.
END

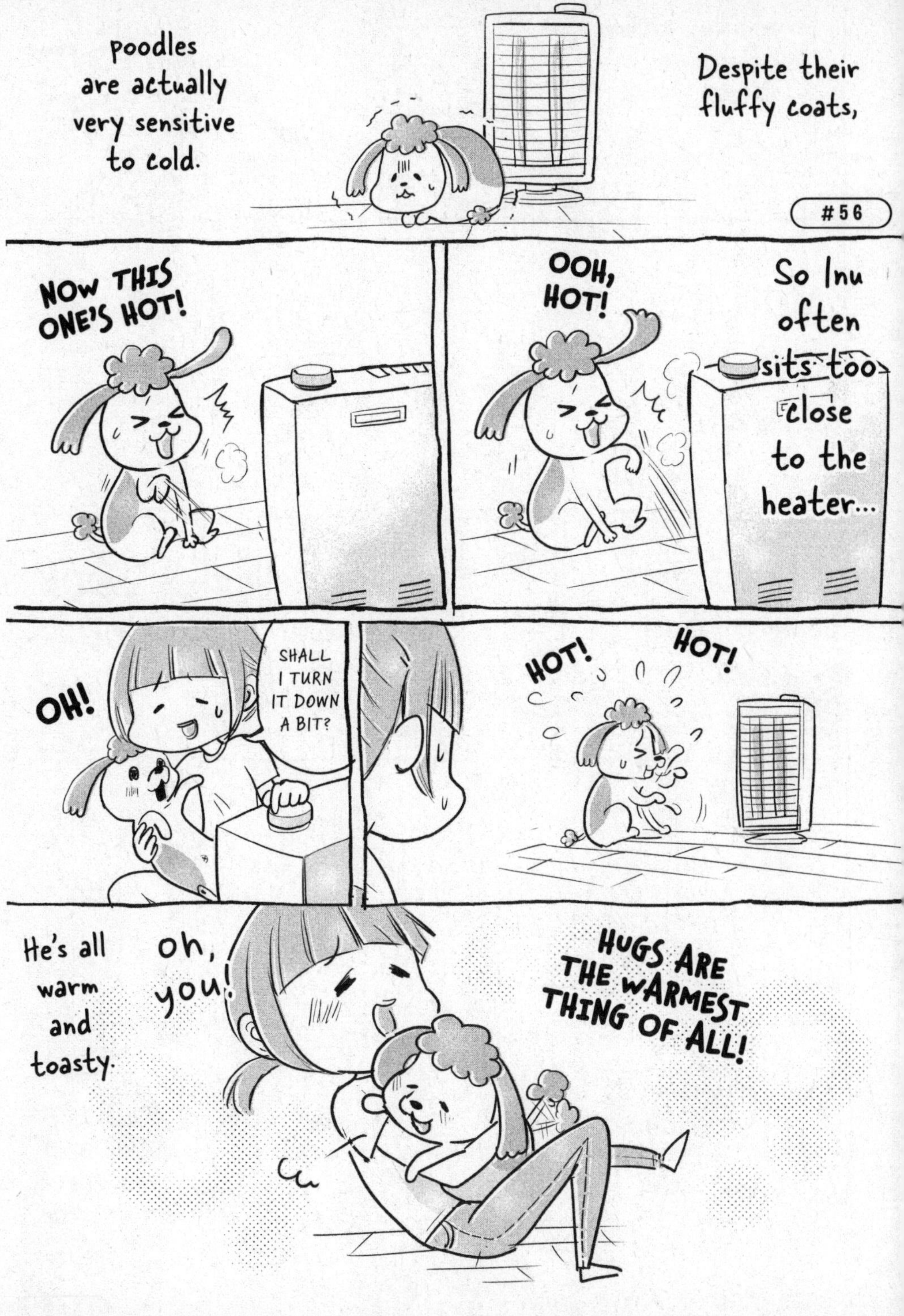

#56
Despite their fluffy coats,
poodles are actually very sensitive to cold.
So Inu often sits too close to the heater...
OOH, HOT!
NOW THIS ONE'S HOT!
HOT!
HOT!
SHALL I TURN IT DOWN A BIT?
OH!
HUGS ARE THE WARMEST THING OF ALL!
oh, you!
He's all warm and toasty.

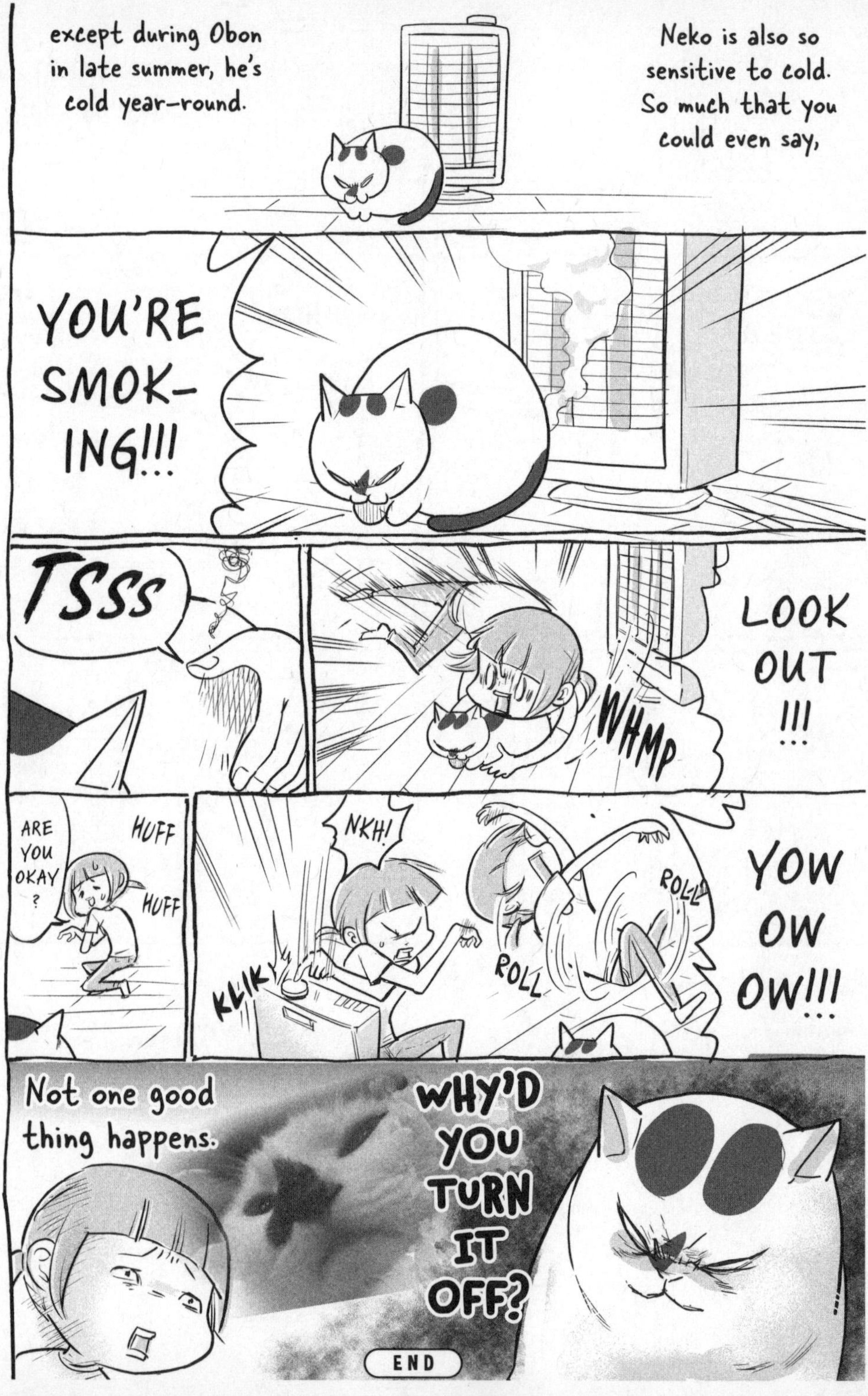
except during Obon in late summer, he's cold year-round.
Neko is also so sensitive to cold. So much that you could even say,
YOU'RE SMOK-ING!!!...
TSSS
WHMP
LOOK OUT!!!...
ARE YOU OKAY?
HUFF
HUFF
NKH!
KLIK
ROLL
ROLL
YOW OW OW!!!...
Not one good thing happens.
WHY'D YOU TURN IT OFF?
END

The height of peacefulness. An angelic smile.

Newly-Drawn 4-Panel Strip

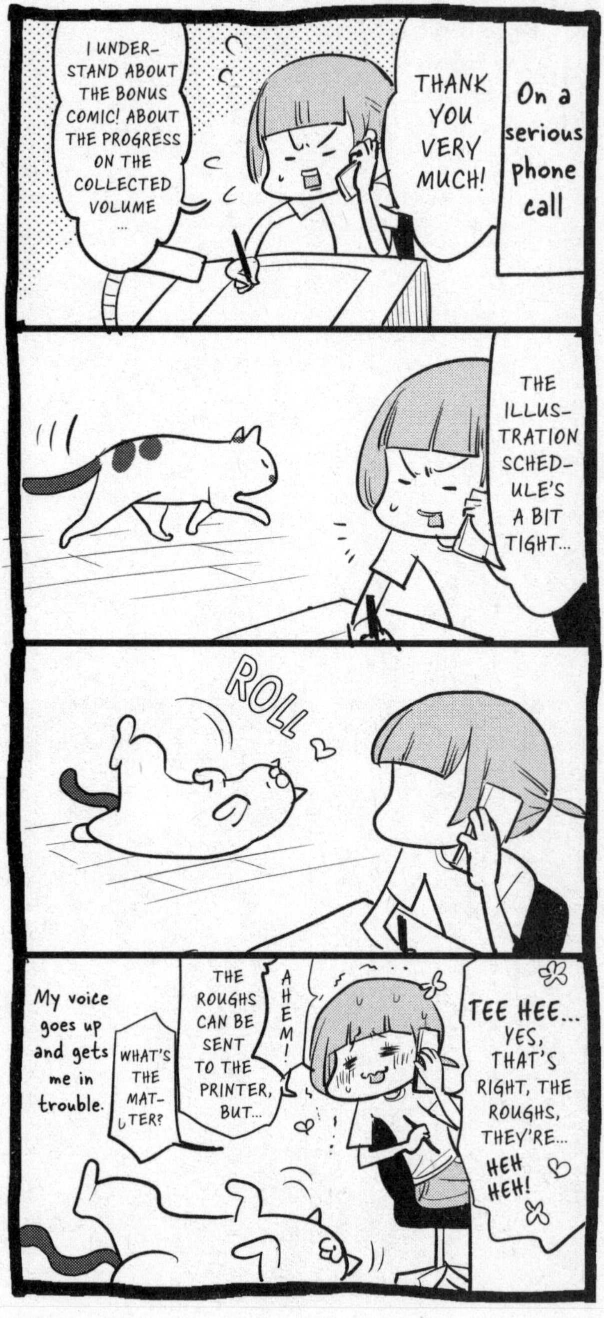
On a serious phone call
THANK YOU VERY MUCH!
I UNDERSTAND ABOUT THE BONUS COMIC! ABOUT THE PROGRESS ON THE COLLECTED VOLUME ...
THE ILLUSTRATION SCHEDULE'S A BIT TIGHT...
ROLL
TEE HEE... YES, THAT'S RIGHT, THE ROUGHS, THEY'RE... HEH HEH!
AHEM!
THE ROUGHS CAN BE SENT TO THE PRINTER, BUT...
WHAT'S THE MATTER?
My voice goes up and gets me in trouble.

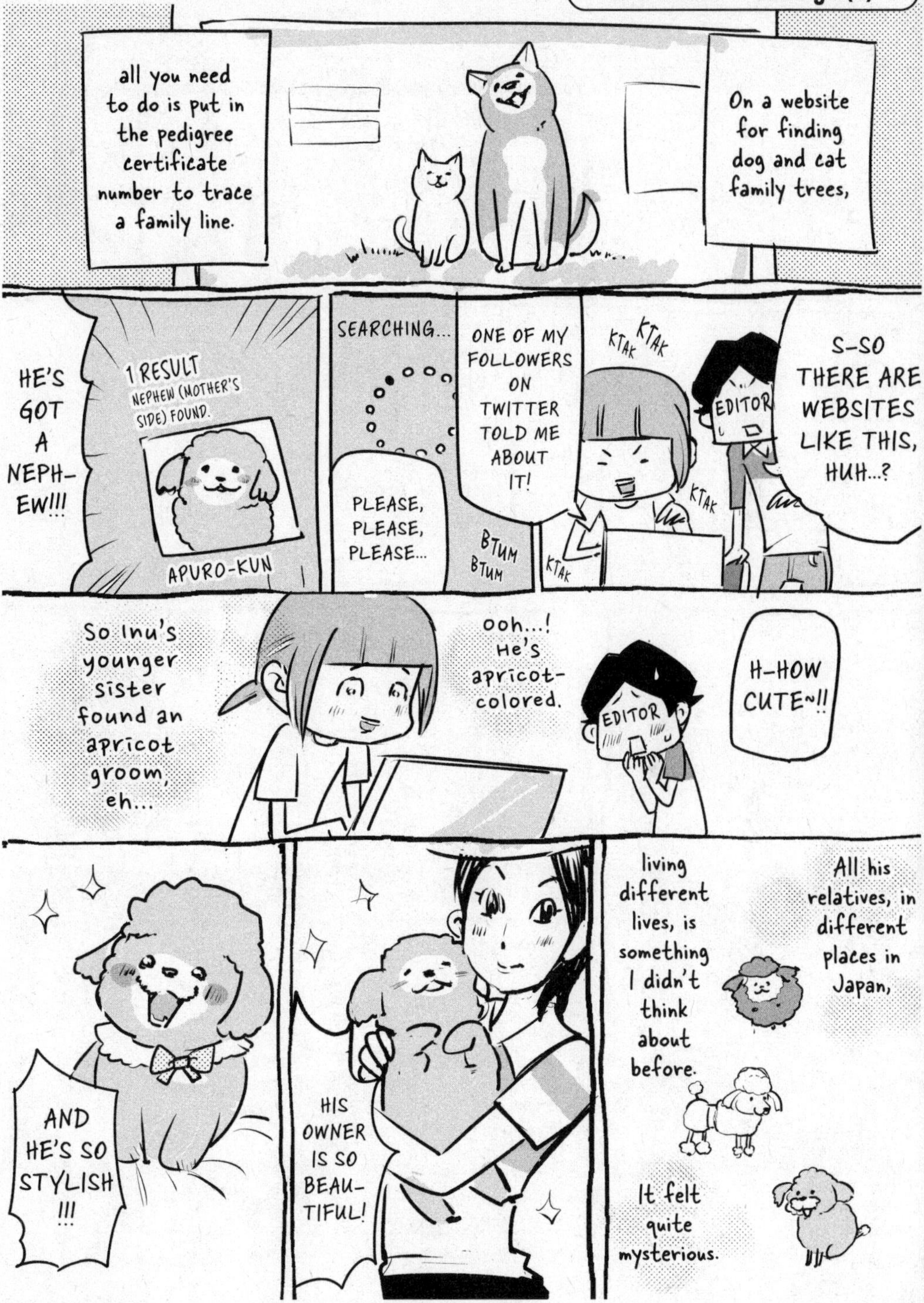
On a website for finding dog and cat family trees,
all you need to do is put in the pedigree certificate number to trace a family line.
S-SO THERE ARE WEBSITES LIKE THIS, HUH...?
KTAK KTAK
EDITOR
ONE OF MY FOLLOWERS ON TWITTER TOLD ME ABOUT IT!
KTAK
KTAK
SEARCHING...
PLEASE, PLEASE, PLEASE...
BTUM BTUM
1 RESULT
NEPHEW (MOTHER'S SIDE) FOUND.
APURO-KUN
HE'S GOT A NEPH-EW!!!
H-HOW CUTE~!!
EDITOR
ooh...! He's apricot-colored.
So Inu's younger sister found an apricot groom, eh...
All his relatives, in different places in Japan,
living different lives, is something I didn't think about before.
It felt quite mysterious.
HIS OWNER IS SO BEAU-TIFUL!
AND HE'S SO STYLISH!!!

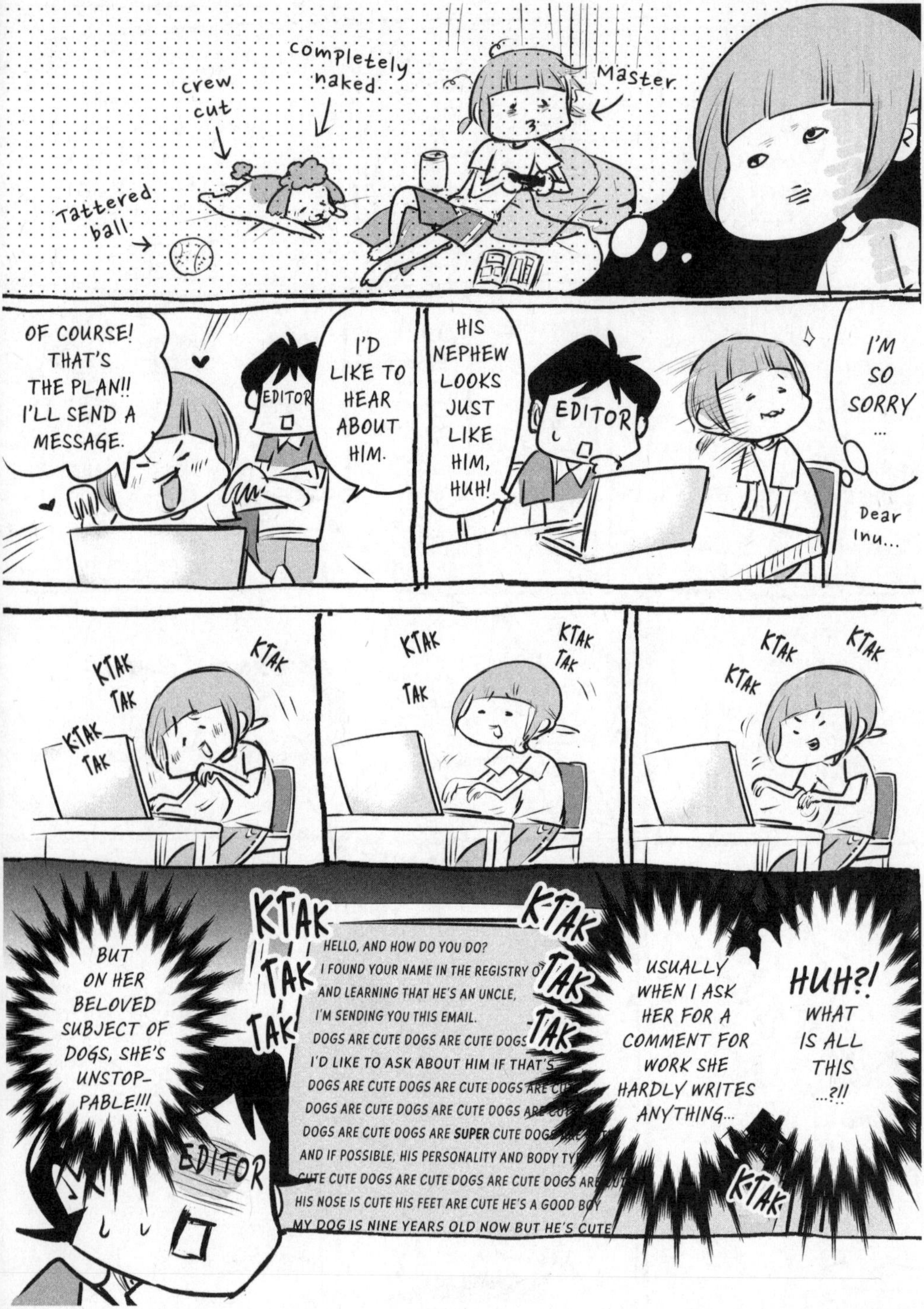
Master
completely naked
crew cut
Tattered ball
I'M SO SORRY ...
Dear Inu...
EDITOR
HIS NEPHEW LOOKS JUST LIKE HIM, HUH!
I'D LIKE TO HEAR ABOUT HIM.
EDITOR
OF COURSE! THAT'S THE PLAN!! I'LL SEND A MESSAGE.
KTAK
KTAK TAK
KTAK
KTAK TAK
TAK
KTAK
KTAK TAK
KTAK TAK
HUH?! WHAT IS ALL THIS ...?!!
USUALLY WHEN I ASK HER FOR A COMMENT FOR WORK SHE HARDLY WRITES ANYTHING...
KTAK
K-TAK TAK TAK
HELLO, AND HOW DO YOU DO?
I FOUND YOUR NAME IN THE REGISTRY O
AND LEARNING THAT HE'S AN UNCLE,
I'M SENDING YOU THIS EMAIL.
DOGS ARE CUTE DOGS ARE CUTE DOGS
I'D LIKE TO ASK ABOUT HIM IF THAT'S
DOGS ARE CUTE DOGS ARE CUTE DOGS ARE CU
DOGS ARE CUTE DOGS ARE CUTE DOGS ARE CUTE
DOGS ARE CUTE DOGS ARE SUPER CUTE DOGS
AND IF POSSIBLE, HIS PERSONALITY AND BODY TY
CUTE CUTE DOGS ARE CUTE DOGS ARE CUTE DOGS ARE
HIS NOSE IS CUTE HIS FEET ARE CUTE HE'S A GOOD BOY
MY DOG IS NINE YEARS OLD NOW BUT HE'S CUTE
KTAK TAK TAK
BUT ON HER BELOVED SUBJECT OF DOGS, SHE'S UNSTOP-PABLE!!!
EDITOR

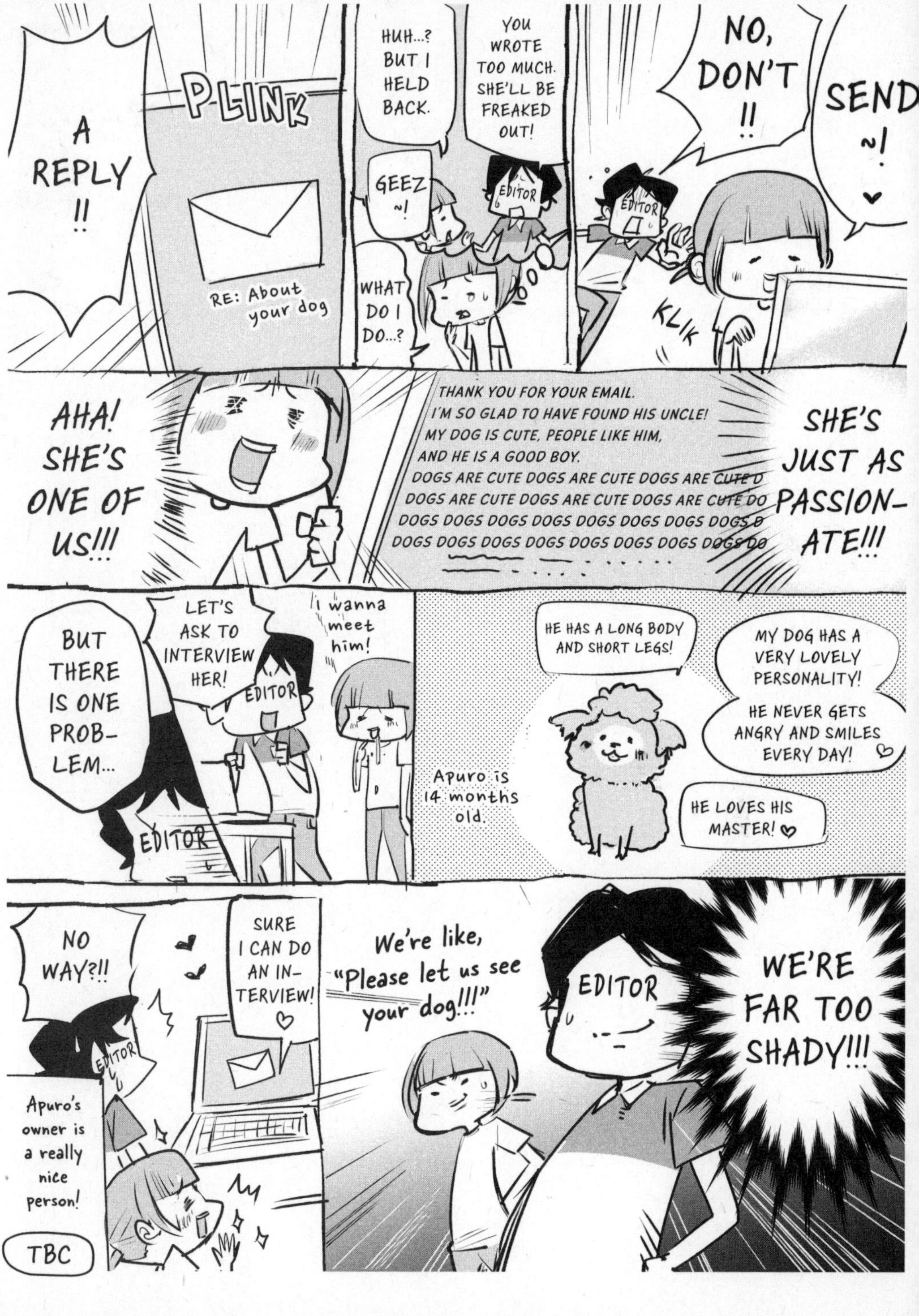
SEND ~! ♥
NO, DON'T !!
EDITOR
KLIK
YOU WROTE TOO MUCH. SHE'LL BE FREAKED OUT!
HUH...? BUT I HELD BACK.
EDITOR
GEEZ ~!
WHAT DO I DO...?
PLINK
A REPLY !!
RE: About your dog
SHE'S JUST AS PASSION-ATE!!!
THANK YOU FOR YOUR EMAIL.
I'M SO GLAD TO HAVE FOUND HIS UNCLE!
MY DOG IS CUTE, PEOPLE LIKE HIM,
AND HE IS A GOOD BOY.
DOGS ARE CUTE DOGS ARE CUTE DOGS ARE CUTE D
DOGS ARE CUTE DOGS ARE CUTE DOGS ARE CUTE DO
DOGS DOGS DOGS DOGS DOGS DOGS DOGS DOGS D
DOGS DOGS DOGS DOGS DOGS DOGS DOGS DOGS DO
AHA! SHE'S ONE OF US!!!
MY DOG HAS A VERY LOVELY PERSONALITY!
HE HAS A LONG BODY AND SHORT LEGS!
HE NEVER GETS ANGRY AND SMILES EVERY DAY! ♡
Apuro is 14 months old.
HE LOVES HIS MASTER! ♡
I wanna meet him!
LET'S ASK TO INTERVIEW HER!
EDITOR
BUT THERE IS ONE PROB-LEM...
EDITOR
WE'RE FAR TOO SHADY!!!
EDITOR
We're like, "Please let us see your dog!!!"
SURE I CAN DO AN IN-TERVIEW! ♡
NO WAY?!!
EDITOR
Apuro's owner is a really nice person!
TBC

#57

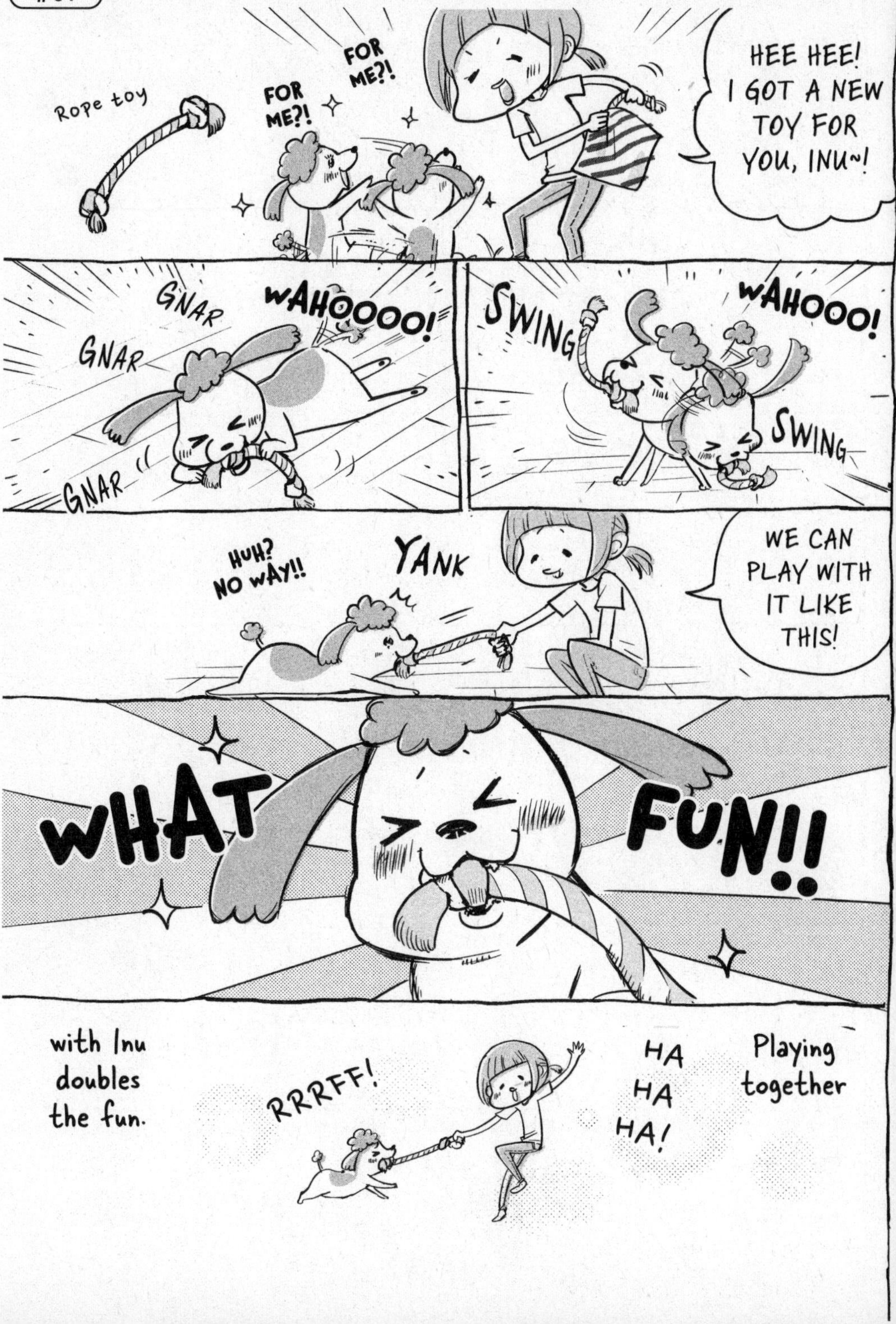
HEE HEE! I GOT A NEW TOY FOR YOU, INU~!
FOR ME?!
FOR ME?!
Rope toy
WAHOOO!
SWING
SWING
WAHOOOO!
GNAR
GNAR
GNAR
WE CAN PLAY WITH IT LIKE THIS!
YANK
HUH? NO WAY!!
WHAT FUN!!
Playing together
HA HA HA!
RRRFF!
with Inu doubles the fun.

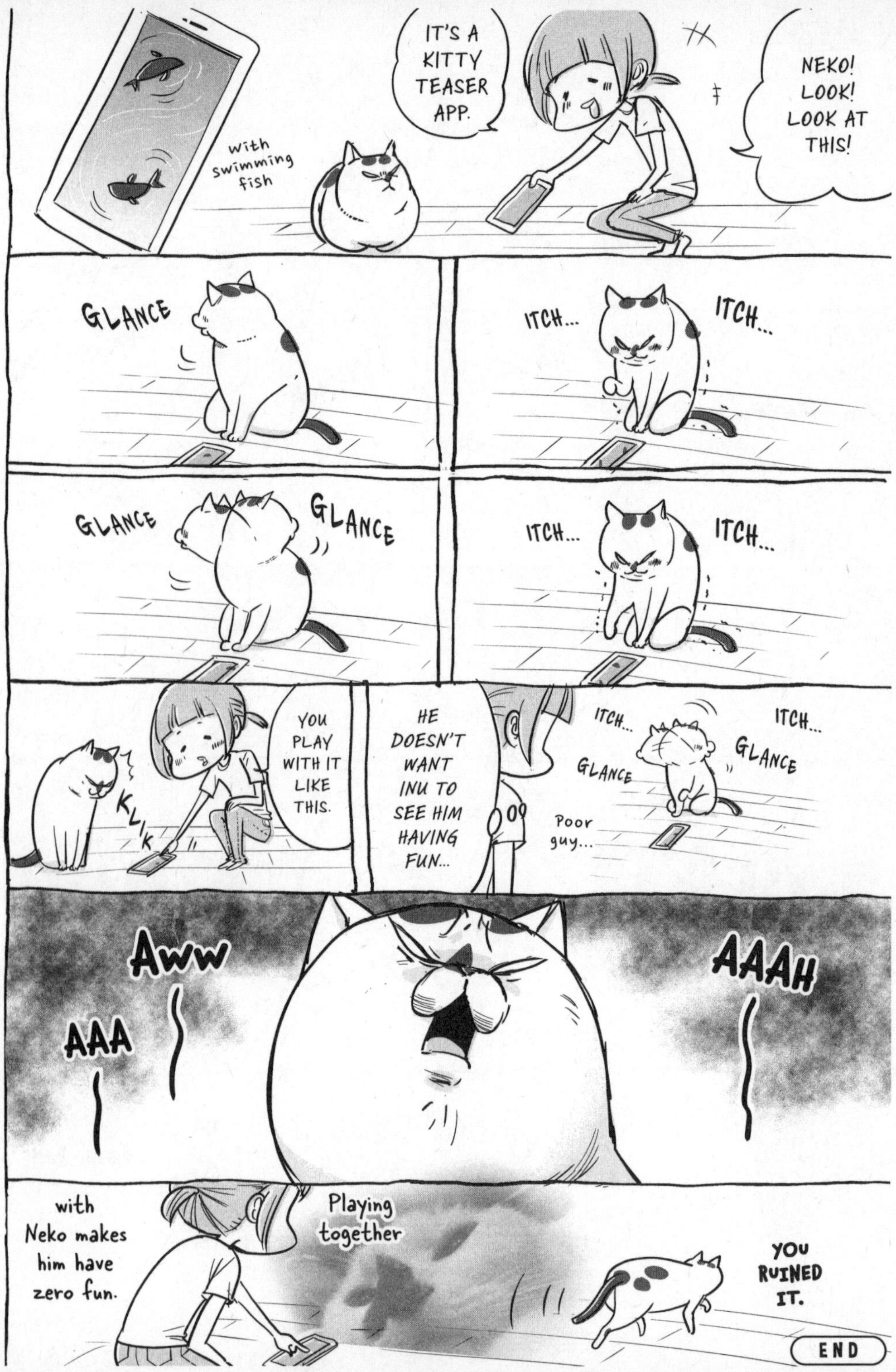
NEKO! LOOK! LOOK AT THIS!
IT'S A KITTY TEASER APP.
with swimming fish
ITCH...
ITCH...
GLANCE
ITCH...
ITCH...
GLANCE
GLANCE
ITCH...
GLANCE
ITCH...
HE DOESN'T WANT INU TO SEE HIM HAVING FUN...
GLANCE
Poor guy...
YOU PLAY WITH IT LIKE THIS.
KLIK
AAAH
Aww
AAA
YOU RUINED IT.
Playing together
with Neko makes him have zero fun.
END

#58

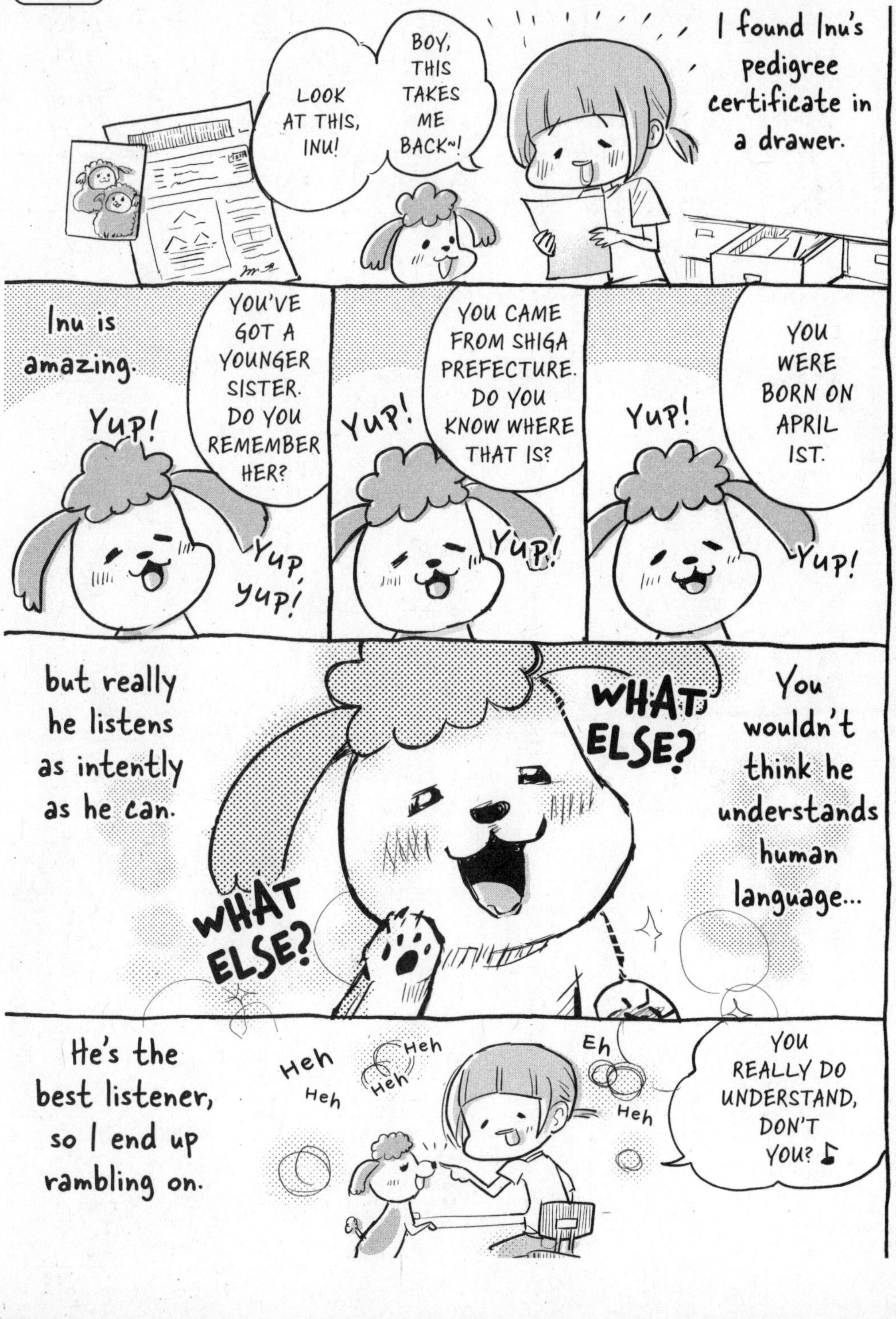

I found Inu's pedigree certificate in a drawer.
LOOK AT THIS, INU! BOY, THIS TAKES ME BACK~!
YOU WERE BORN ON APRIL 1ST.
Yup!
Yup!
YOU CAME FROM SHIGA PREFECTURE. DO YOU KNOW WHERE THAT IS?
Yup!
Yup!
Inu is amazing.
YOU'VE GOT A YOUNGER SISTER. DO YOU REMEMBER HER?
Yup!
Yup, yup!
You wouldn't think he understands human language...
WHAT ELSE?
WHAT ELSE?
but really he listens as intently as he can.
YOU REALLY DO UNDERSTAND, DON'T YOU? ♪
Eh
Heh
Heh
Heh
Heh
Heh
Heh
He's the best listener, so I end up rambling on.

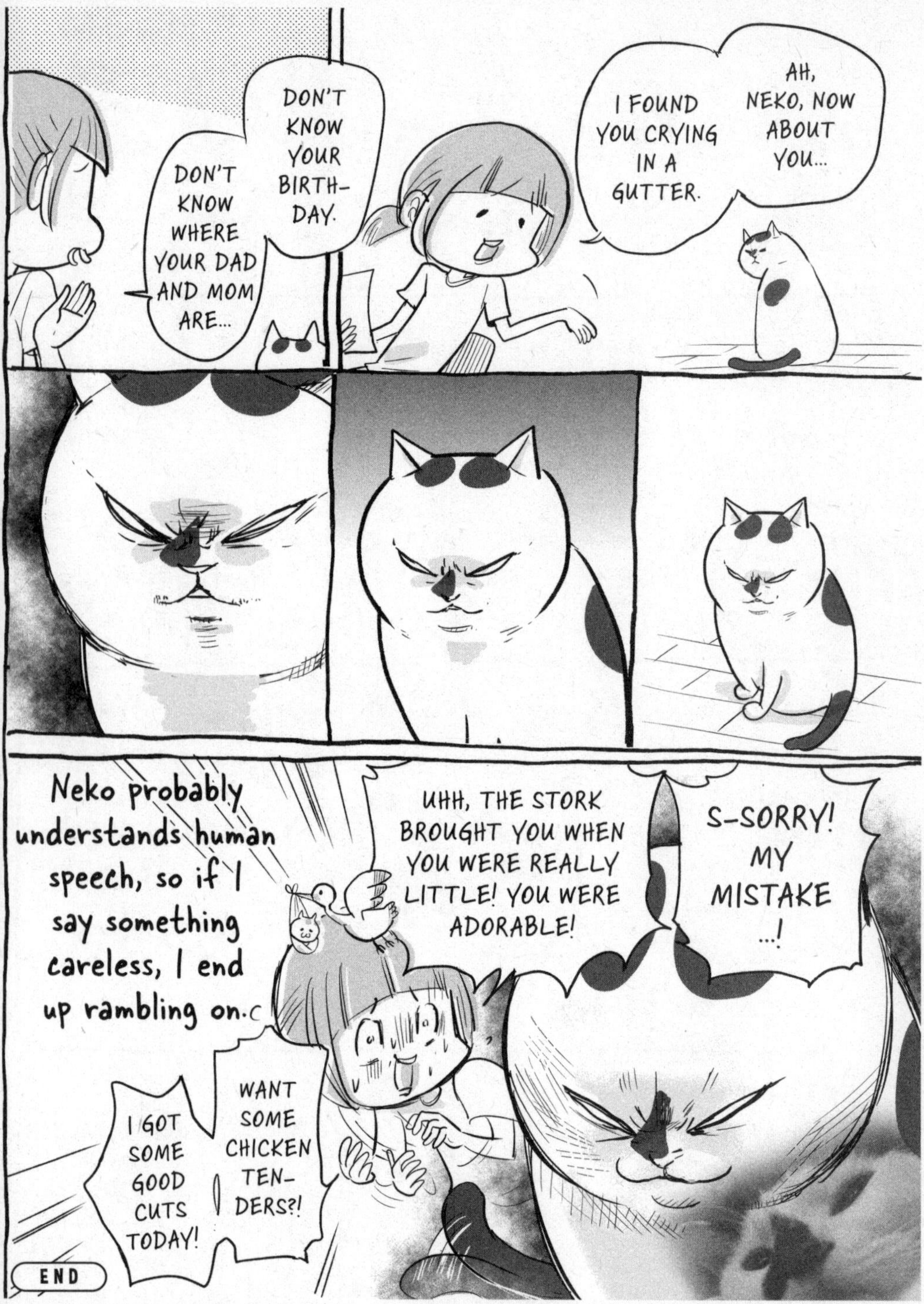
AH, NEKO, NOW ABOUT YOU...
I FOUND YOU CRYING IN A GUTTER.
DON'T KNOW YOUR BIRTH-DAY.
DON'T KNOW WHERE YOUR DAD AND MOM ARE...
S-SORRY! MY MISTAKE ...!
UHH, THE STORK BROUGHT YOU WHEN YOU WERE REALLY LITTLE! YOU WERE ADORABLE!
Neko probably understands human speech, so if I say something careless, I end up rambling on.
WANT SOME CHICKEN TEN-DERS?!
I GOT SOME GOOD CUTS TODAY!
END

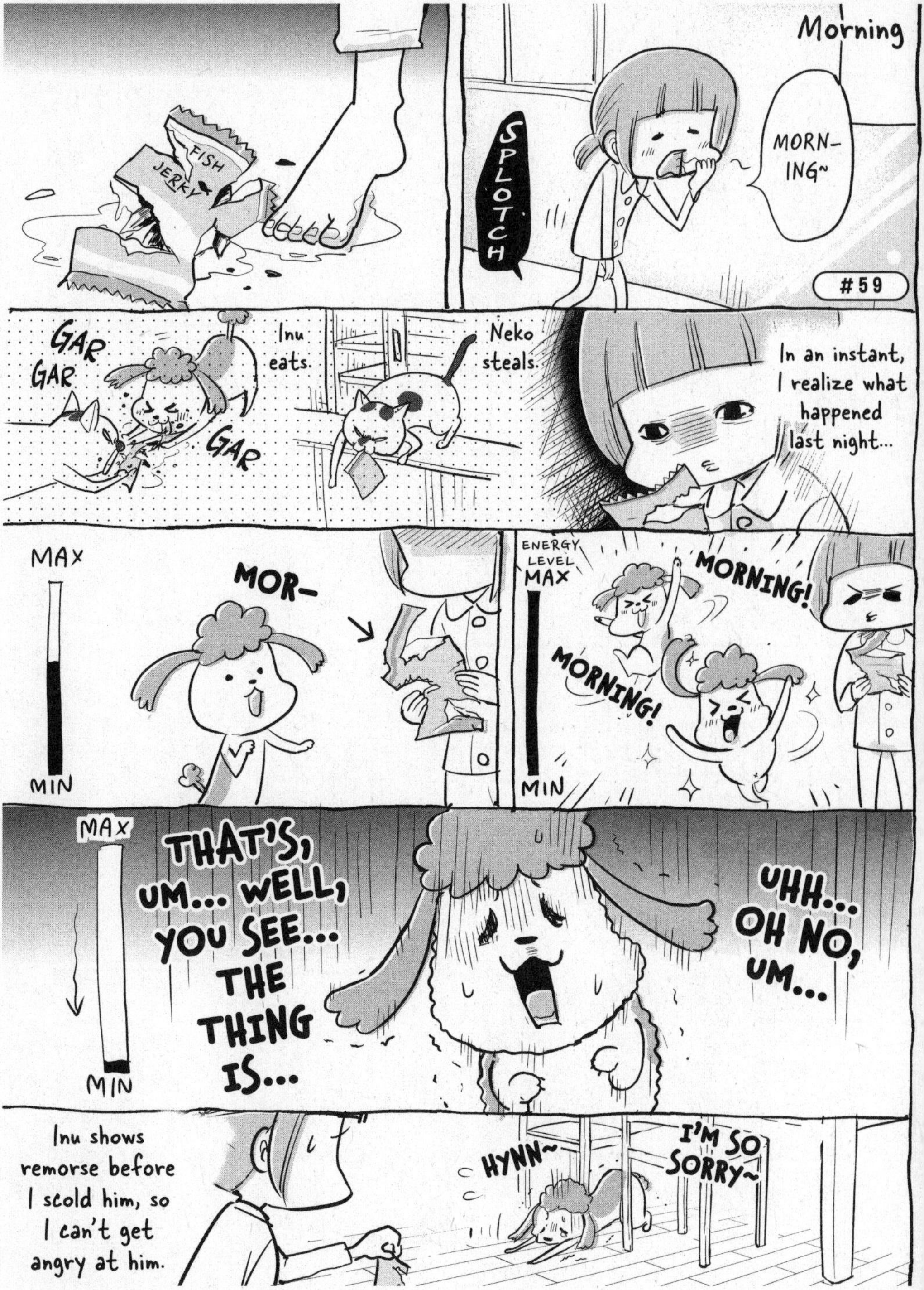
Morning
#59
MORN-ING~
SPLOTCH
FISH JERKY
In an instant, I realize what happened last night...
Neko steals.
Inu eats.
GAR
GAR
GAR
ENERGY LEVEL
MAX
MORNING!
MORNING!
MIN
MAX
MOR-
MIN
UHH... OH NO, UM...
THAT'S, UM... WELL, YOU SEE... THE THING IS...
MAX
MIN
I'M SO SORRY~
HYNN~
Inu shows remorse before I scold him, so I can't get angry at him.

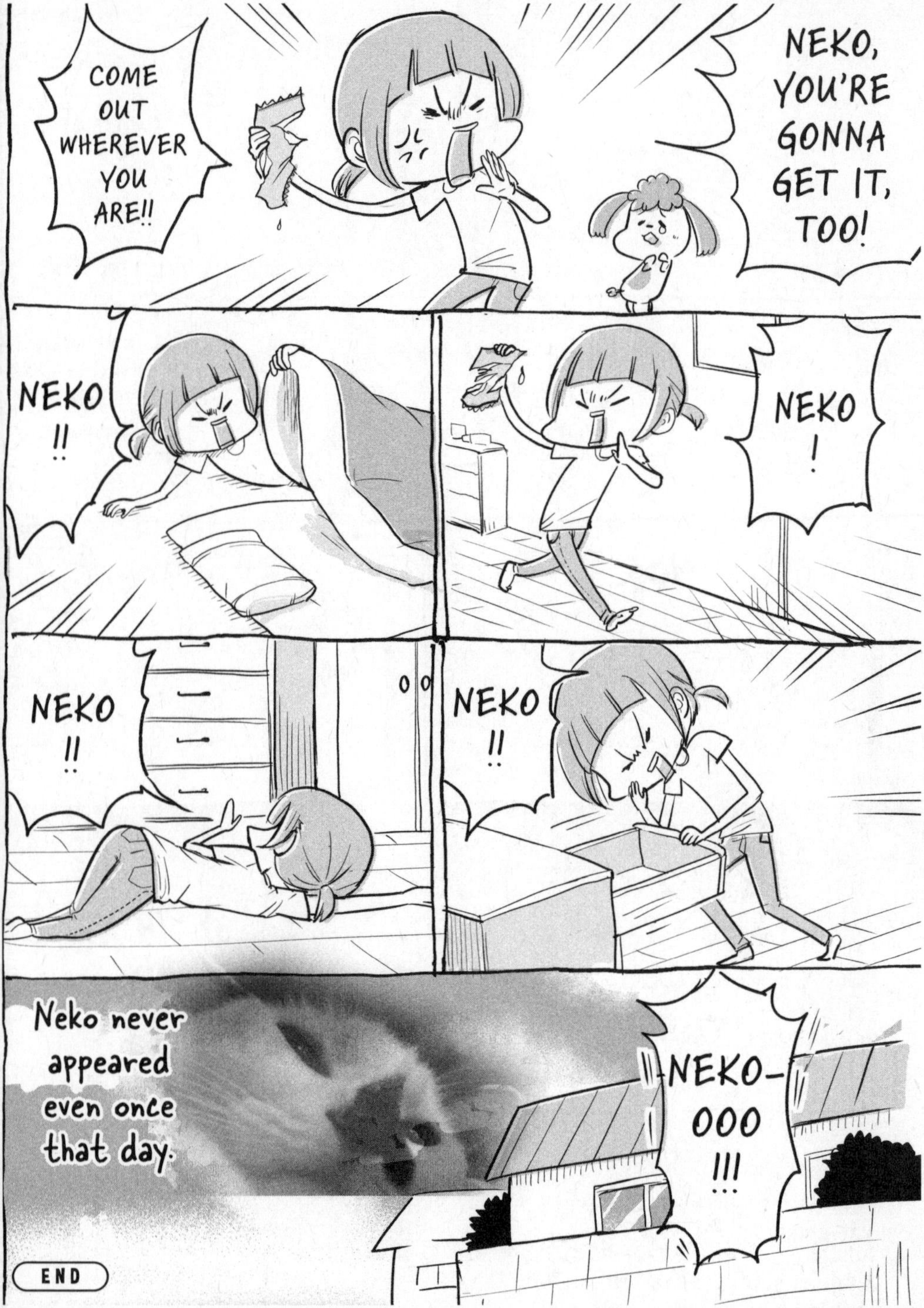
NEKO, YOU'RE GONNA GET IT, TOO!
COME OUT WHEREVER YOU ARE!!
NEKO!
NEKO!!
NEKO!!
NEKO!!
NEKO-OOO!!!
Neko never appeared even once that day.
END

Magical goblin cat to the extreme. Looks like he should be in an *ukiyoe* painting.

Newly-Drawn 4-Panel Strip

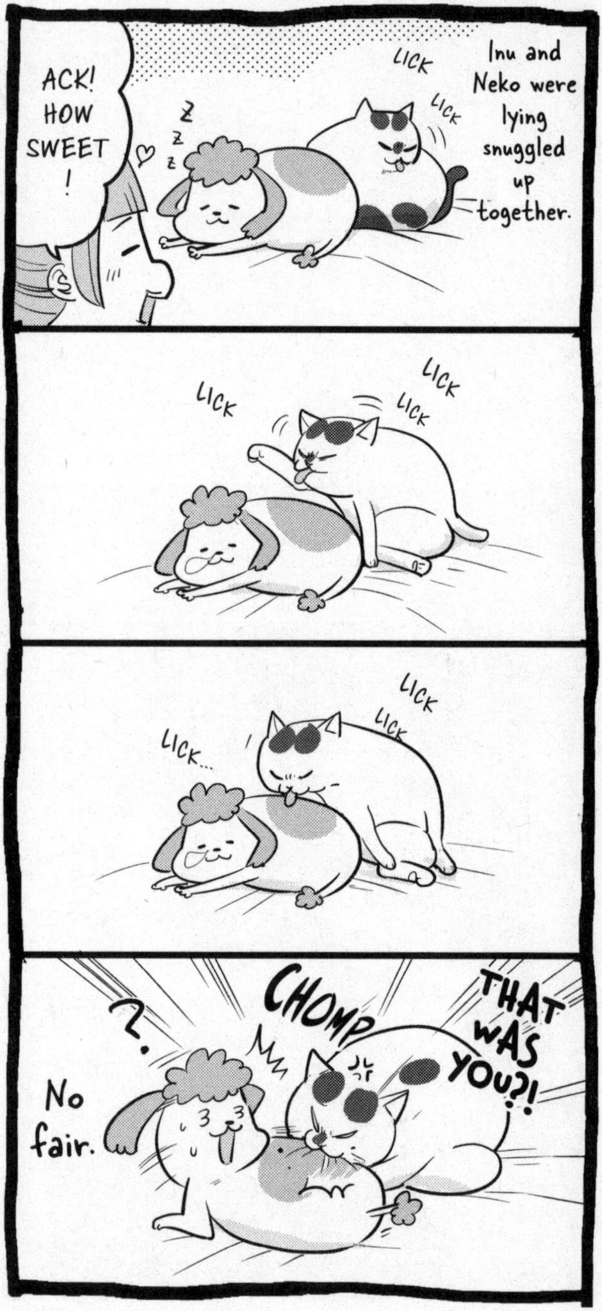
Inu and Neko were lying snuggled up together.
LICK
LICK
ACK! HOW SWEET!
LICK
LICK
LICK
LICK
LICK
LICK...
THAT WAS YOU?!
CHOMP
No fair.

#60

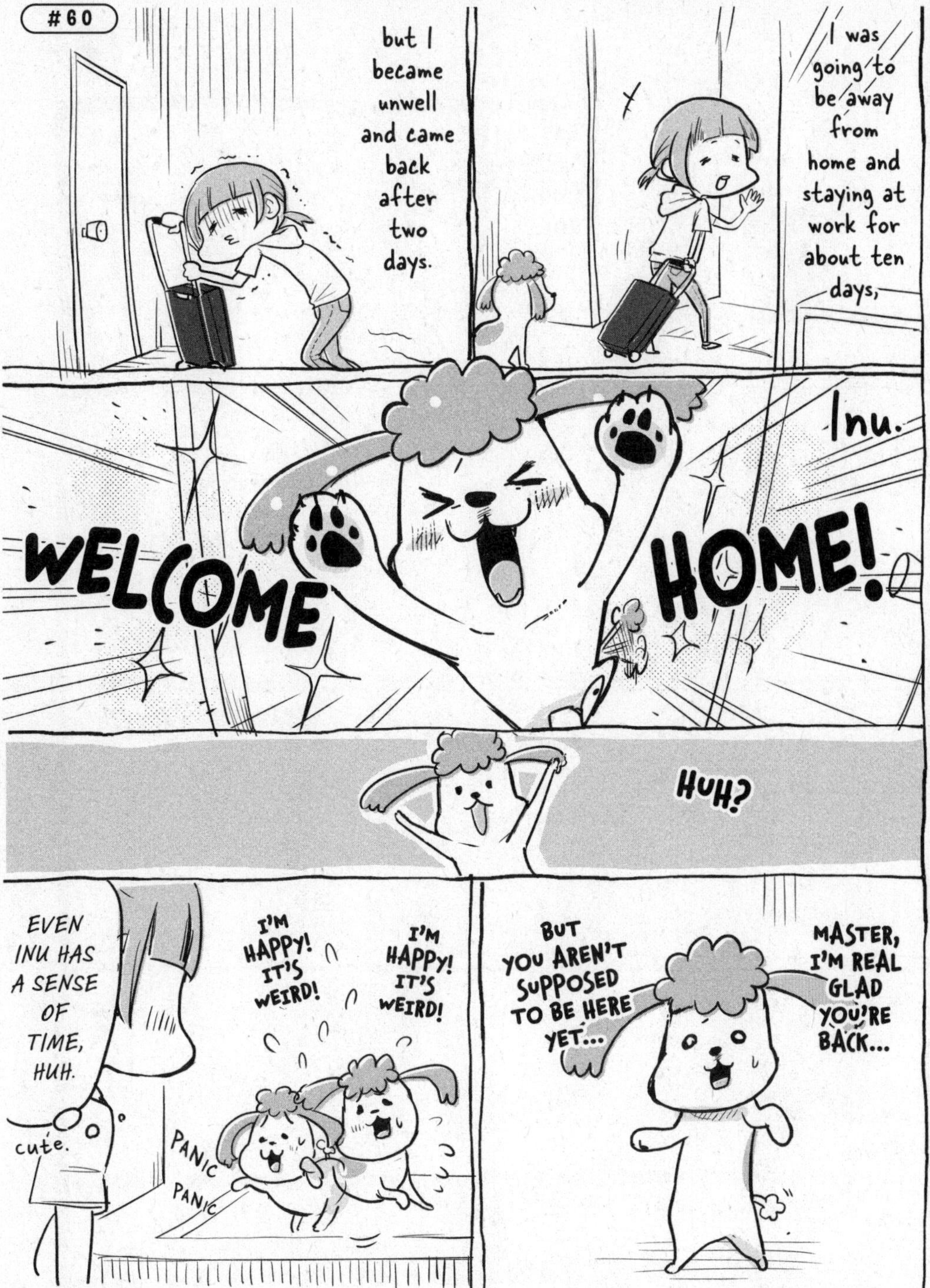
I was going to be away from home and staying at work for about ten days,
but I became unwell and came back after two days.
Inu.
WELCOME HOME!
HUH?
MASTER, I'M REAL GLAD YOU'RE BACK...
BUT YOU AREN'T SUPPOSED TO BE HERE YET...
I'M HAPPY! IT'S WEIRD!
I'M HAPPY! IT'S WEIRD!
EVEN INU HAS A SENSE OF TIME, HUH.
cute.
PANIC
PANIC

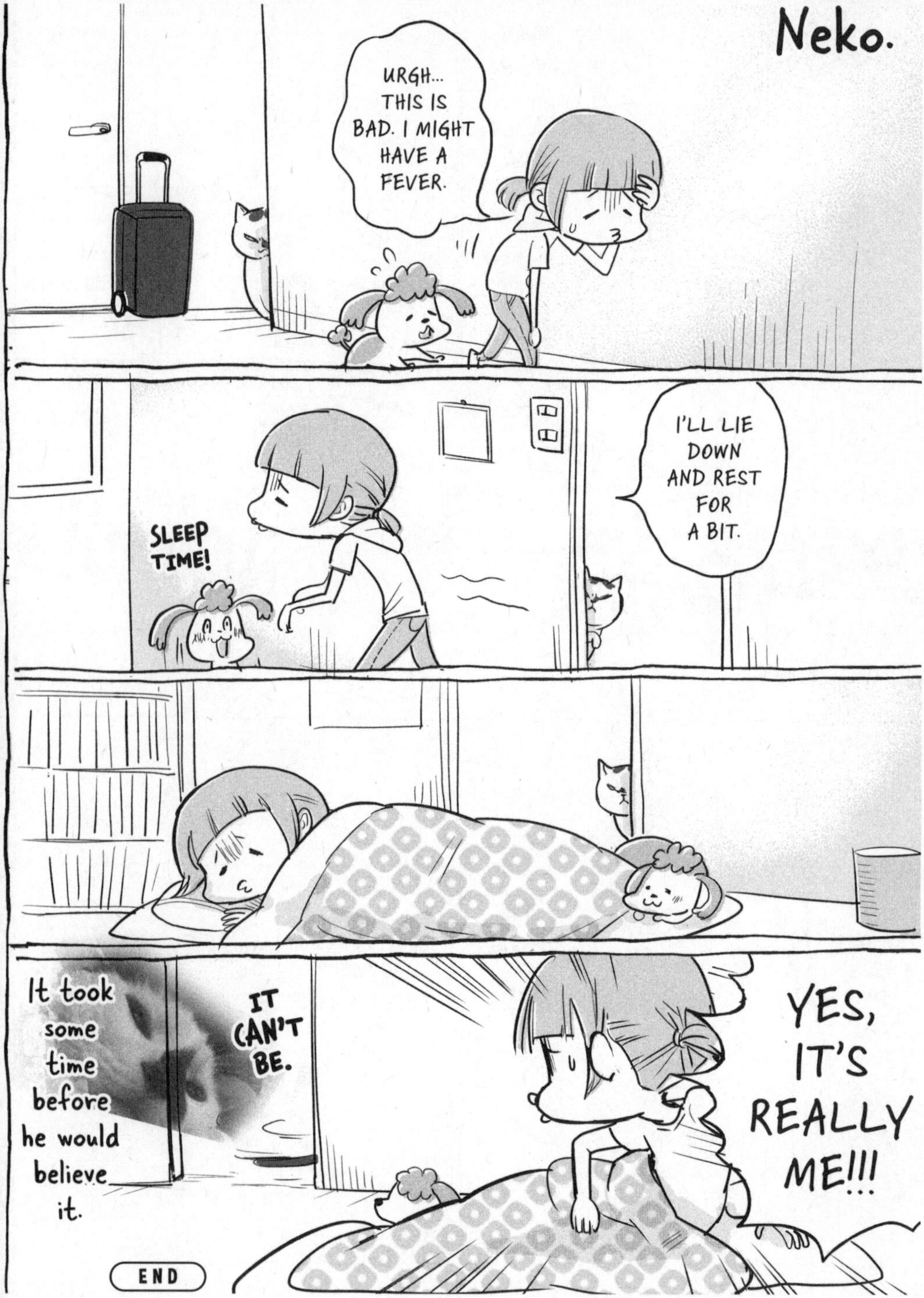
Neko.
URGH... THIS IS BAD. I MIGHT HAVE A FEVER.
I'LL LIE DOWN AND REST FOR A BIT.
SLEEP TIME!
YES, IT'S REALLY ME!!!...
IT CAN'T BE.
It took some time before he would believe it.
END

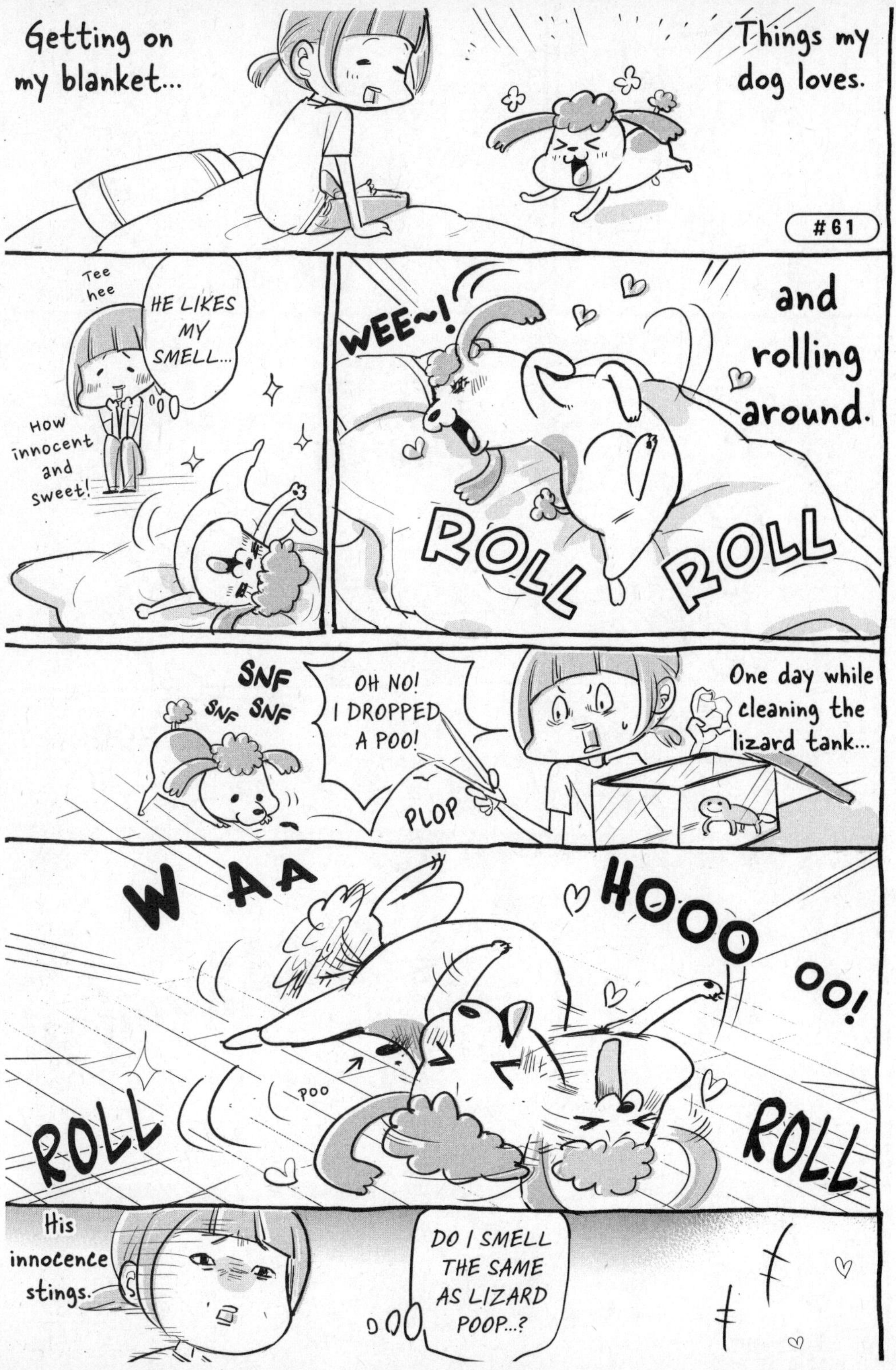

Things my dog loves.
Getting on my blanket...
#61
and rolling around.
WEE~!
ROLL ROLL
Tee hee
HE LIKES MY SMELL...
How innocent and sweet!
One day while cleaning the lizard tank...
OH NO! I DROPPED A POO!
PLOP
SNF SNF SNF
W AA HOOO OO!
ROLL
POO
ROLL
DO I SMELL THE SAME AS LIZARD POOP...?
His innocence stings.

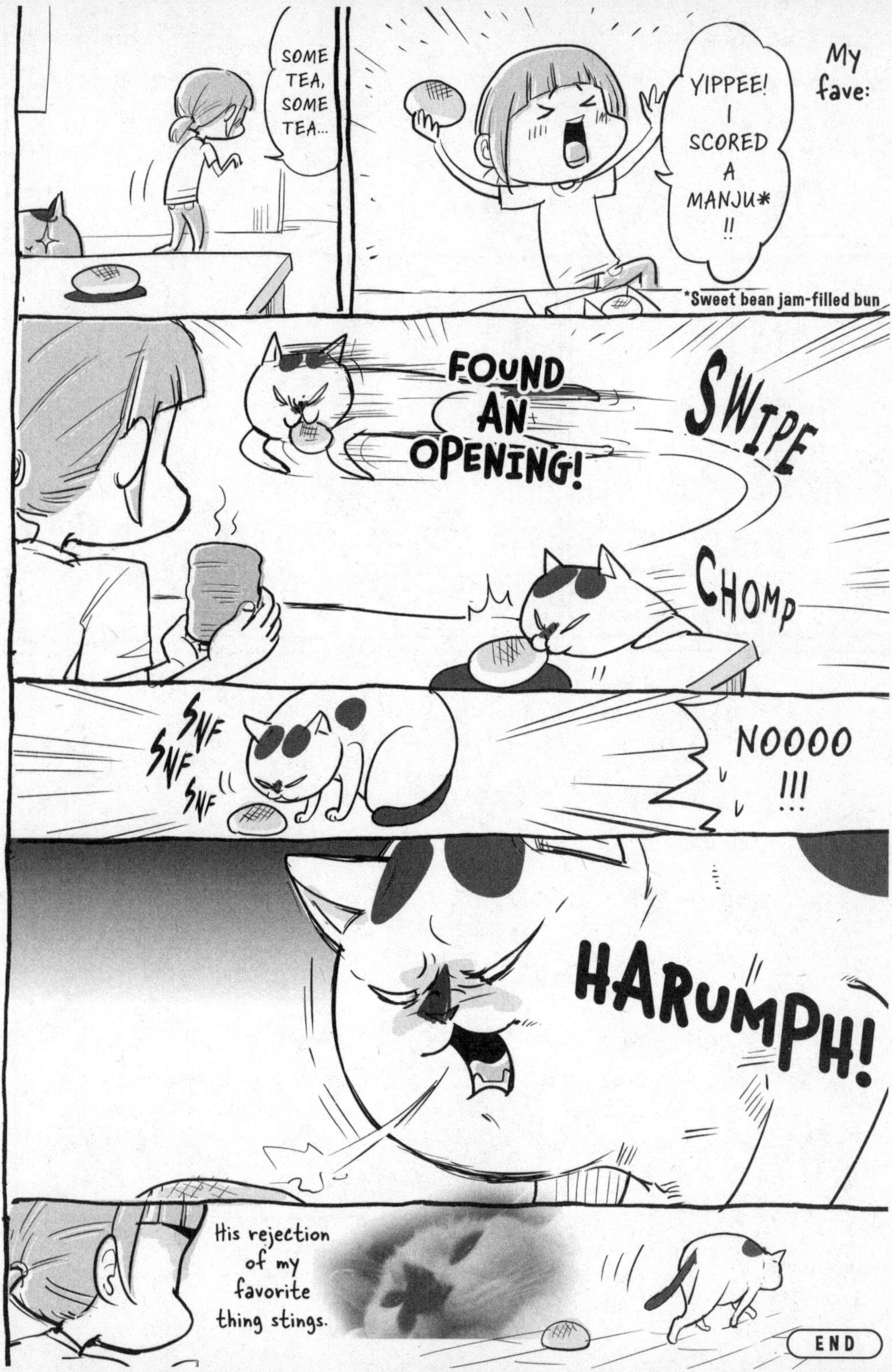

My fave:
YIPPEE! I SCORED A MANJU* !!
*Sweet bean jam-filled bun
SOME TEA, SOME TEA...
SWIPE
FOUND AN OPENING!
CHOMP
NOOOO !!!...
SNF SNF SNF
HARUMPH!
His rejection of my favorite thing stings.
END

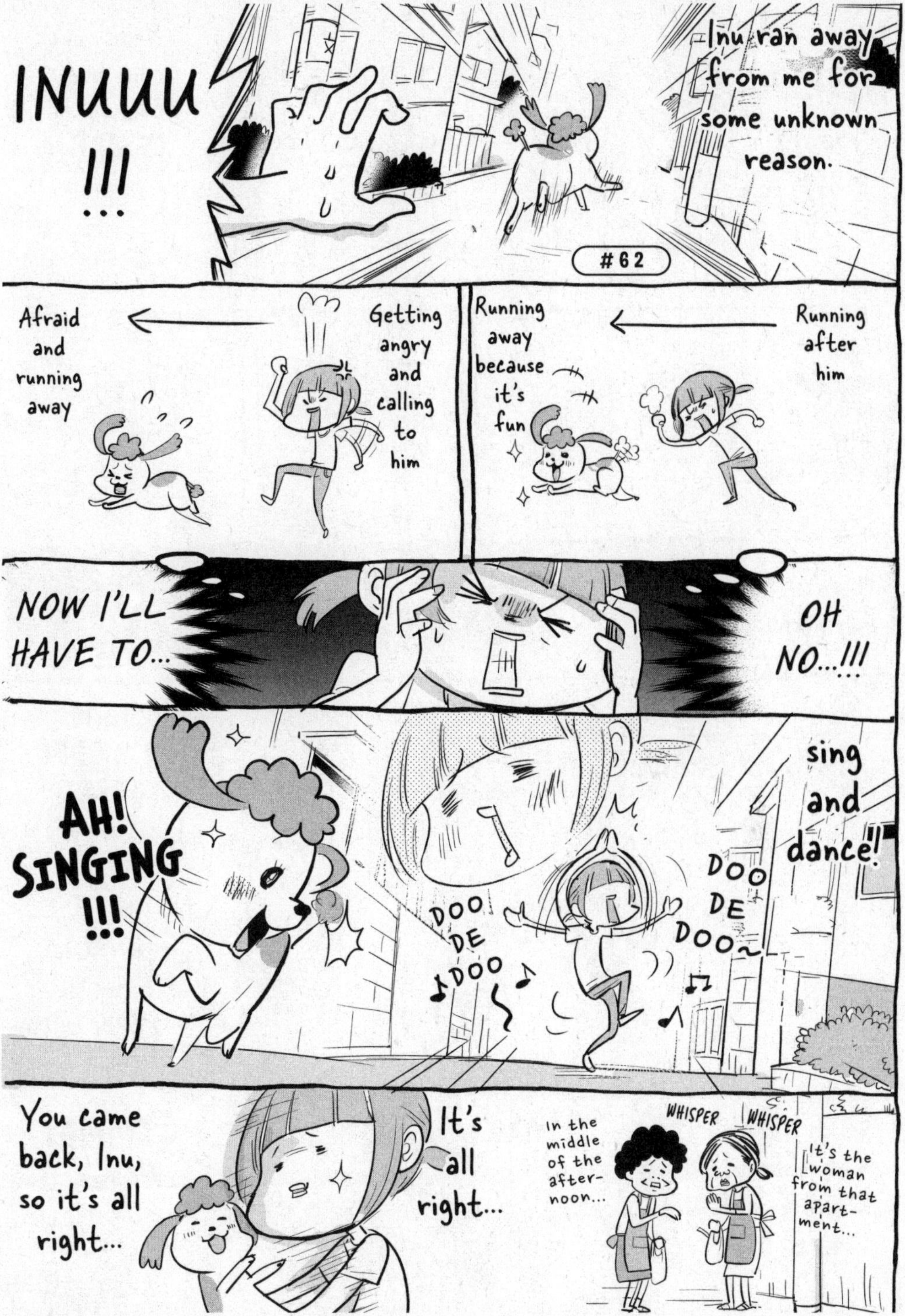
Inu ran away from me for some unknown reason.
INUUU !!! ...
#62
Running after him
Running away because it's fun
Getting angry and calling to him
Afraid and running away
OH NO...!!!
NOW I'LL HAVE TO...
sing and dance!
DOO DE DOO~
DOO DE DOO
AH! SINGING !!!
WHISPER WHISPER
It's the woman from that apart-ment...
In the middle of the after-noon...
It's all right...
You came back, Inu, so it's all right...

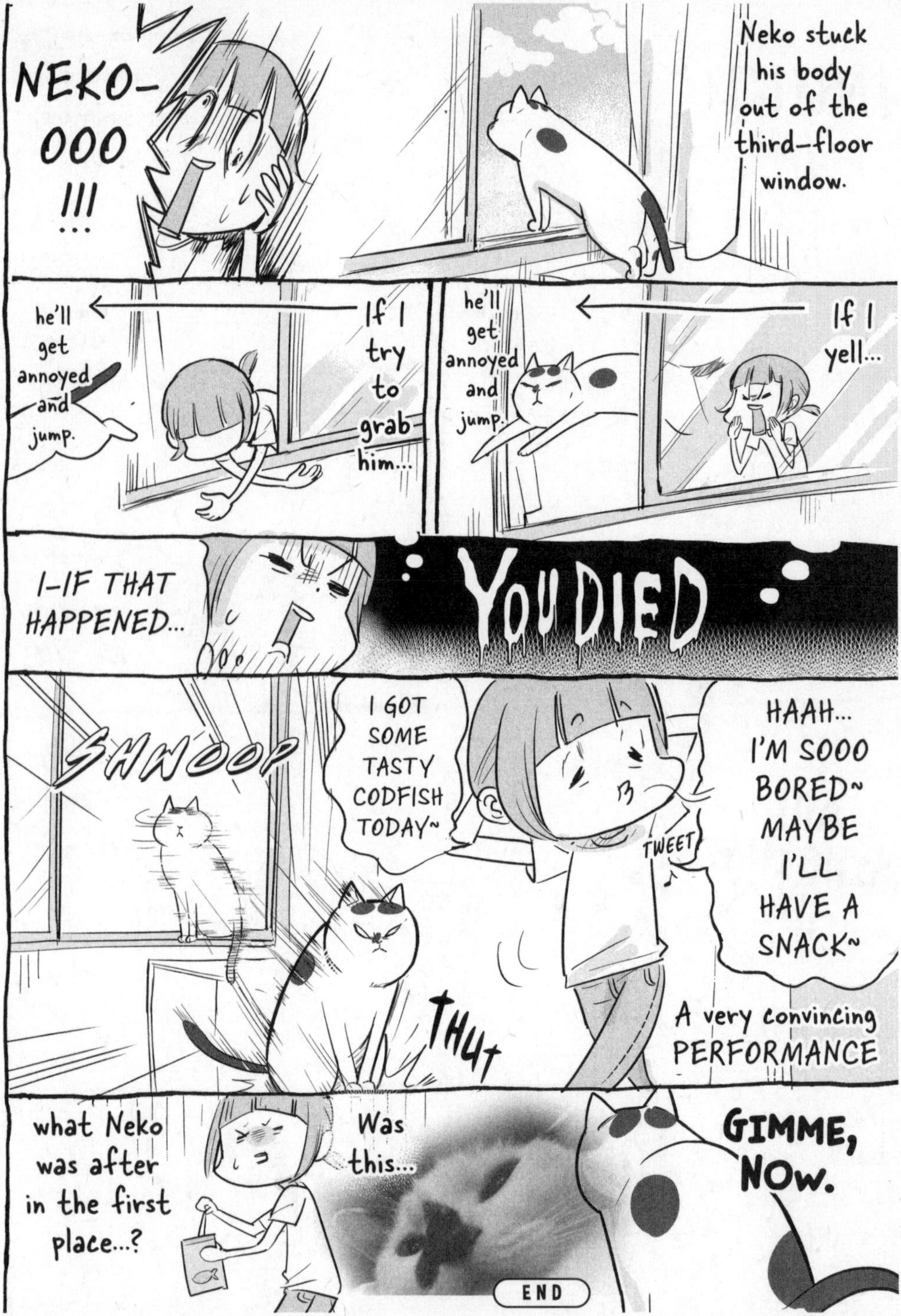
Neko stuck his body out of the third-floor window.
NEKO-OOO !!!...
If I yell...
he'll get annoyed and jump.
If I try to grab him...
he'll get annoyed and jump.
YOU DIED
I-IF THAT HAPPENED...
HAAH... I'M SOOO BORED~ MAYBE I'LL HAVE A SNACK~
I GOT SOME TASTY CODFISH TODAY~
TWEET
A very convincing PERFORMANCE
SHWOOP
THUT
GIMME, NOW.
Was this...
what Neko was after in the first place...?
END

Bonus

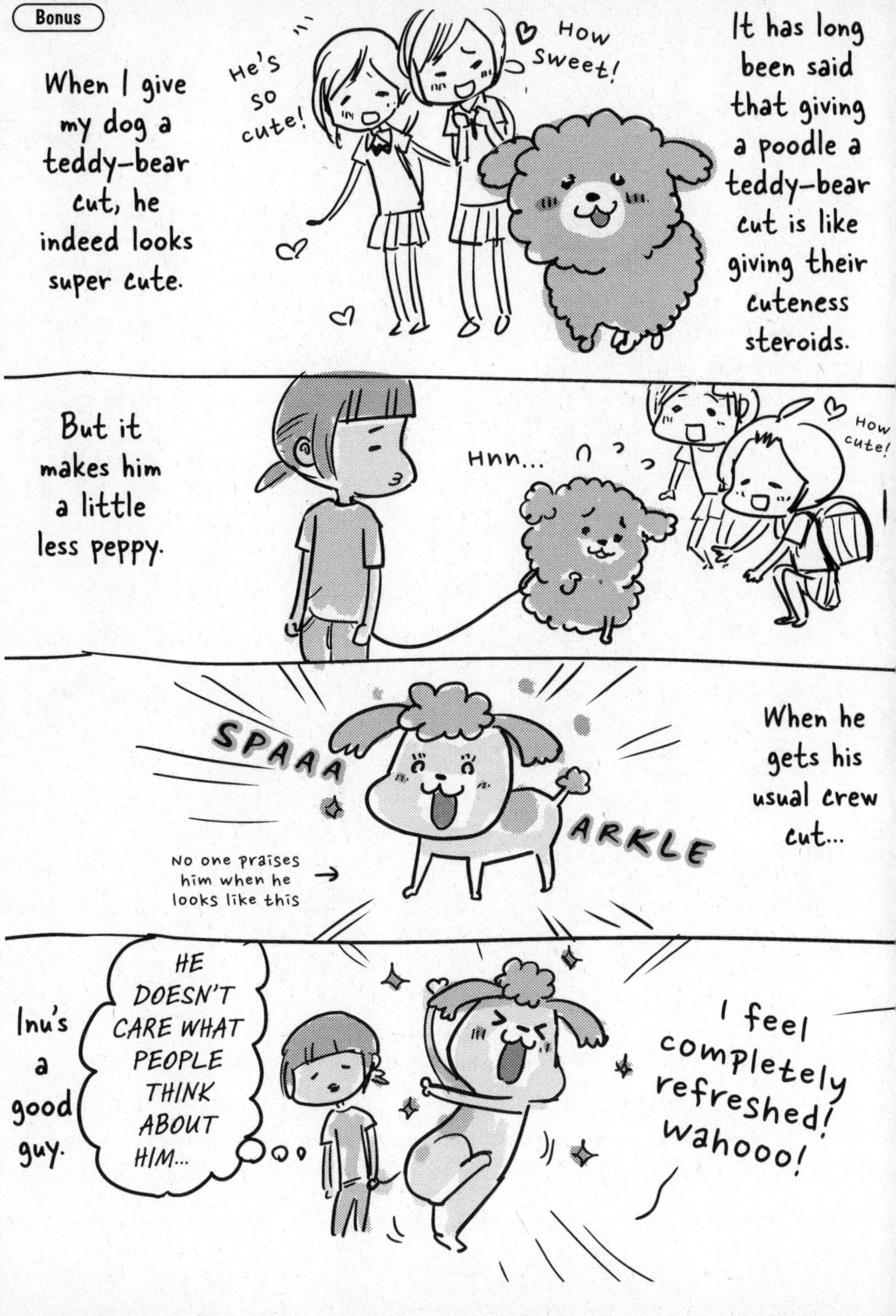

It has long been said that giving a poodle a teddy-bear cut is like giving their cuteness steroids.
How Sweet!
He's so cute!
When I give my dog a teddy-bear cut, he indeed looks super cute.
How cute!
Hnn...
But it makes him a little less peppy.
When he gets his usual crew cut...
SPAAAARKLE
No one praises him when he looks like this
I feel completely refreshed! Wahooo!
HE DOESN'T CARE WHAT PEOPLE THINK ABOUT HIM...
Inu's a good guy.

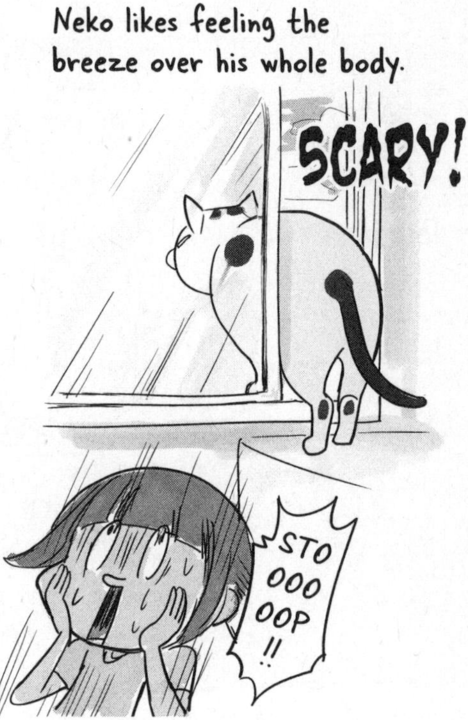

Neko likes feeling the breeze over his whole body.
SCARY!
STOOOOOOP!!

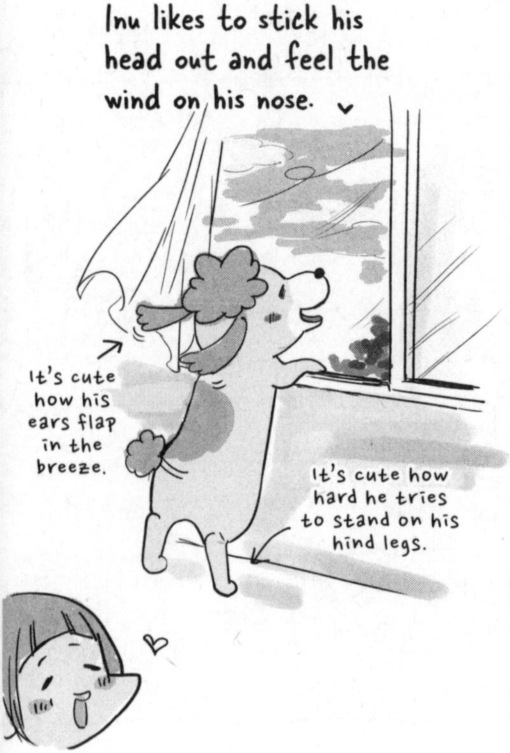

Inu likes to stick his head out and feel the wind on his nose.
It's cute how his ears flap in the breeze.
It's cute how hard he tries to stand on his hind legs.

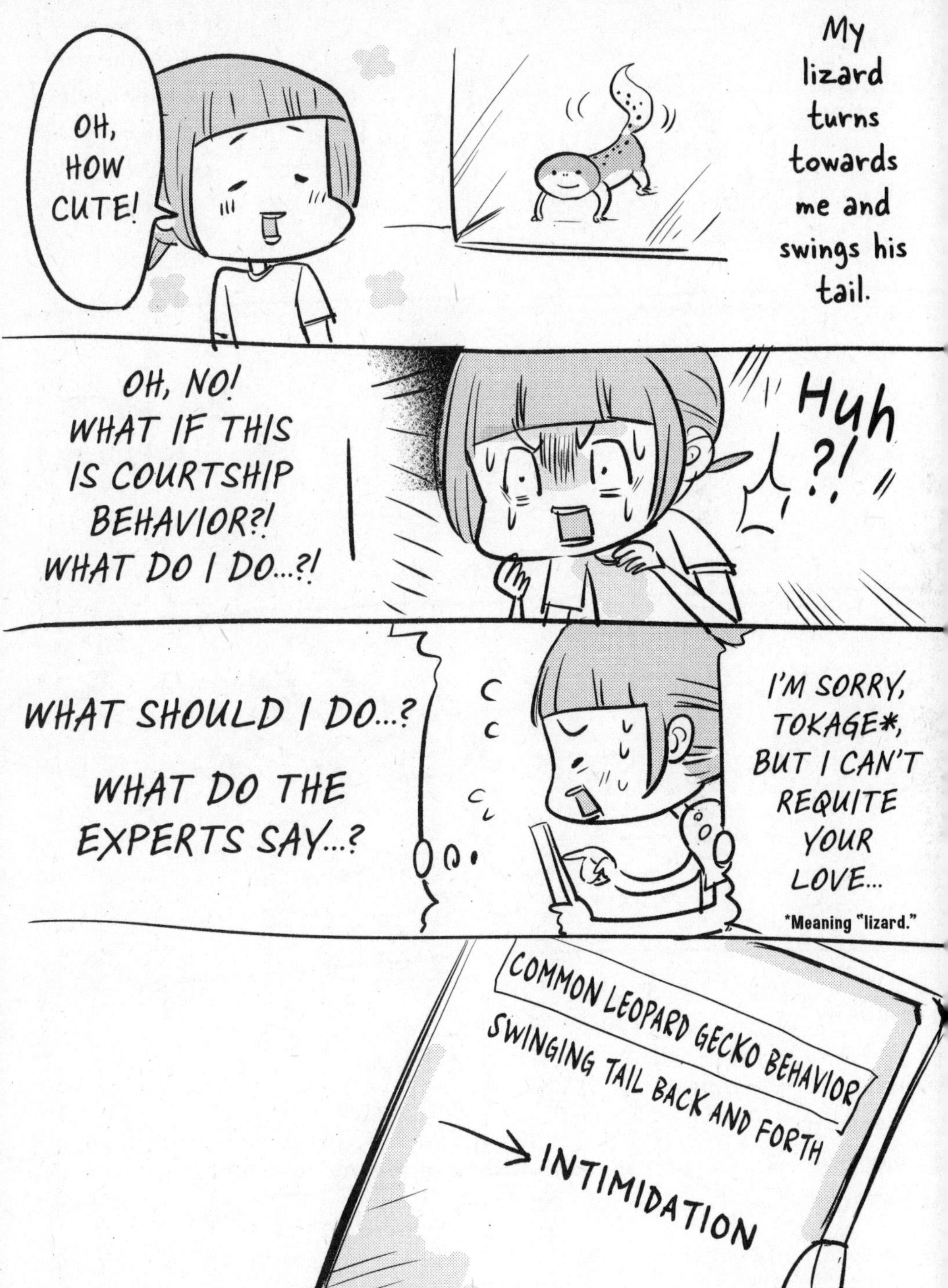
My lizard turns towards me and swings his tail.
OH, HOW CUTE!
Huh?!
OH, NO! WHAT IF THIS IS COURTSHIP BEHAVIOR?! WHAT DO I DO...?!
I'M SORRY, TOKAGE*, BUT I CAN'T REQUITE YOUR LOVE...
WHAT SHOULD I DO...?
WHAT DO THE EXPERTS SAY...?
COMMON LEOPARD GECKO BEHAVIOR
SWINGING TAIL BACK AND FORTH
→ INTIMIDATION
*Meaning "lizard."

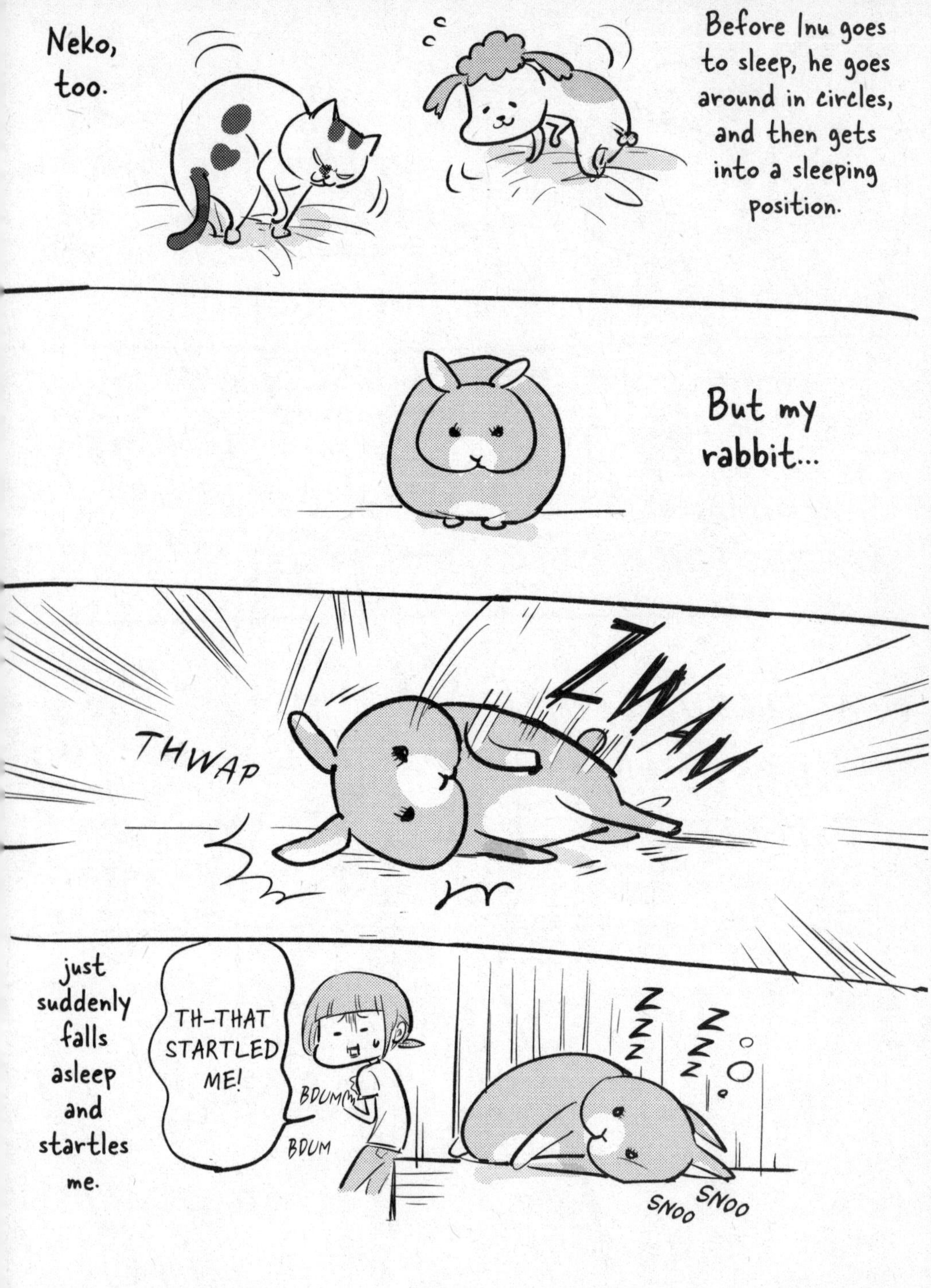

Before Inu goes to sleep, he goes around in circles, and then gets into a sleeping position.
Neko, too.
But my rabbit...
ZWAM
THWAP
ZZZ
ZZZ
SNOO SNOO
BDUM BDUM
TH-THAT STARTLED ME!
just suddenly falls asleep and startles me.

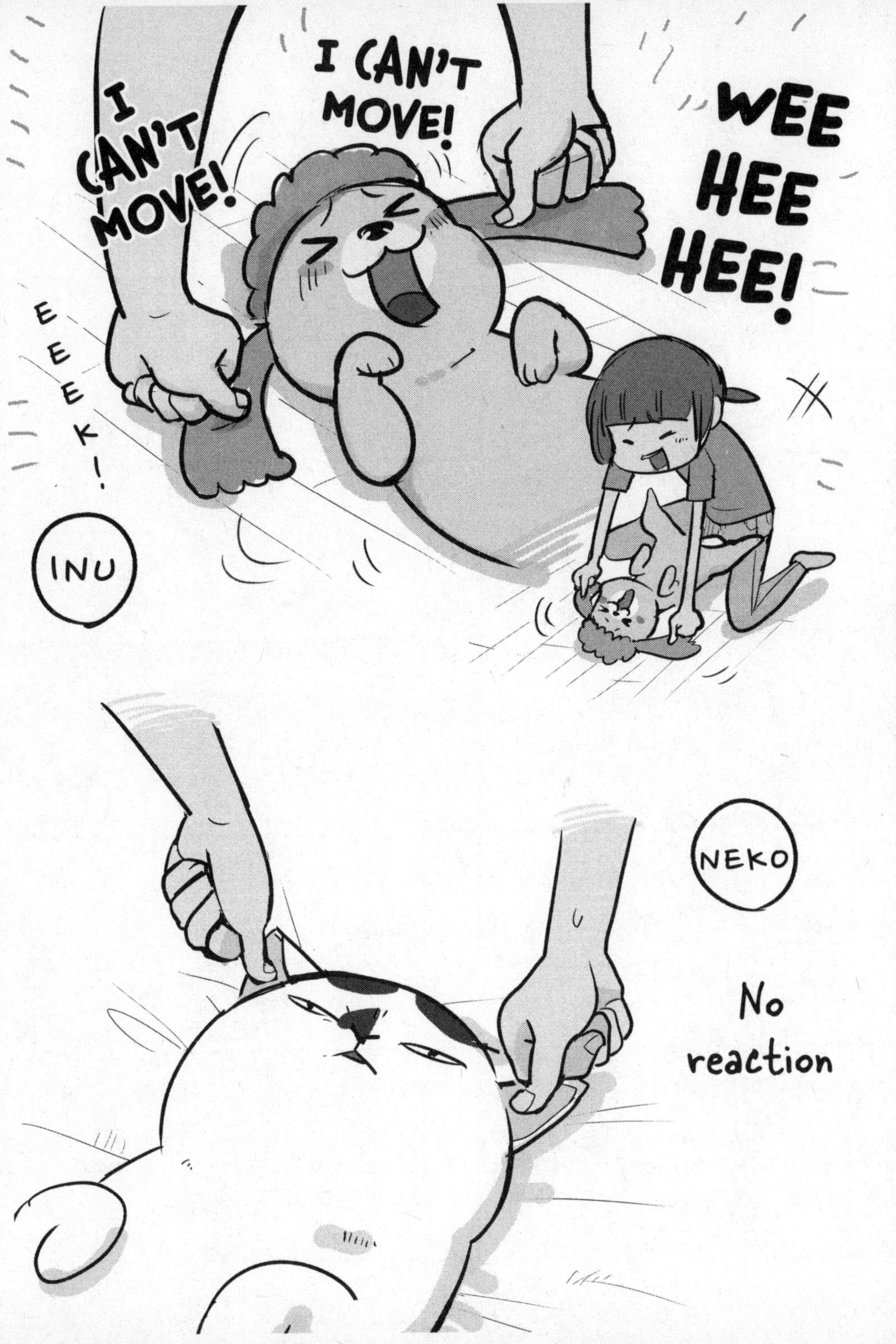
WEE HEE HEE!
I CAN'T MOVE!
I CAN'T MOVE!
EEEEK!
INU
NEKO
No reaction

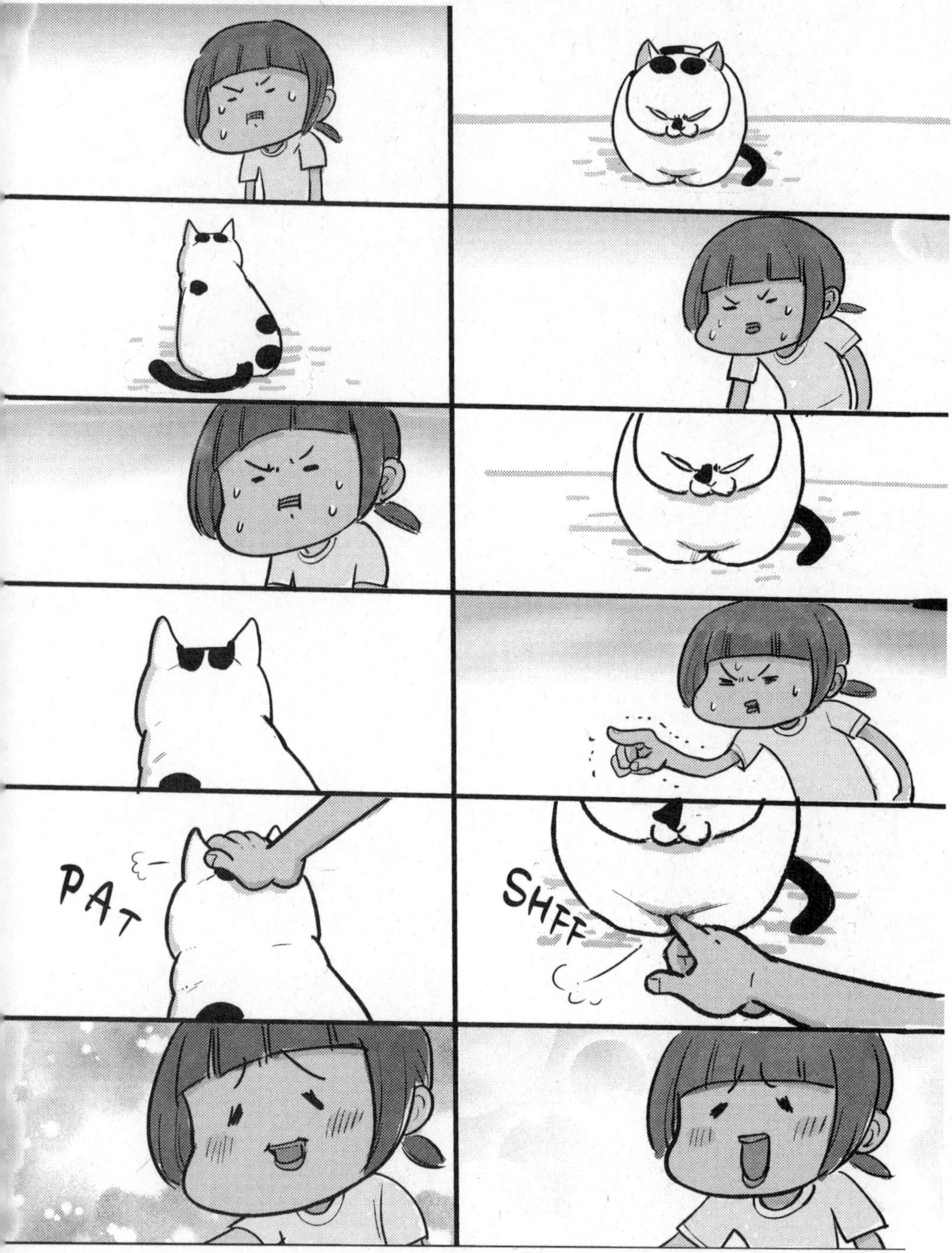
SHFF
PAT

Neko in a spot he's recently taken to. Inu taking interest.

Newly-Drawn 4-Panel Strip

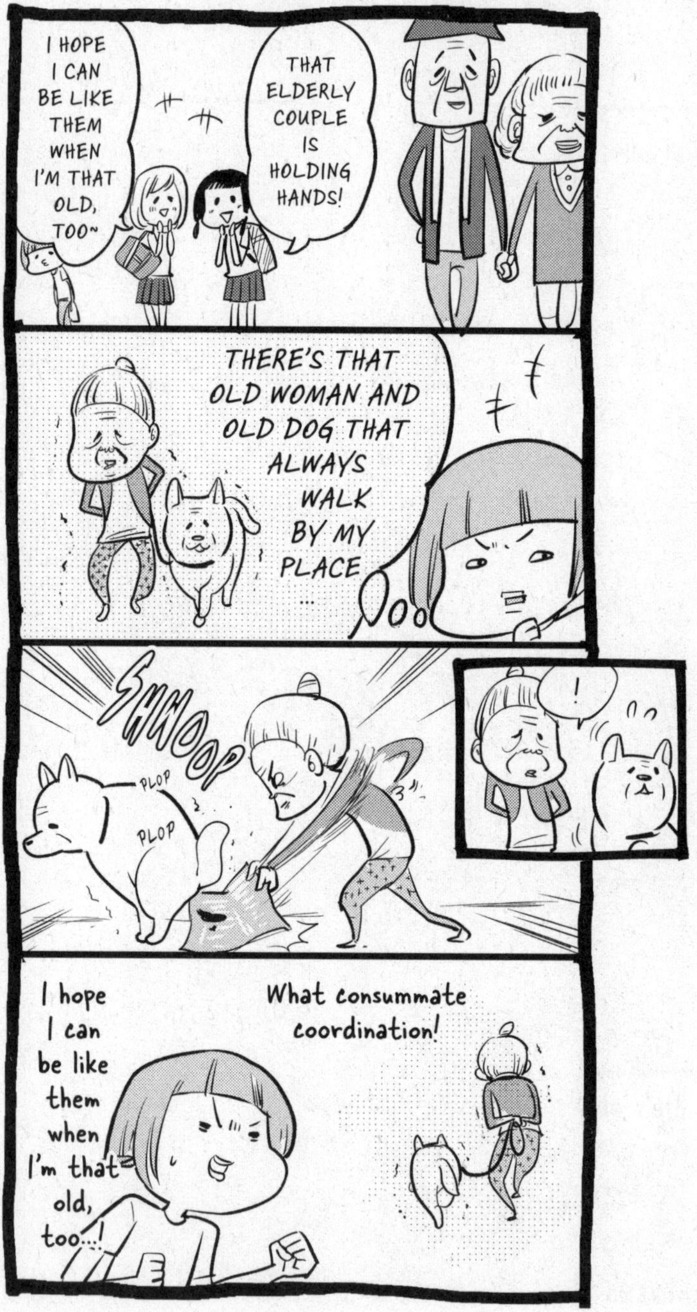
THAT ELDERLY COUPLE IS HOLDING HANDS!
I HOPE I CAN BE LIKE THEM WHEN I'M THAT OLD, TOO~
THERE'S THAT OLD WOMAN AND OLD DOG THAT ALWAYS WALK BY MY PLACE ...
!
SHWOOP
PLOP
PLOP
What consummate coordination!
I hope I can be like them when I'm that old, too...!

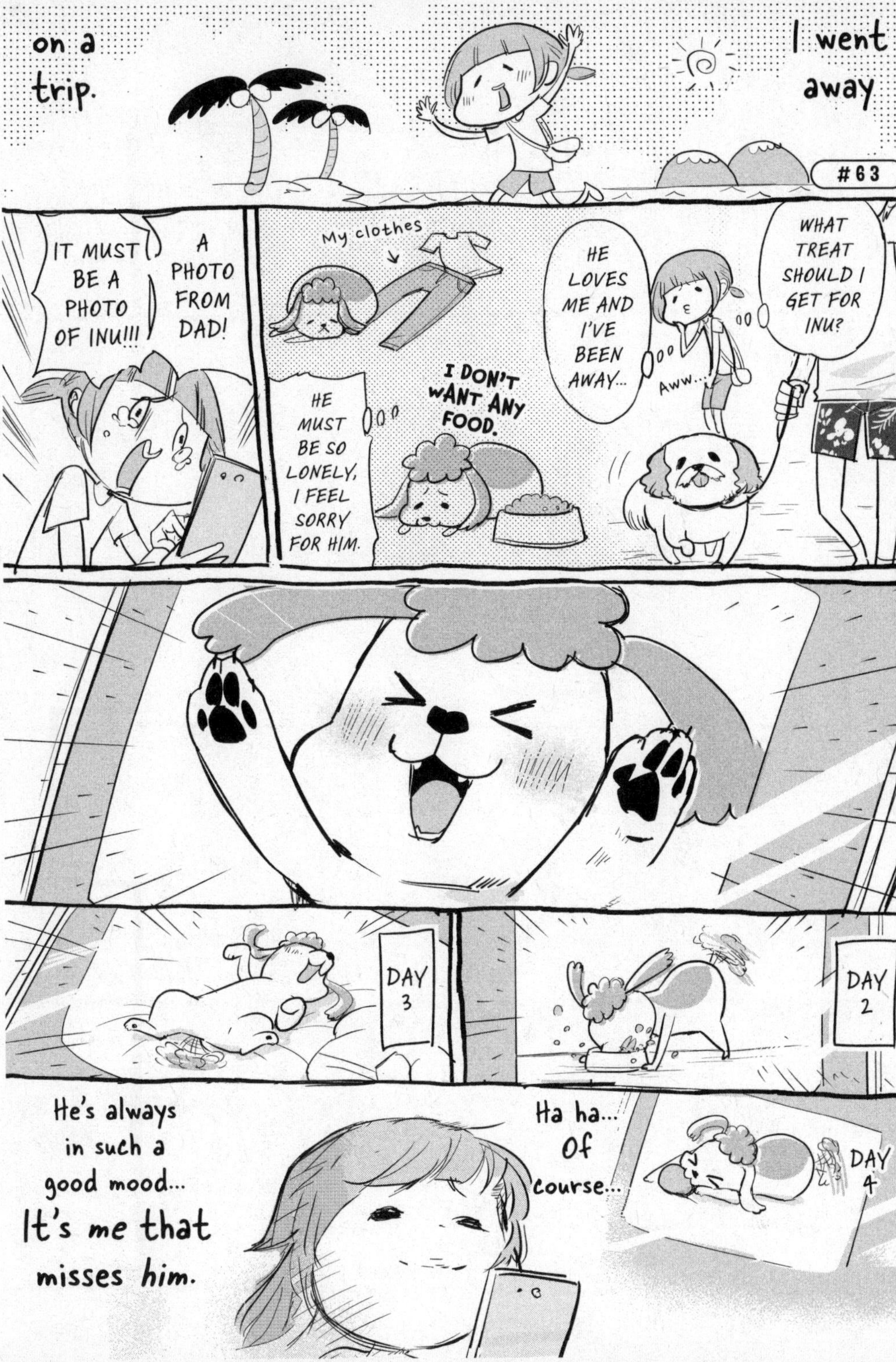
I went away
on a trip.
#63
WHAT TREAT SHOULD I GET FOR INU?
HE LOVES ME AND I'VE BEEN AWAY...
Aww...
My clothes
I DON'T WANT ANY FOOD.
HE MUST BE SO LONELY, I FEEL SORRY FOR HIM.
A PHOTO FROM DAD!
IT MUST BE A PHOTO OF INU!!!
DAY 2
DAY 3
DAY 4
Ha ha... Of course...
He's always in such a good mood...
It's me that misses him.

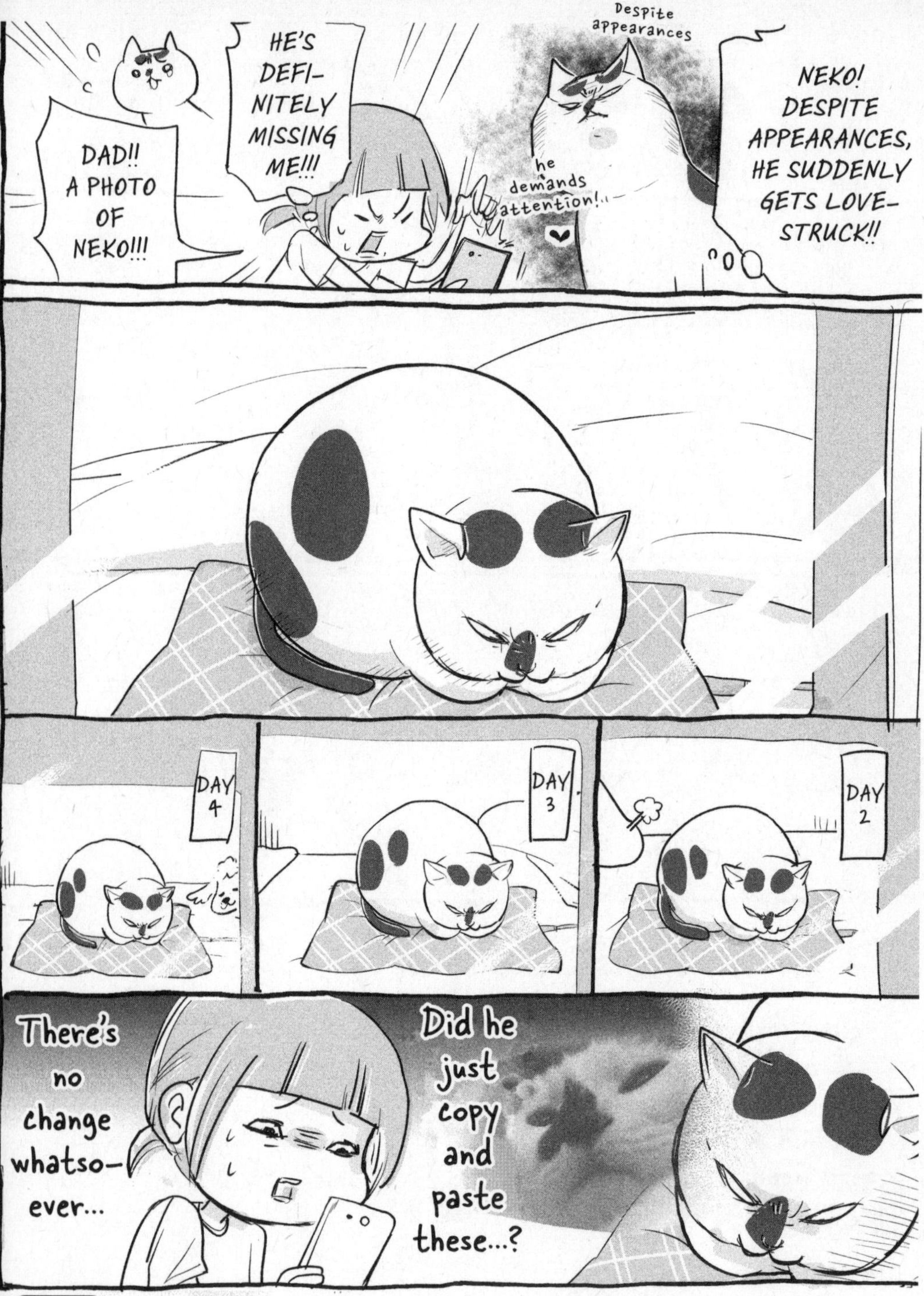
Despite appearances
NEKO! DESPITE APPEARANCES, HE SUDDENLY GETS LOVE-STRUCK!!
he demands attention!..
HE'S DEFI-NITELY MISSING ME!!!
DAD!! A PHOTO OF NEKO!!!
DAY 2
DAY 3
DAY 4
Did he just copy and paste these...?
There's no change whatso-ever...

END

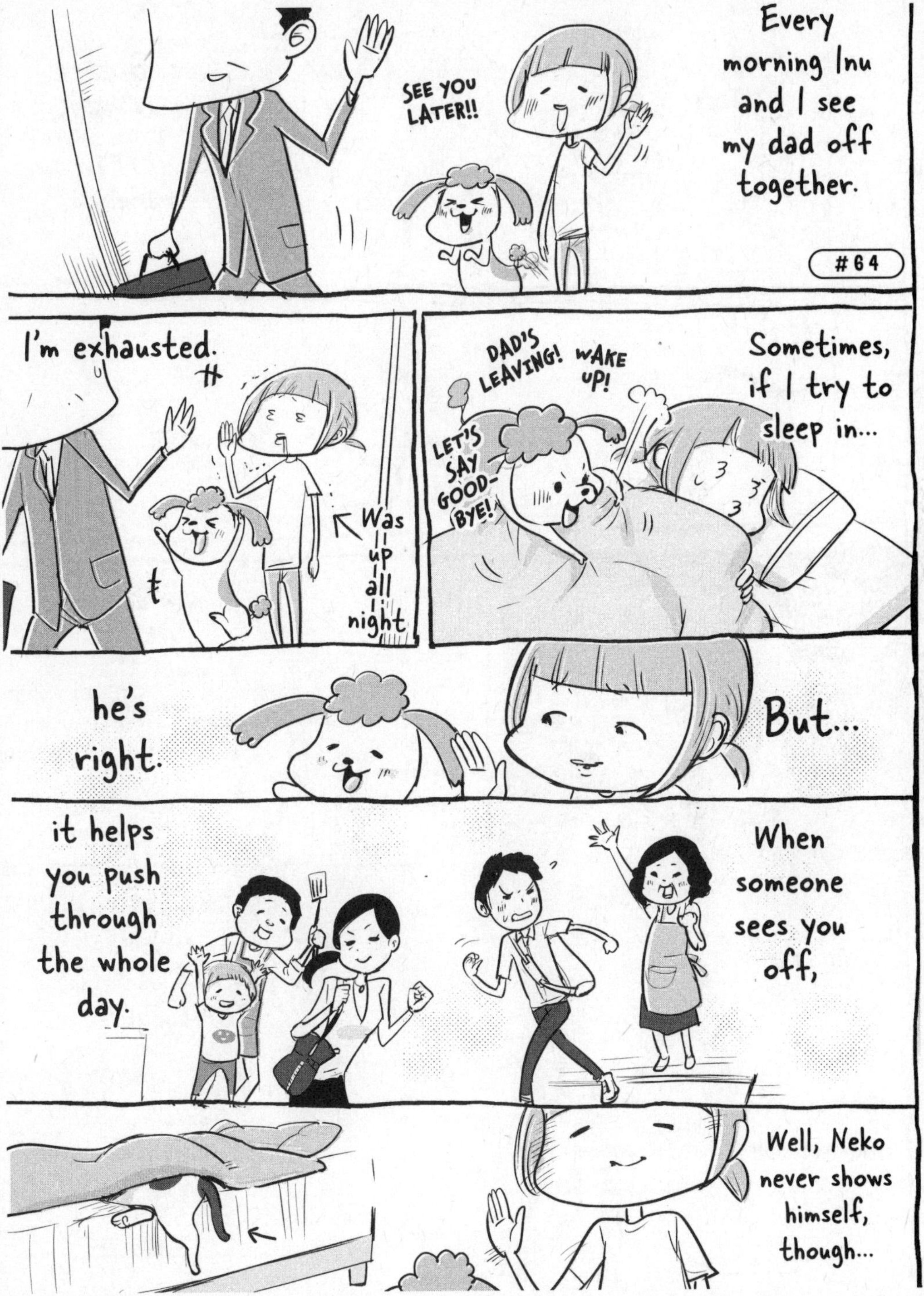
Every morning Inu and I see my dad off together.
#64
SEE YOU LATER!!
Sometimes, if I try to sleep in...
WAKE UP!
DAD'S LEAVING!
LET'S SAY GOOD-BYE!
I'm exhausted.
Was up all night
But...
he's right.
When someone sees you off,
it helps you push through the whole day.
Well, Neko never shows himself, though...

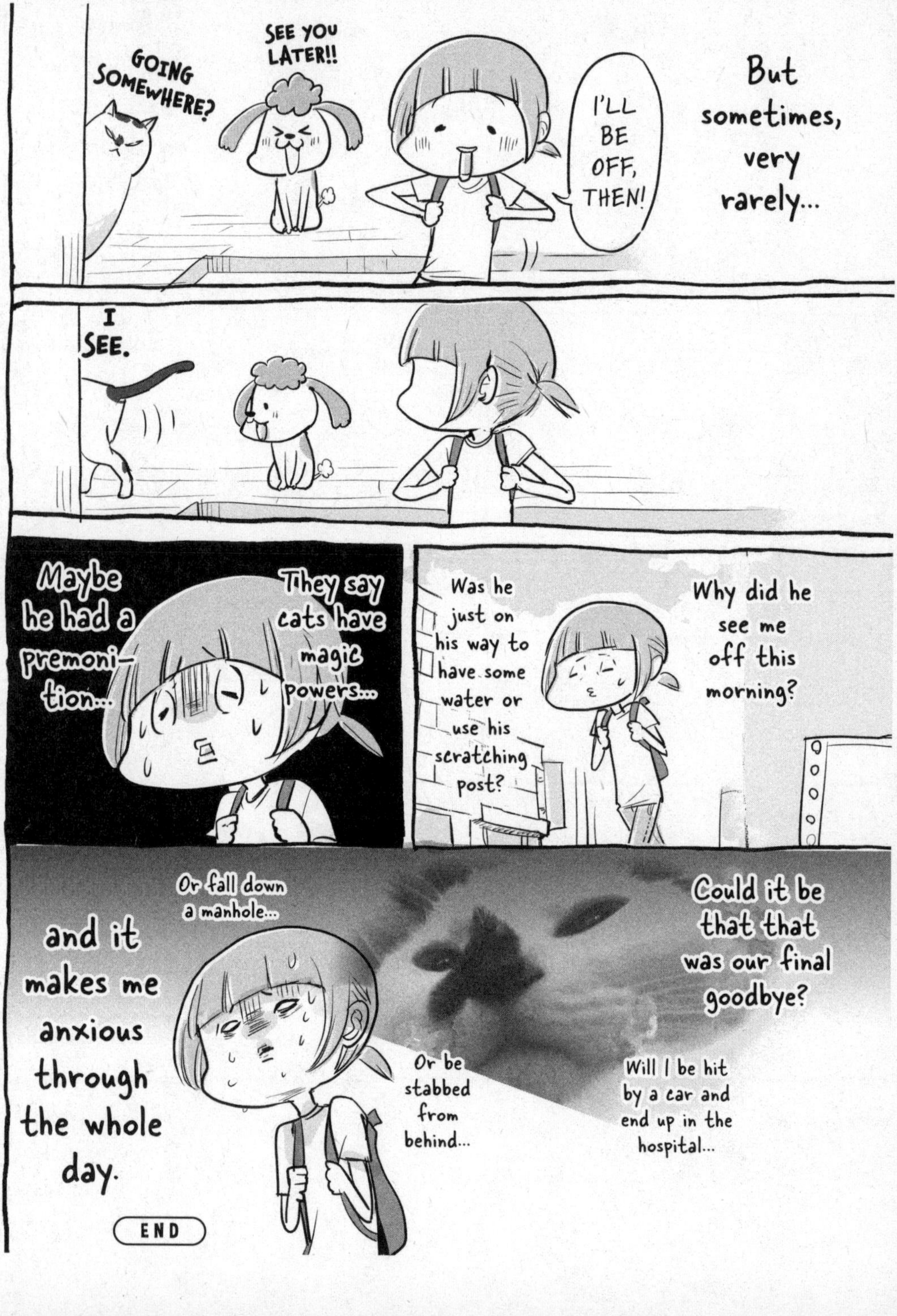

But sometimes, very rarely...
I'LL BE OFF, THEN!
SEE YOU LATER!!
GOING SOMEWHERE?
I SEE.
Why did he see me off this morning?
Was he just on his way to have some water or use his scratching post?
They say cats have magic powers...
Maybe he had a premoni-tion...
Could it be that that was our final goodbye?
Will I be hit by a car and end up in the hospital...
Or be stabbed from behind...
Or fall down a manhole...
and it makes me anxious through the whole day.
END

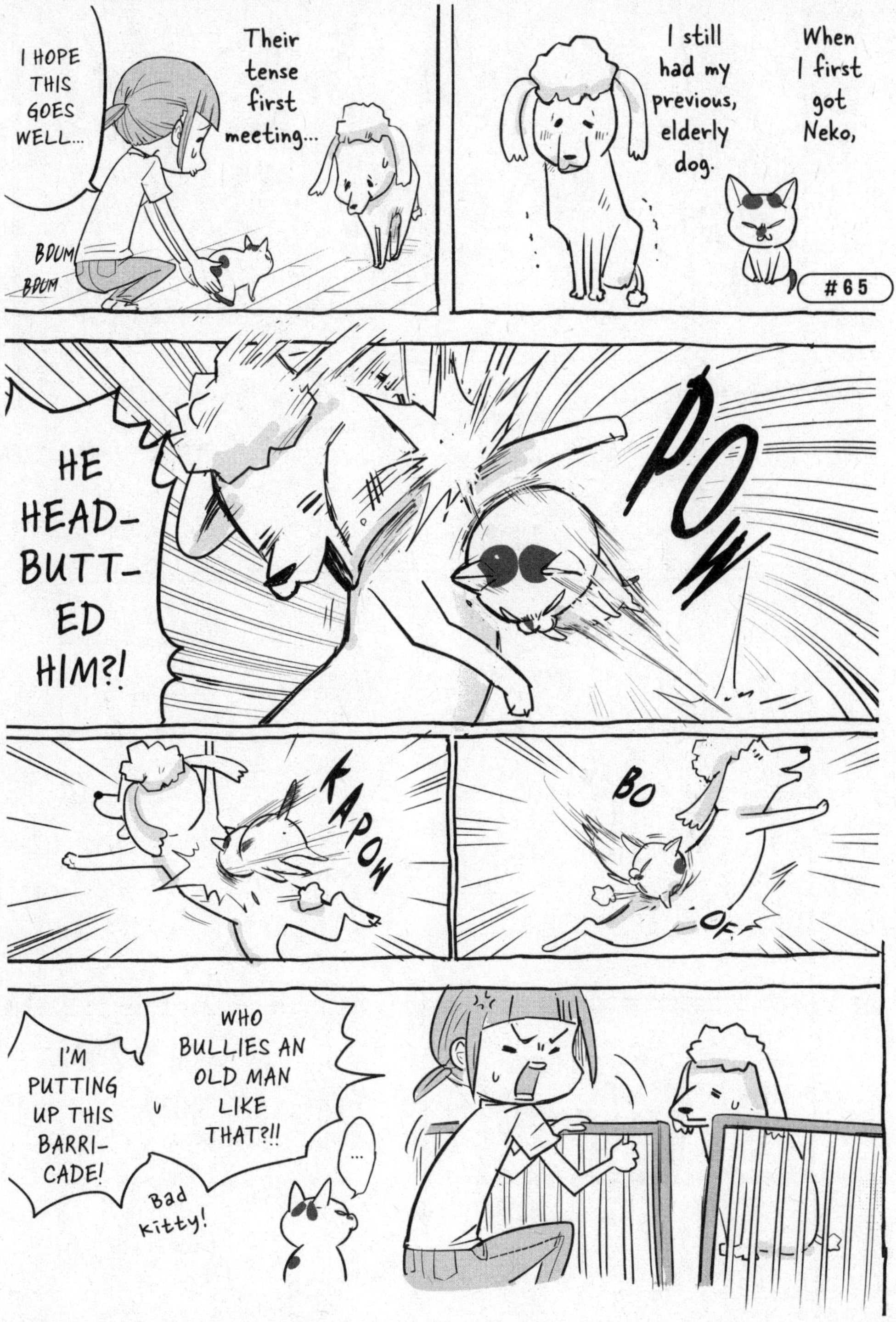
When I first got Neko,
I still had my previous, elderly dog.
#65
Their tense first meeting...
I HOPE THIS GOES WELL...
BDUM BDUM
POW
HE HEAD-BUTT-ED HIM?!
BO
OF
KAPOW
WHO BULLIES AN OLD MAN LIKE THAT?!!
I'M PUTTING UP THIS BARRI-CADE!
...
Bad kitty!

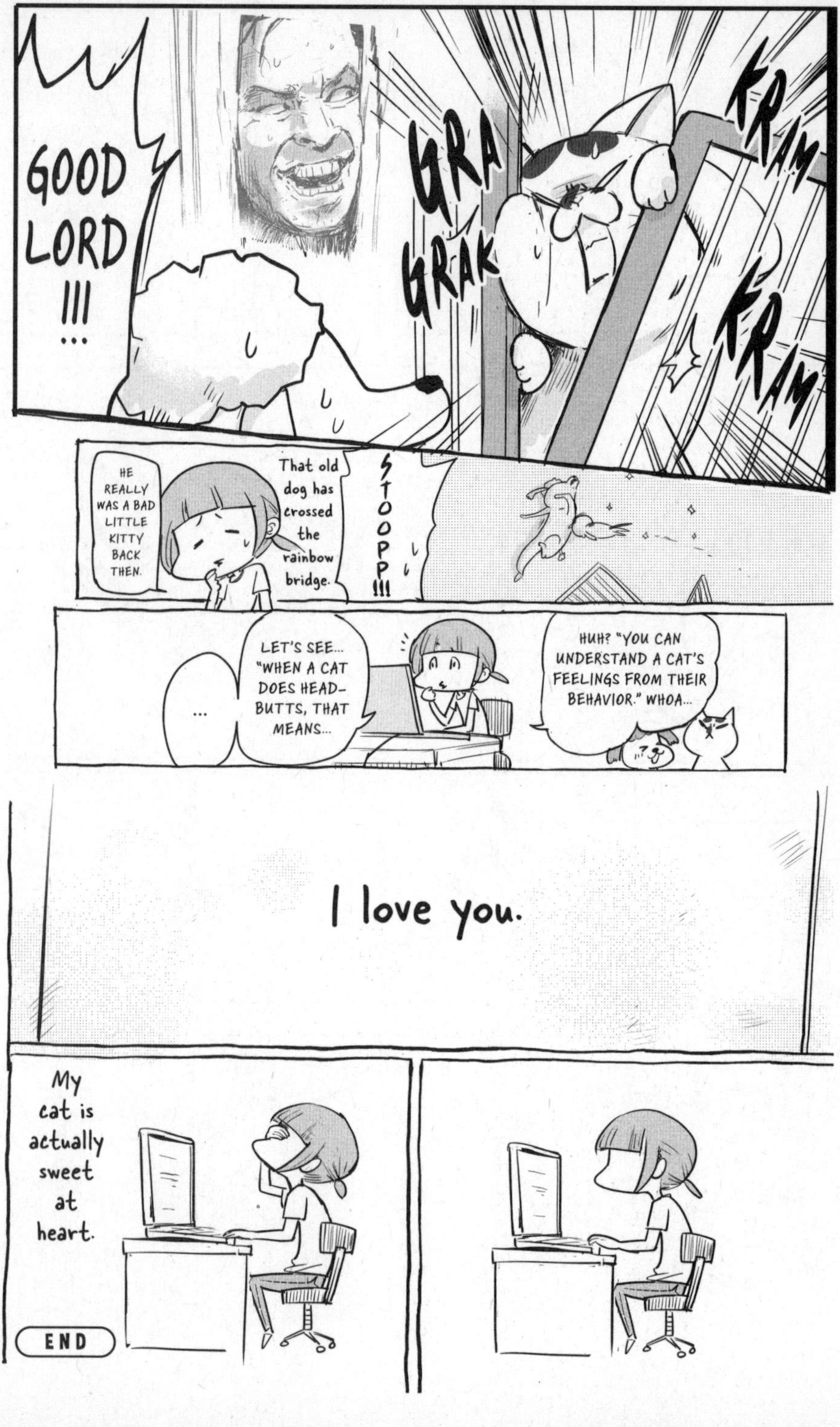
KRAM KRAM
GRA GRAK
GOOD LORD!!! ...
STOOPP!!!
That old dog has crossed the rainbow bridge.
HE REALLY WAS A BAD LITTLE KITTY BACK THEN.
HUH? "YOU CAN UNDERSTAND A CAT'S FEELINGS FROM THEIR BEHAVIOR." WHOA...
LET'S SEE... "WHEN A CAT DOES HEAD-BUTTS, THAT MEANS...
...
I love you.
My cat is actually sweet at heart.
END

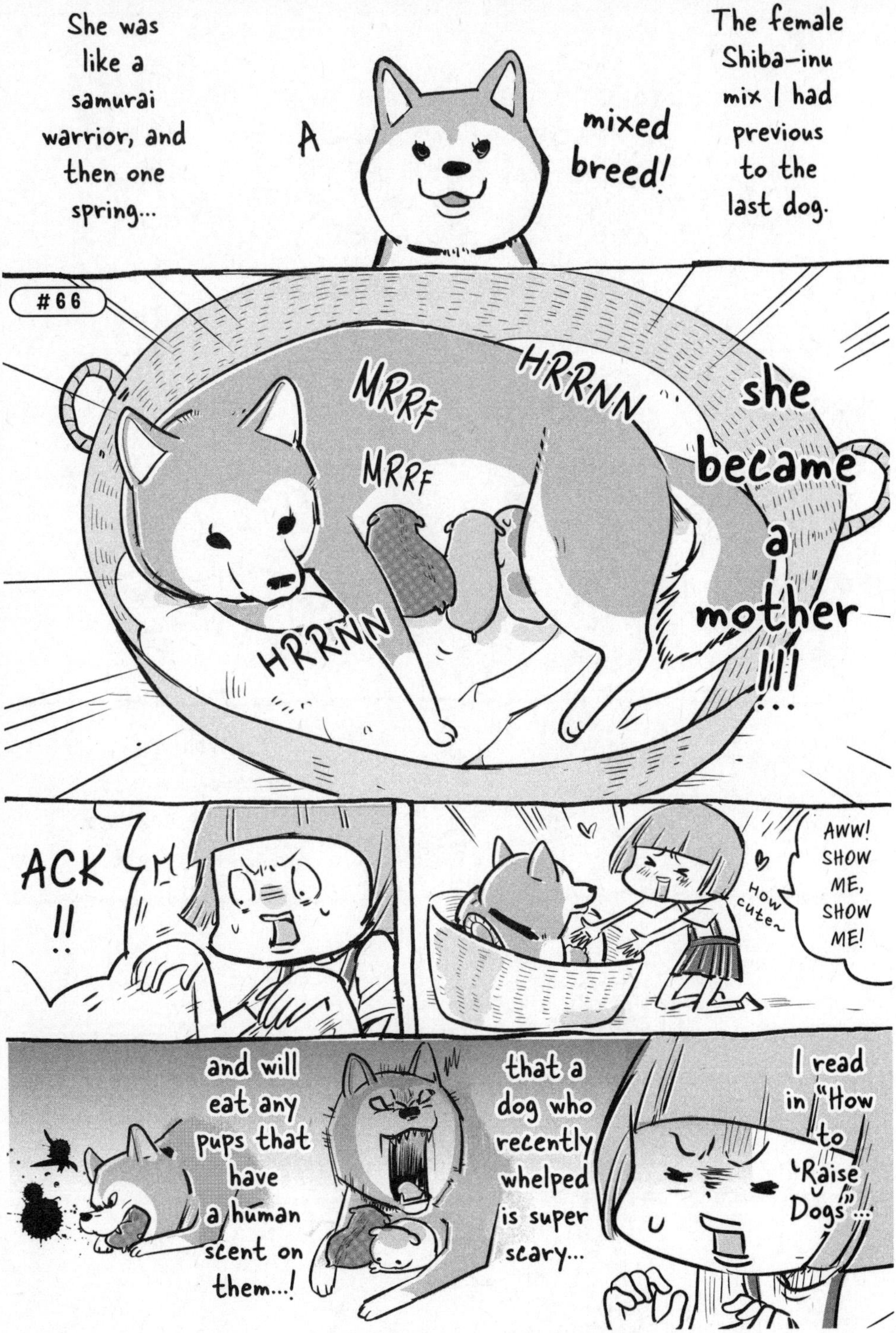
The female Shiba-inu mix I had previous to the last dog.
A mixed breed!
She was like a samurai warrior, and then one spring...
#66
she became a mother!!!...
HRRNN
MRRF
MRRF
HRRNN
AWW! SHOW ME, SHOW ME!
How cute~
ACK!!
I read in "How to Raise Dogs"...
that a dog who recently whelped is super scary...
and will eat any pups that have a human scent on them...!

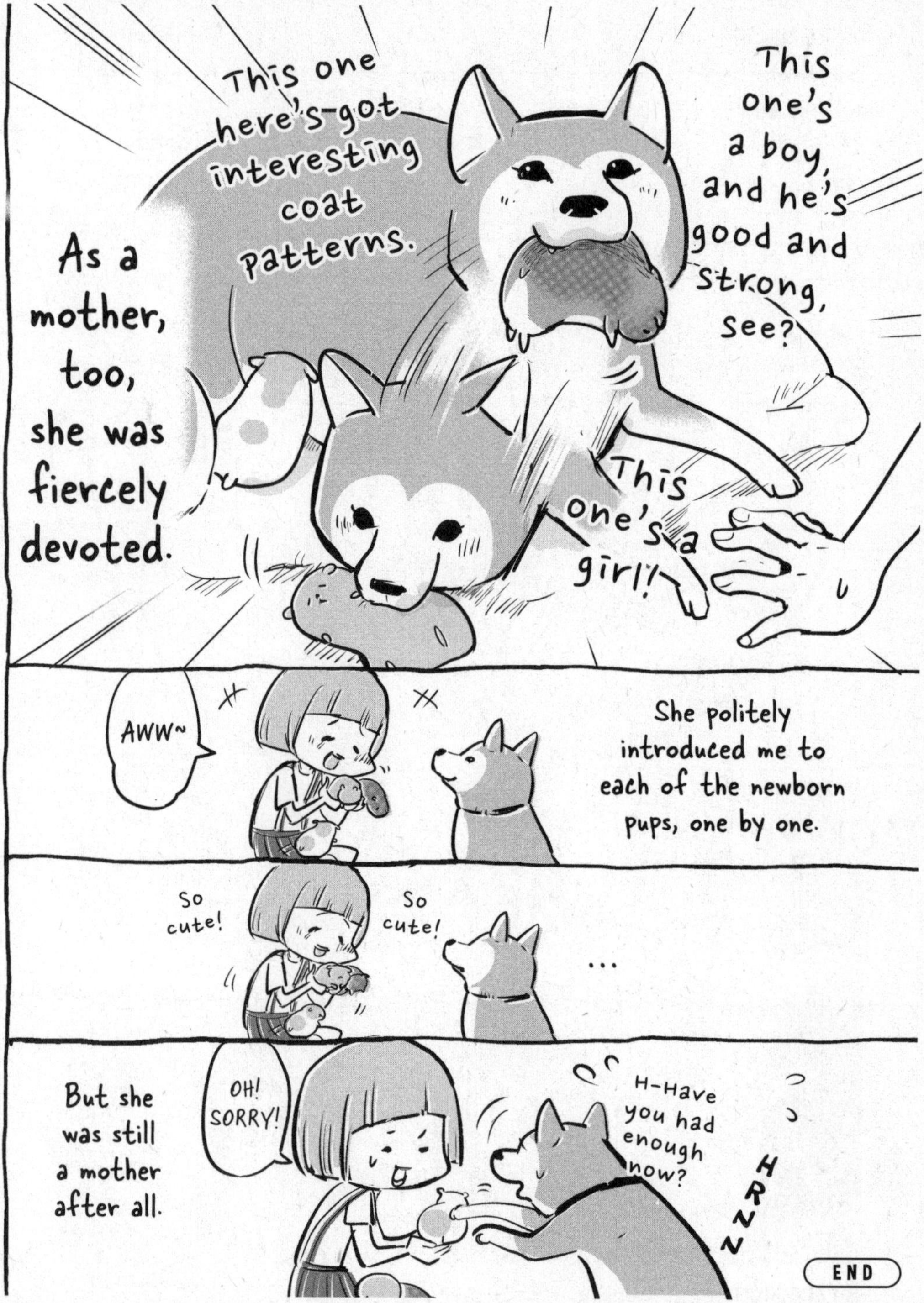
This one's a boy, and he's good and strong, see?
This one here's got interesting coat patterns.
This one's a girl!
As a mother, too, she was fiercely devoted.
She politely introduced me to each of the newborn pups, one by one.
AWW~
...
So cute!
So cute!
HRNN
H-Have you had enough now?
OH! SORRY!
But she was still a mother after all.
END

A rare instance of the pair together and not bickering.

Newly-Drawn 4-Panel Strip

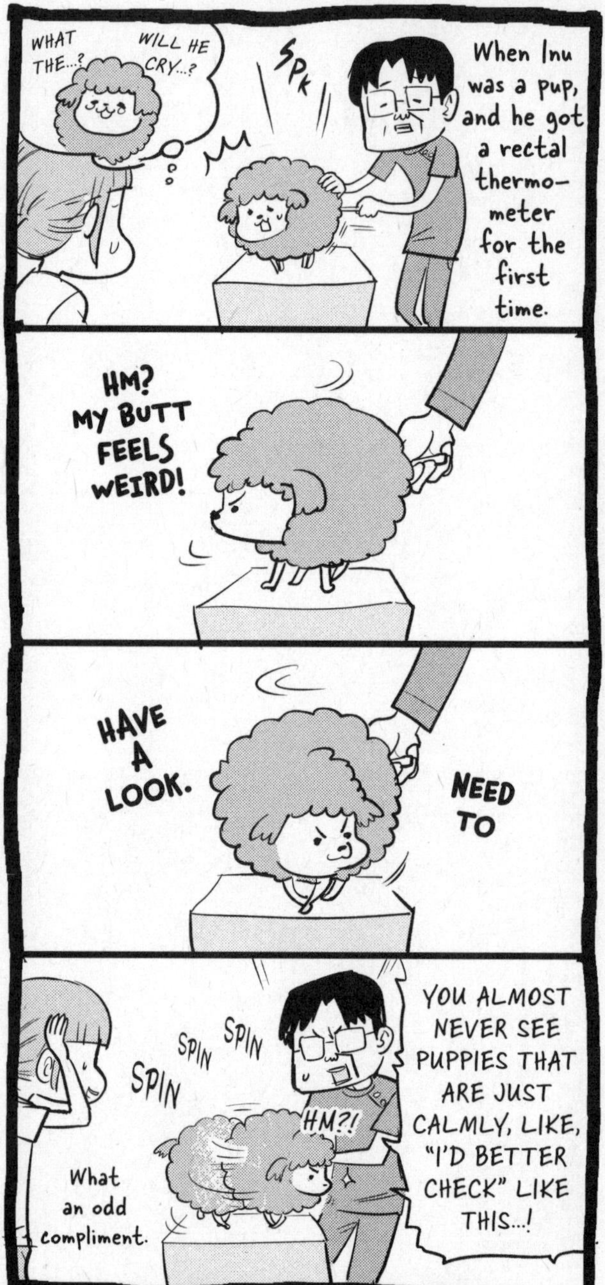

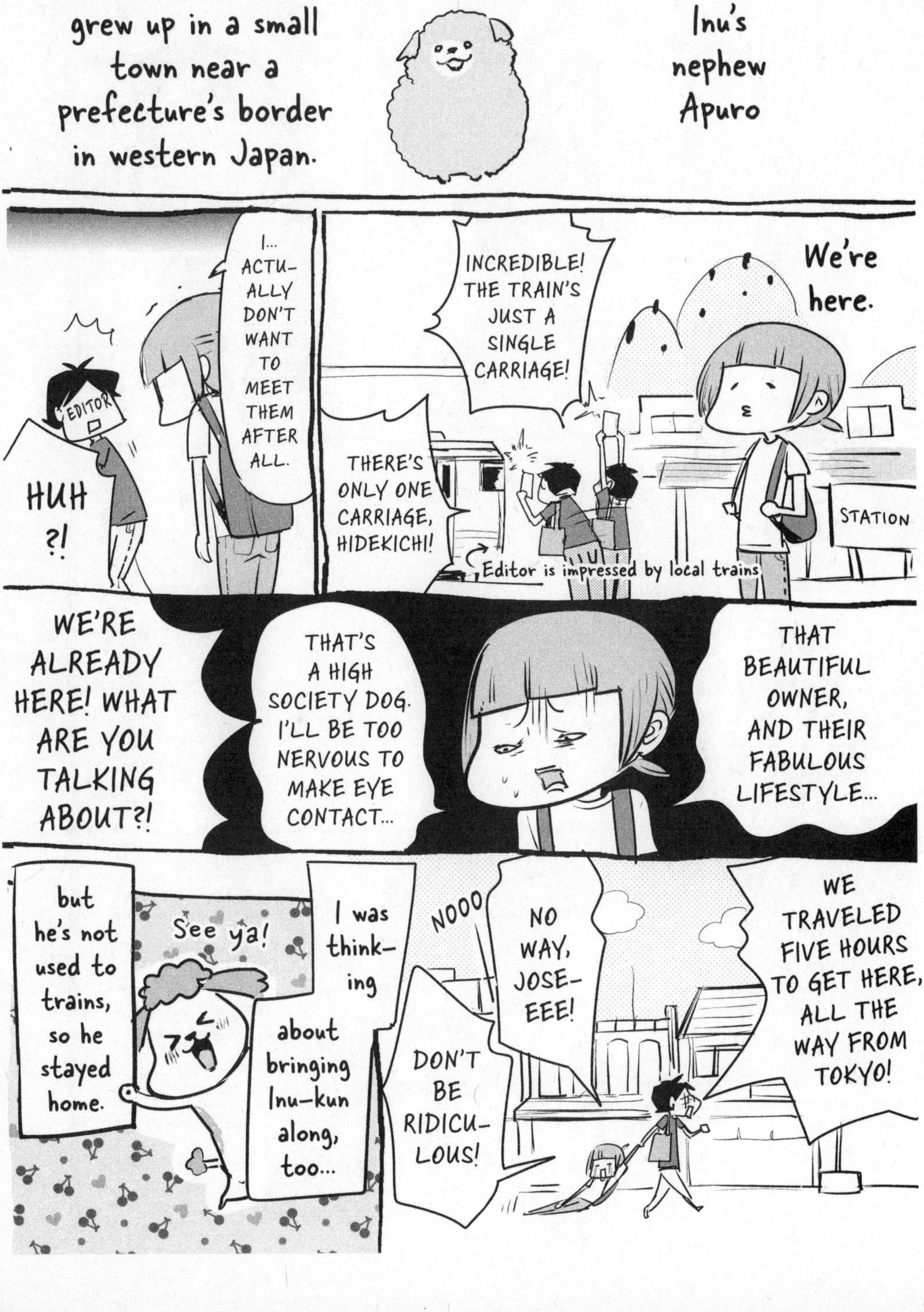
Inu's nephew Apuro
grew up in a small town near a prefecture's border in western Japan.
We're here.
INCREDIBLE! THE TRAIN'S JUST A SINGLE CARRIAGE!
THERE'S ONLY ONE CARRIAGE, HIDEKICHI!
STATION
Editor is impressed by local trains
I... ACTU-ALLY DON'T WANT TO MEET THEM AFTER ALL.
EDITOR
HUH ?!
THAT BEAUTIFUL OWNER, AND THEIR FABULOUS LIFESTYLE...
THAT'S A HIGH SOCIETY DOG. I'LL BE TOO NERVOUS TO MAKE EYE CONTACT...
WE'RE ALREADY HERE! WHAT ARE YOU TALKING ABOUT?!
WE TRAVELED FIVE HOURS TO GET HERE, ALL THE WAY FROM TOKYO!
NO WAY, JOSE-EEE!
NOOO
DON'T BE RIDICU-LOUS!
I was think-ing
about bringing Inu-kun along, too...
See ya!
but he's not used to trains, so he stayed home.

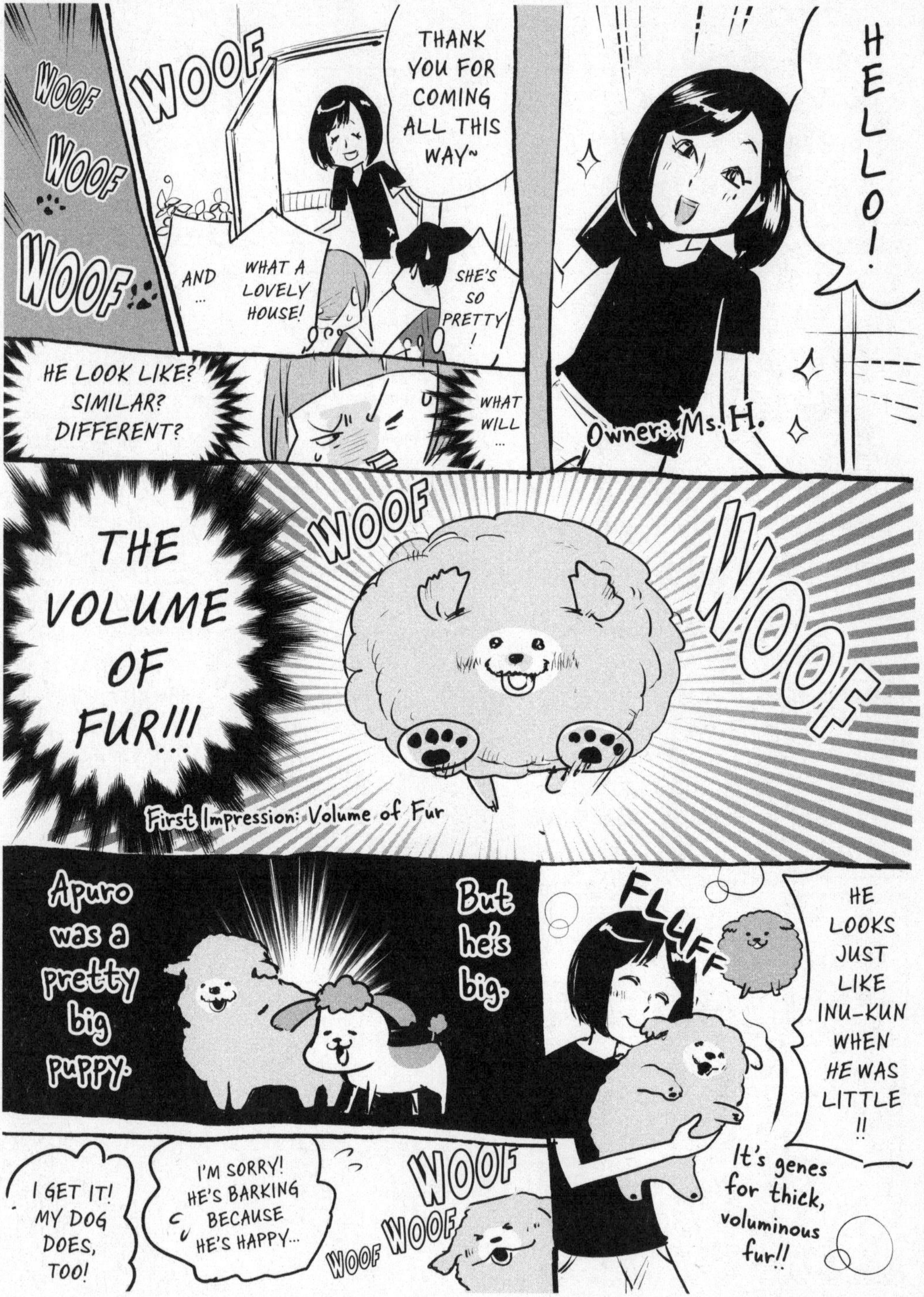

HELLO!
Owner: Ms. H.
THANK YOU FOR COMING ALL THIS WAY~
WOOF
WOOF
WOOF
WOOF
SHE'S SO PRETTY!
WHAT A LOVELY HOUSE!
AND ...
WHAT WILL ...
HE LOOK LIKE? SIMILAR? DIFFERENT?
WOOF
WOOF
THE VOLUME OF FUR!!!
First Impression: Volume of Fur
HE LOOKS JUST LIKE INU-KUN WHEN HE WAS LITTLE!!
FLUFF
It's genes for thick, voluminous fur!!
But he's big.
Apuro was a pretty big puppy.
WOOF
WOOF
WOOF
I'M SORRY! HE'S BARKING BECAUSE HE'S HAPPY...
I GET IT! MY DOG DOES, TOO!

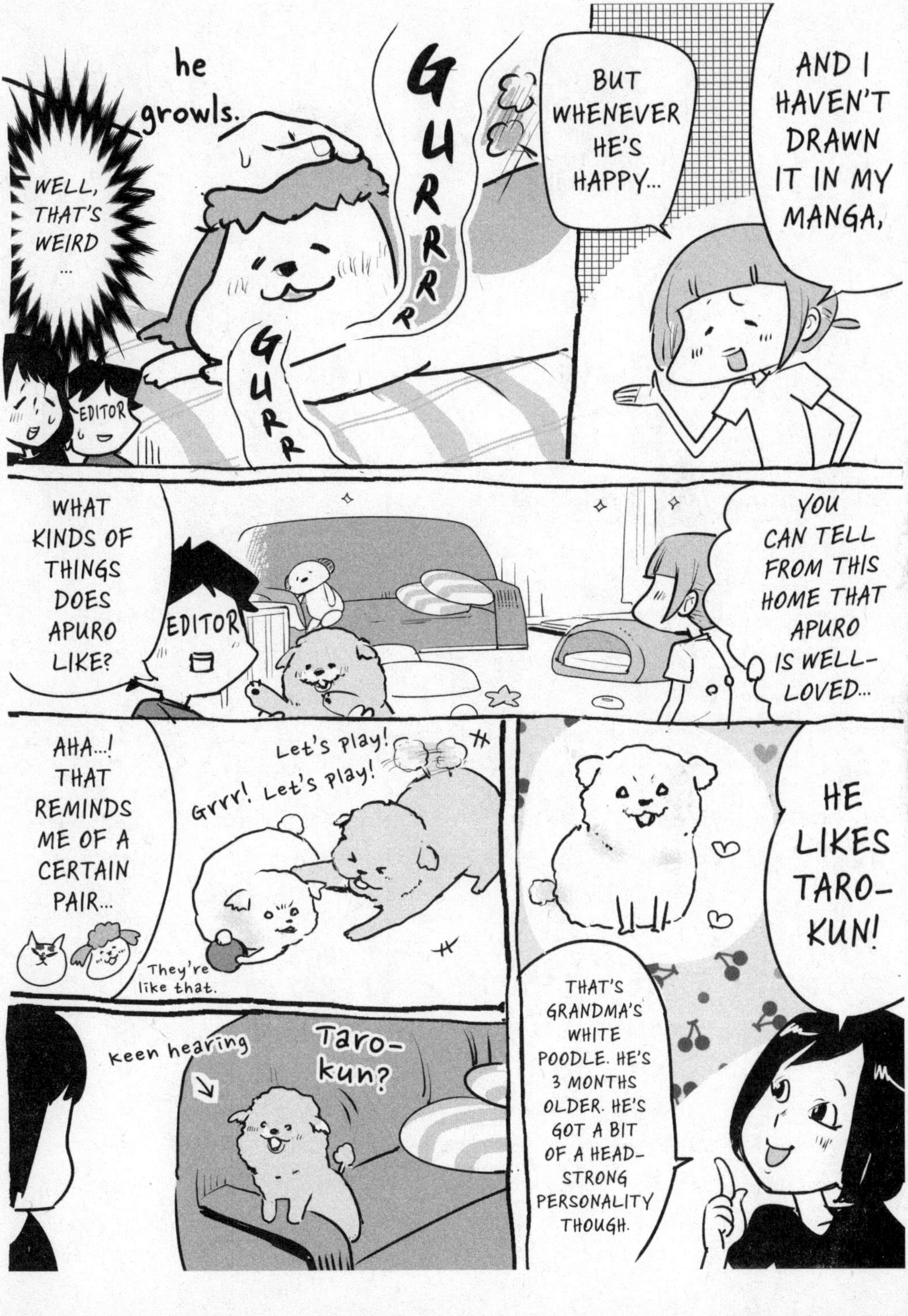
AND I HAVEN'T DRAWN IT IN MY MANGA,
BUT WHENEVER HE'S HAPPY...
GURRR
he growls.
GURR
WELL, THAT'S WEIRD ...
EDITOR
YOU CAN TELL FROM THIS HOME THAT APURO IS WELL-LOVED...
WHAT KINDS OF THINGS DOES APURO LIKE?
EDITOR
HE LIKES TARO-KUN!
THAT'S GRANDMA'S WHITE POODLE. HE'S 3 MONTHS OLDER. HE'S GOT A BIT OF A HEAD-STRONG PERSONALITY THOUGH.
AHA...! THAT REMINDS ME OF A CERTAIN PAIR...
Let's play!
Grrr! Let's play!
They're like that.
Taro-kun?
keen hearing

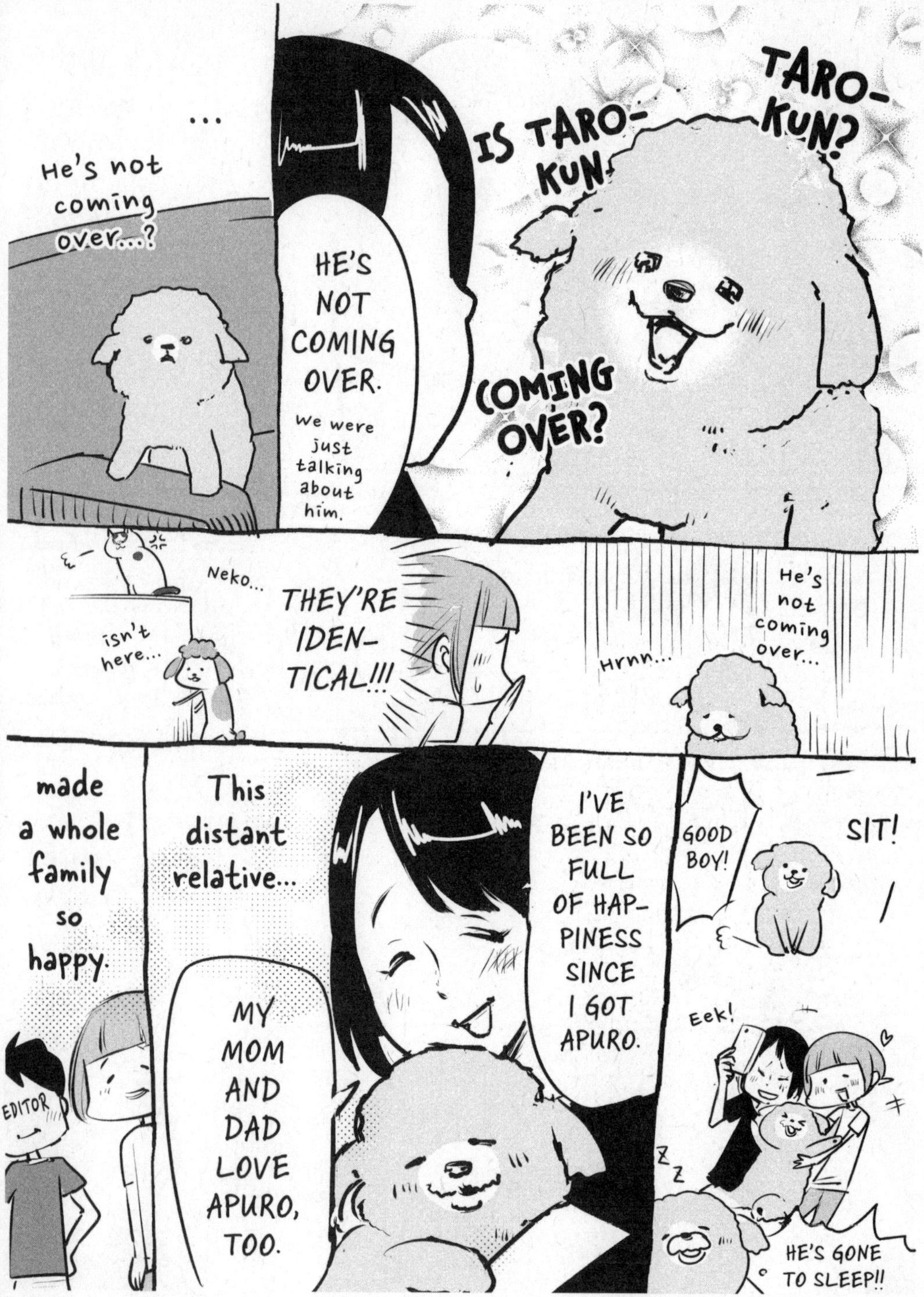

TARO-KUN?
IS TARO-KUN COMING OVER?
HE'S NOT COMING OVER.
We were just talking about him.
...
He's not coming over...?
He's not coming over...
Hrnn...
THEY'RE IDEN-TICAL!!!
Neko...
isn't here...
SIT!
GOOD BOY!
Eek!
Z Z
HE'S GONE TO SLEEP!!
I'VE BEEN SO FULL OF HAP-PINESS SINCE I GOT APURO.
MY MOM AND DAD LOVE APURO, TOO.
This distant relative...
made a whole family so happy.
EDITOR

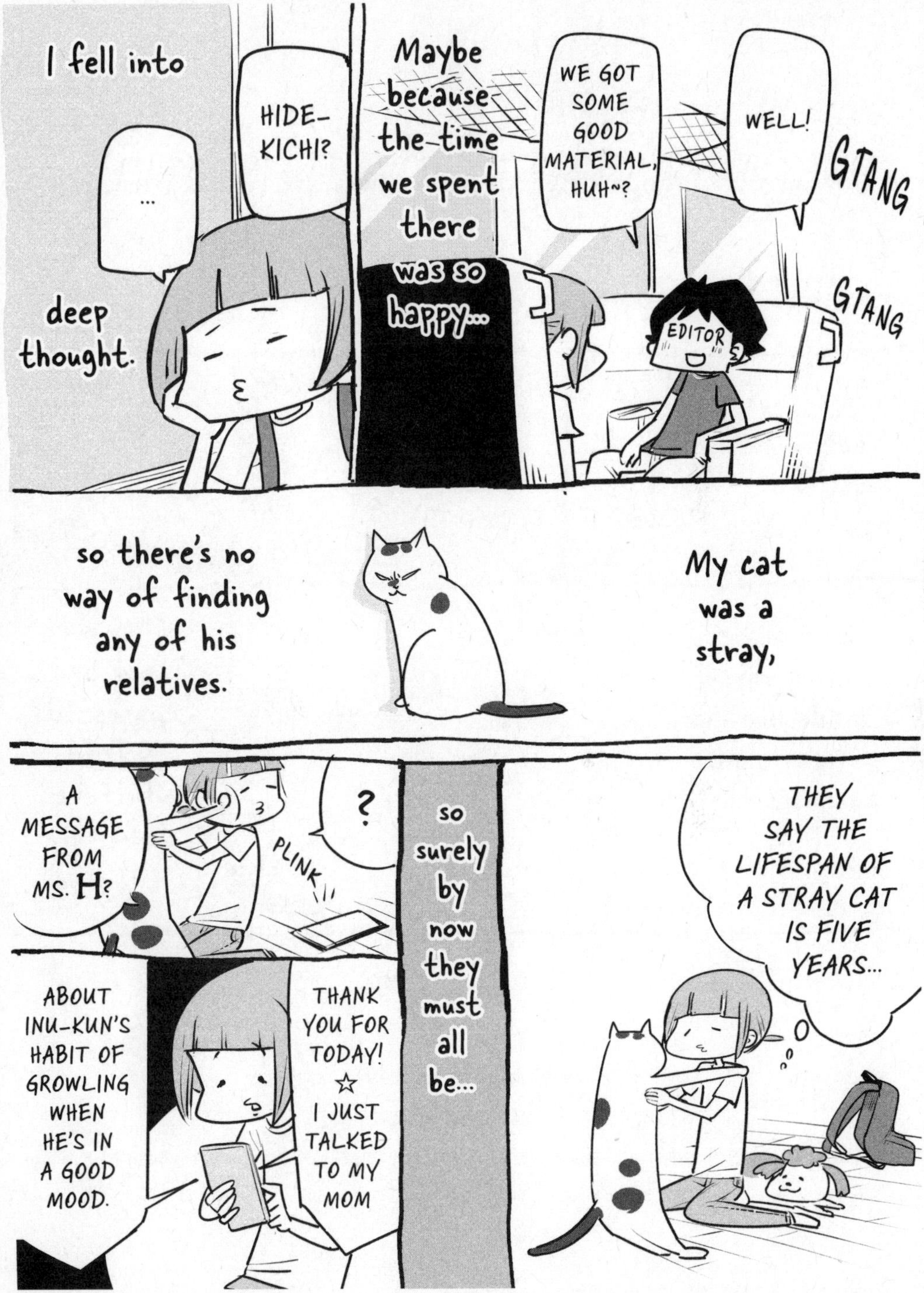
GTANG
GTANG
WELL!
WE GOT SOME GOOD MATERIAL, HUH~?
EDITOR
Maybe because the time we spent there was so happy...
HIDE-KICHI?
...
I fell into deep thought.
My cat was a stray,
so there's no way of finding any of his relatives.
THEY SAY THE LIFESPAN OF A STRAY CAT IS FIVE YEARS...
so surely by now they must all be...
?
PLINK
A MESSAGE FROM MS. H?
THANK YOU FOR TODAY! ☆ I JUST TALKED TO MY MOM
ABOUT INU-KUN'S HABIT OF GROWLING WHEN HE'S IN A GOOD MOOD.

YOU TOLD ME THAT INU GROWLS WHEN HE'S HAPPY, RIGHT? (*'∪'*)

SURELY NEKO MUST HAVE TAUGHT HIM HOW TO DO THAT. ✧

THAT'S WHAT MY MOM SAYS. ♫

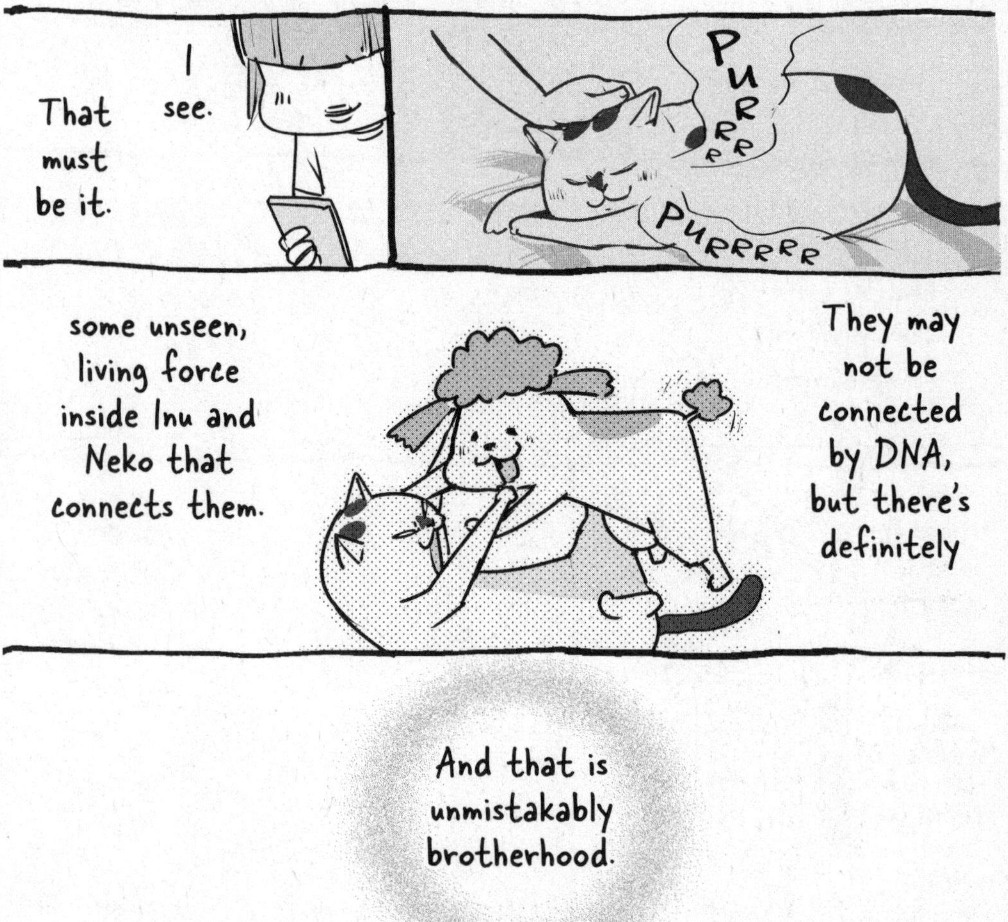
PURRRRR
PURRRRRR
I see.
That must be it.
They may not be connected by DNA, but there's definitely
some unseen, living force inside Inu and Neko that connects them.
And that is unmistakably brotherhood.

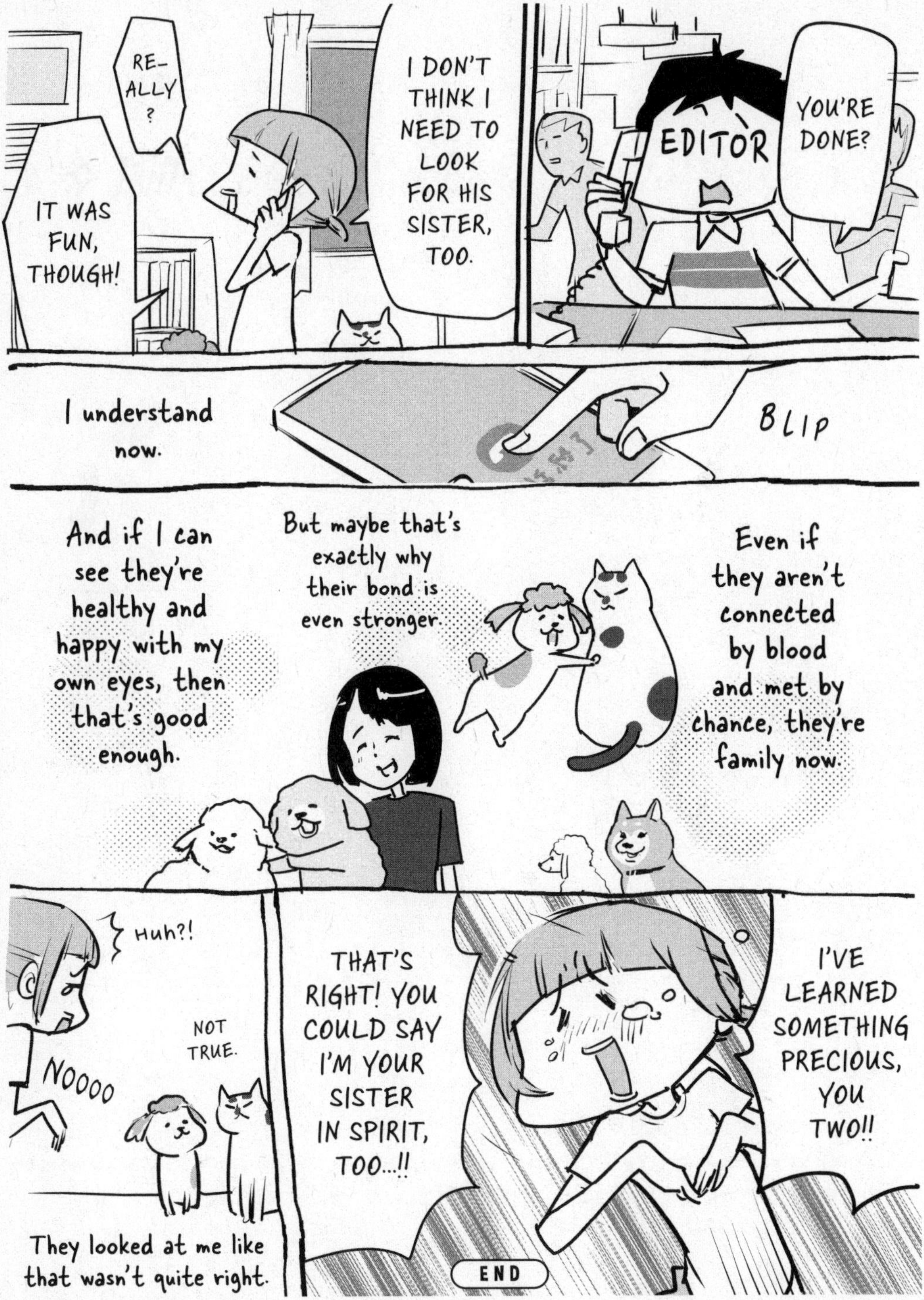
EDITOR
YOU'RE DONE?
I DON'T THINK I NEED TO LOOK FOR HIS SISTER, TOO.
RE-ALLY?
IT WAS FUN, THOUGH!
BLIP
I understand now.
Even if they aren't connected by blood and met by chance, they're family now.
But maybe that's exactly why their bond is even stronger.
And if I can see they're healthy and happy with my own eyes, then that's good enough.
I'VE LEARNED SOMETHING PRECIOUS, YOU TWO!!
THAT'S RIGHT! YOU COULD SAY I'M YOUR SISTER IN SPIRIT, TOO...!!
END
Huh?!
NOT TRUE.
NOOOO
They looked at me like that wasn't quite right.

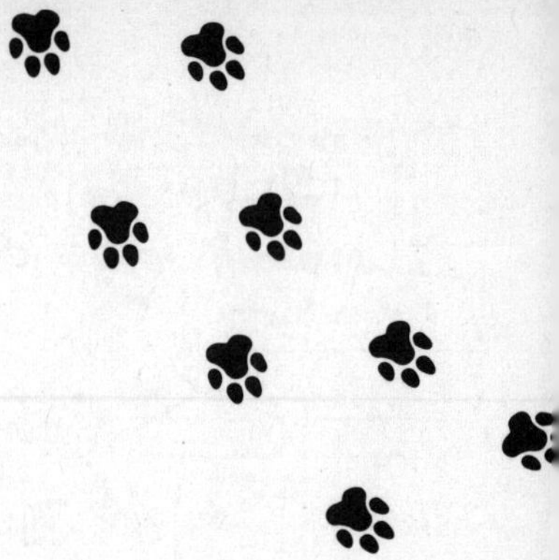

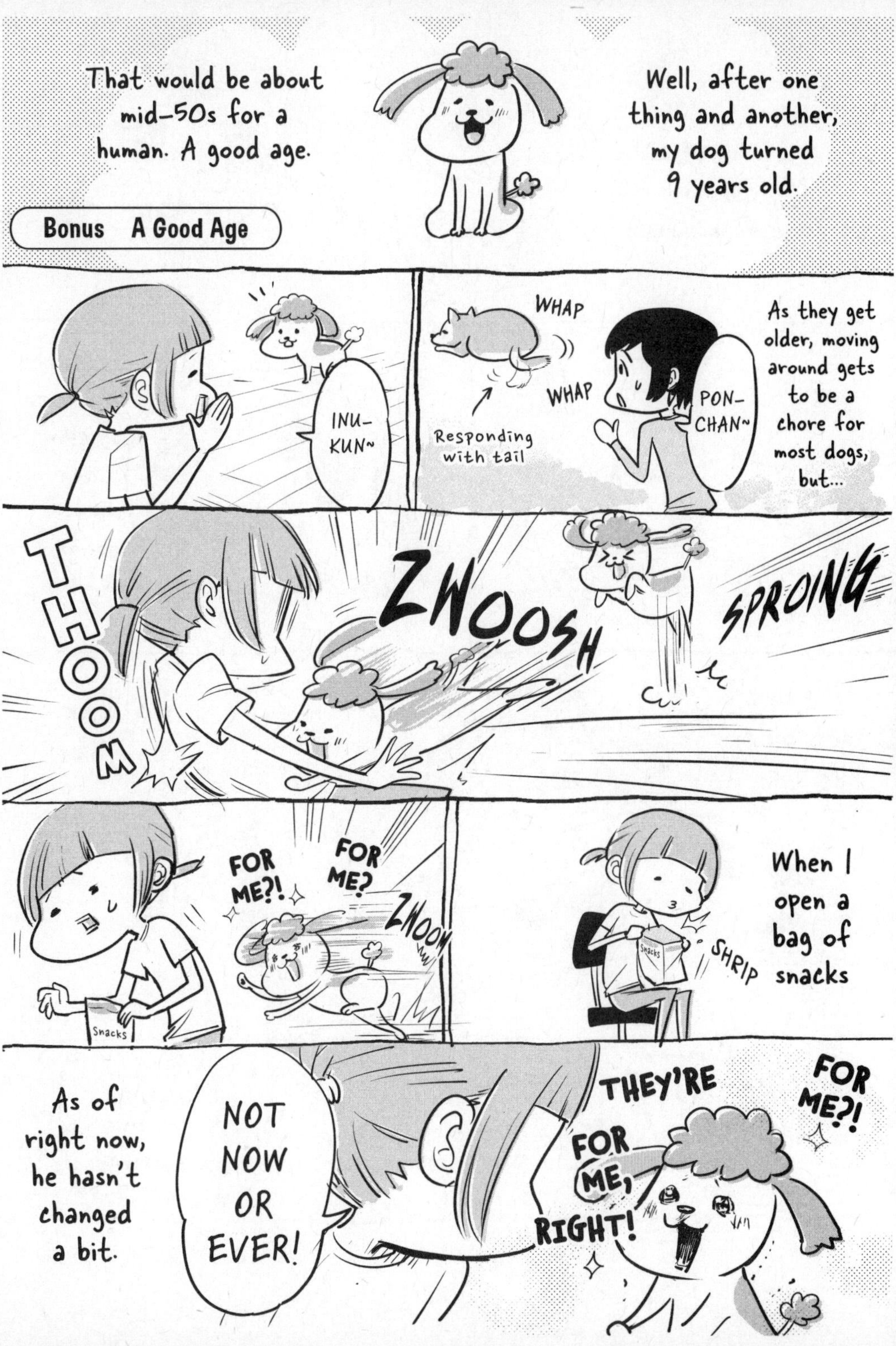
Well, after one thing and another, my dog turned 9 years old.
That would be about mid-50s for a human. A good age.
Bonus A Good Age
As they get older, moving around gets to be a chore for most dogs, but...
PON-CHAN~
WHAP
WHAP
Responding with tail
INU-KUN~
SPROING
ZWOOSH
THOOOM
When I open a bag of snacks
SHRIP
Snacks
FOR ME?
FOR ME?!
ZWOOM
Snacks
FOR ME?!
THEY'RE FOR ME, RIGHT!
NOT NOW OR EVER!
As of right now, he hasn't changed a bit.

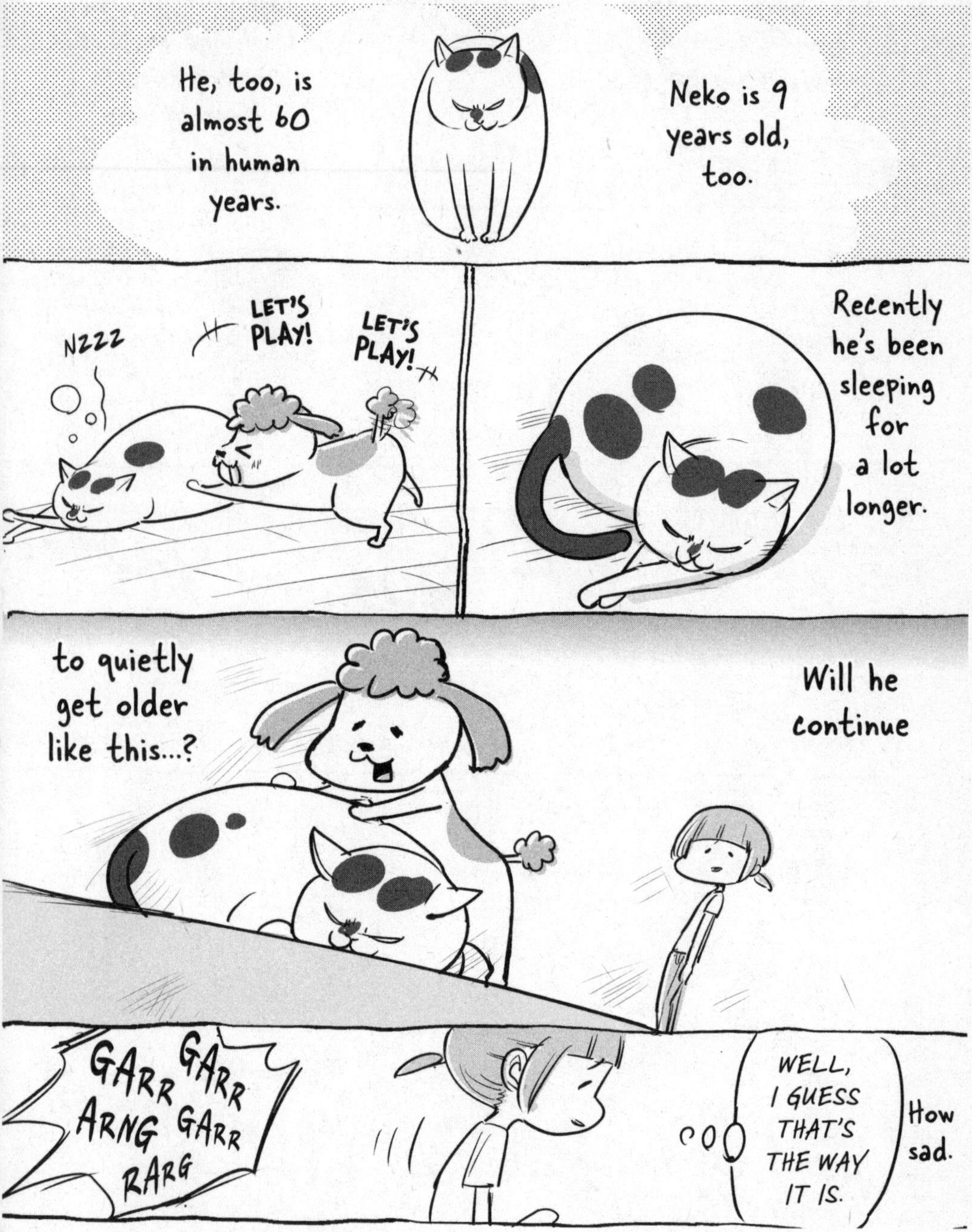
Neko is 9 years old, too.
He, too, is almost 60 in human years.
Recently he's been sleeping for a lot longer.
LET'S PLAY!
LET'S PLAY!
NZZZ
Will he continue
to quietly get older like this...?
How sad.
WELL, I GUESS THAT'S THE WAY IT IS.
GARR GARR ARNG GARR RARG

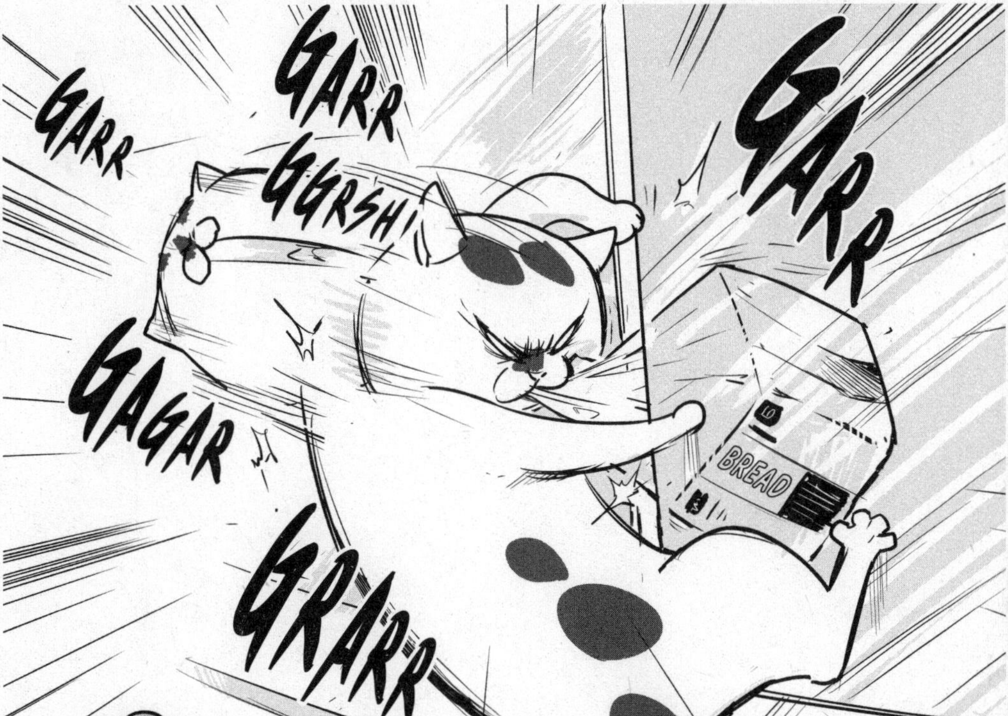
GARR
GARR
GURSH!
GARR
GAGAR
GRARR

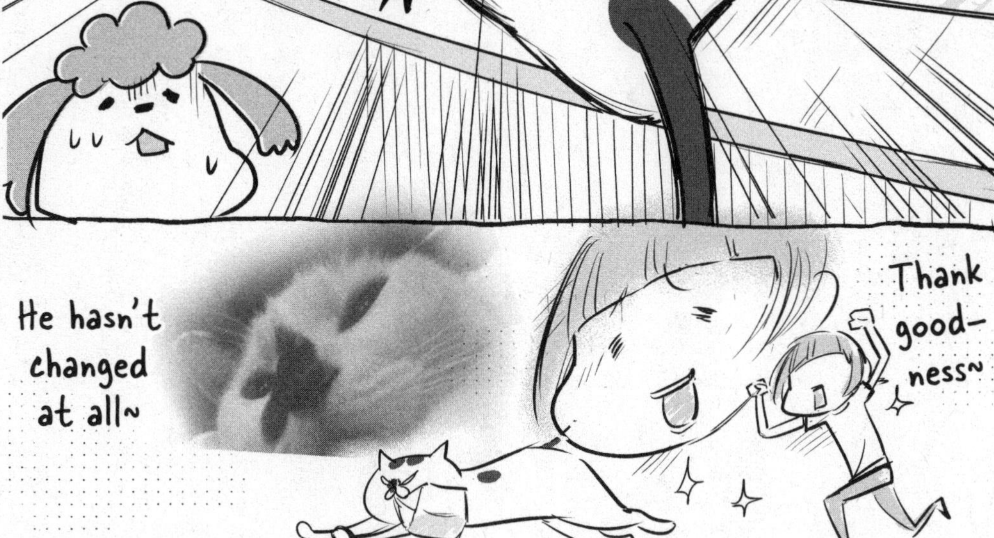
Thank goodness~
He hasn't changed at all~
We are all doing well! Thank you very much~

To be continued in Volume 3

Own this Purr-fect Collection!

The Complete
Chi's Sweet Home
Box Set

The New York Times bestselling cat comic *Chi's Sweet Home* is now available in a complete box set!

Contains all 4 volumes of the series in a cute collector's edition box.

60 cute stickers included!

Available Now!

IS BEING SERIALIZED ON TWITTER! Information

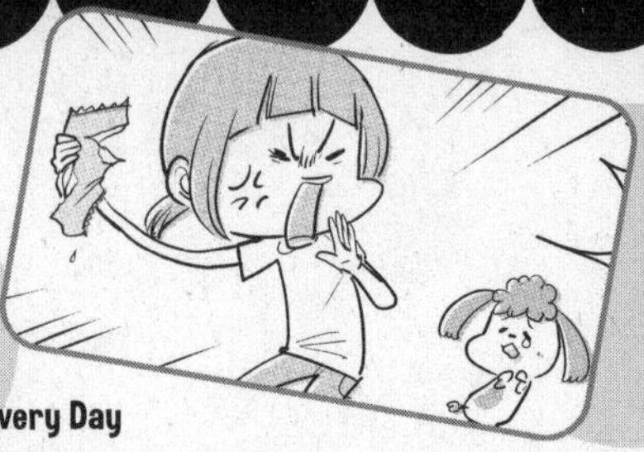

VOLUME 2 EPISODE TITLES WHEN SERIALIZED ON TWITTER

#36	With a Dog AND a Cat,	Their Cute★Reactions Are Fun Every Day
#37	〃	Their Difference in Taste is Remarkable and Fun Every Day
#38	〃	Having Different Dreams is Fun Every Day
#39	〃	The Course of Their Growth is Fun
#40	〃	It's Super Fun Watching Them When They're in a Tizzy
#41	〃	Every Time You Move Your Chair It's Fun
#42	〃	Mindfulness is a Billion Times More Effective, So Every Day is Fun
#43	〃	It's Fun to Scare One but Not the Other, So Every Day is Fun
#44	〃	They Try to Make Their Own Destiny, So Every Day is Fun
#45	〃	Lovely Events Happen at the Vet, Too, So Every Day is Fun
#46	〃	You're Immersed in an Ancient Adventure Even Under a Futon, So Every Day is Fun
#47	〃	They Have Unique Ways of Playing, So Every Day is Fun
#48	〃	One is Good at Seeking Affection and Spoiling You and One is Destructively Bad at It, So Every Day is Fun
#49	〃	One Expresses Their Emotions Directly and the Other is Hopelessly Awkward at It, So Every Day is Fun
#50	〃	Their Store of Patience is So Different, Every Day is Fun

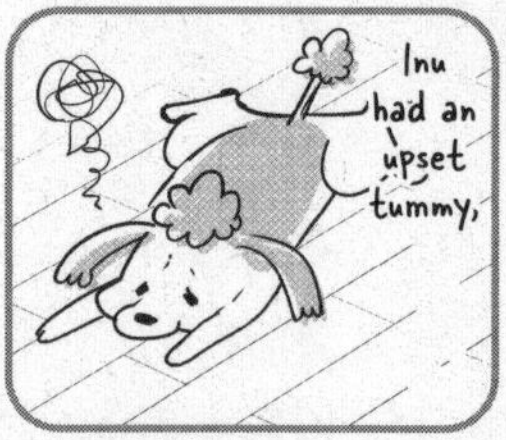
Inu had an upset tummy,

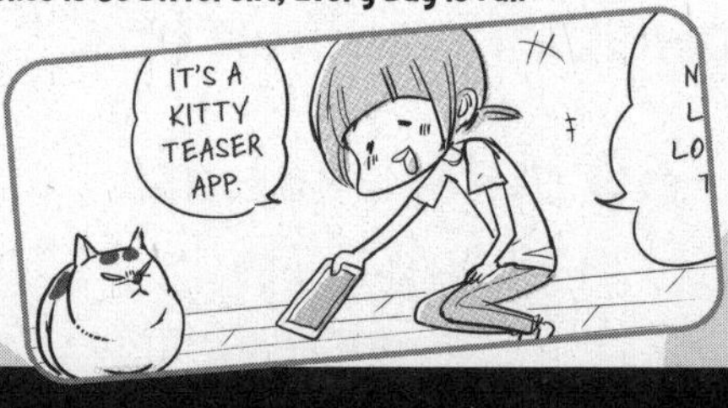
IT'S A KITTY TEASER APP.

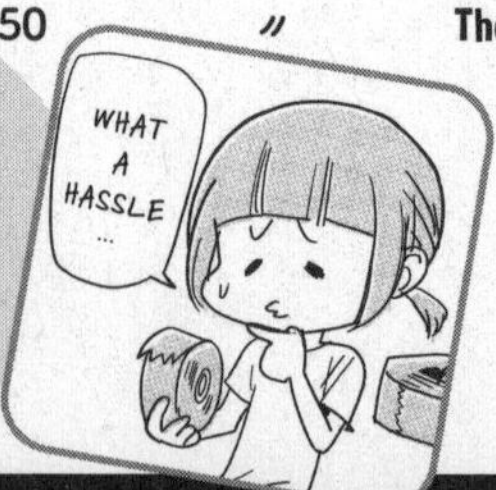
WHAT A HASSLE ...

SUNDAY ☆

(AND TRYING NOT TO TAKE ANY WEEKS OFF!)

"WITH A DOG AND A CAT, EVERY DAY IS FUN"

Twitter @hidekiccan

APPEARING EVERY

With a Dog AND a Cat, Every Day is Fun 2

A Vertical Comics Edition

Translation: Kumar Sivasubramanian
Production: Risa Cho
           Eve Grandt

© 2018 Hidekichi Matsumoto. All rights reserved.
First published in Japan in 2018 by Kodansha, Ltd., Tokyo
Publication rights for this English edition arranged through Kodansha, Ltd., Tokyo
English language version produced by Vertical Comics, an imprint of Kodansha USA Publishing, LLC

Translation provided by Vertical Comics, 2020
Published by Kodansha USA Publishing, LLC, New York

Originally published in Japanese as *Inu to Neko Docchimo Katteru to Mainichi Tanoshii 2* by Kodansha, Ltd., 2018

This is a work of fiction.

ISBN: 978-1-949980-89-9

Manufactured in the United States of America

First Edition

Kodansha USA Publishing, LLC
451 Park Avenue South
7th Floor
New York, NY 10016
www.readvertical.com

Vertical books are distributed through Penguin-Random House Publisher Services.

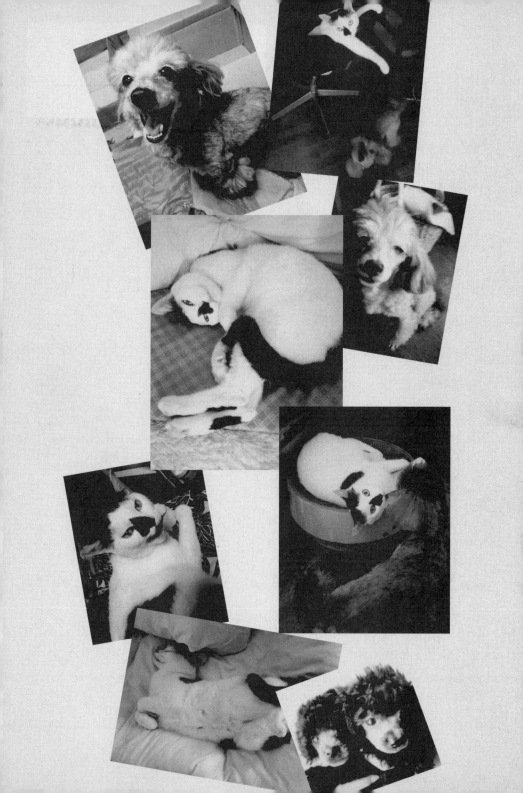

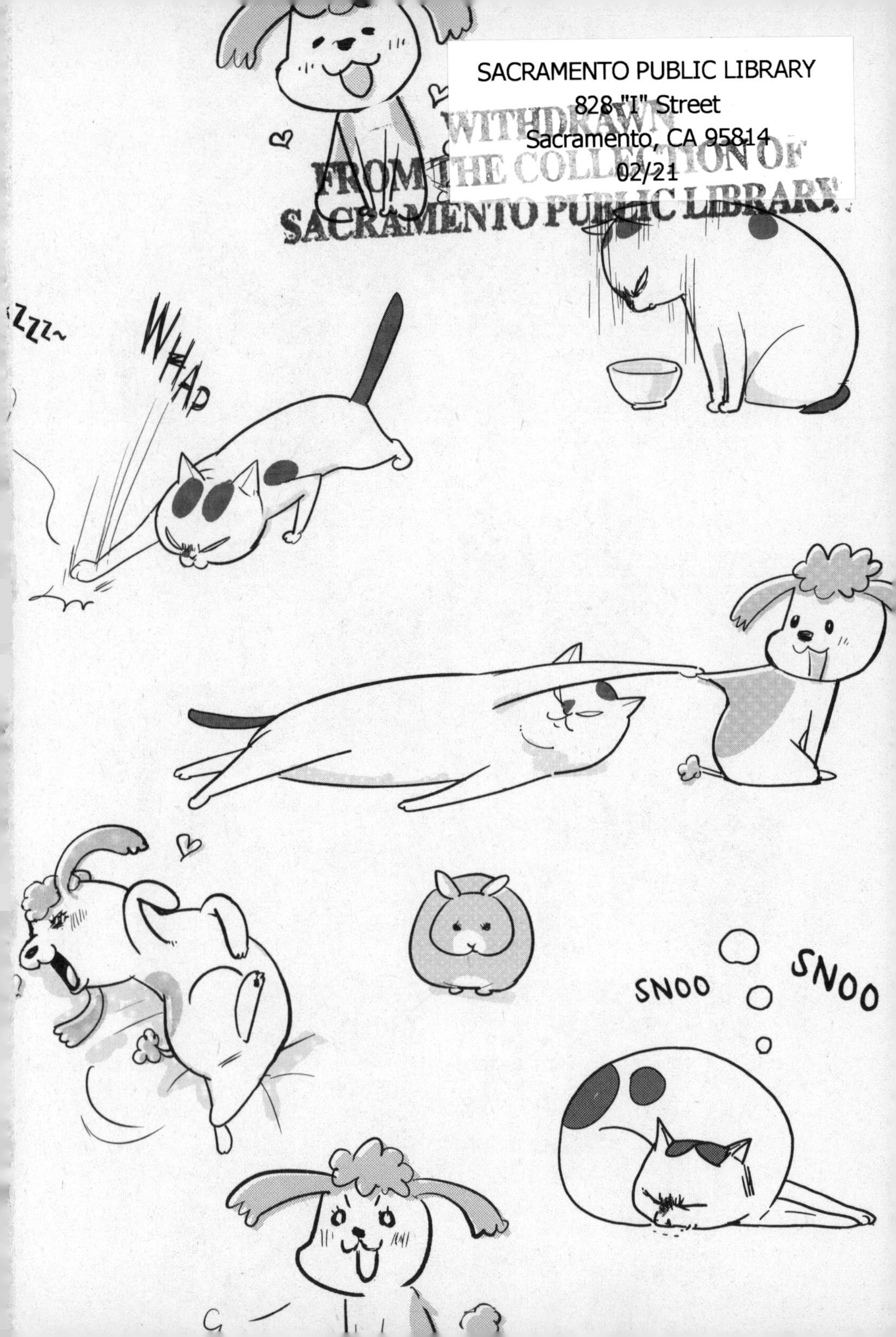
WHAP
ZZZ~
SNOO
SNOO